"*The Warren Buffett Way* outlines his career and presents examples of how his investment techniques and methods evolved and the important individuals in the process. It also details the key investment decisions that produced his unmatched record of performance. Finally, the book contains the thinking and the philosophy of an investor that consistently made money using the tools available to every citizen no matter what their level of wealth."

> Peter S. Lynch
> bestselling author, *One Up On Wall Street*
> and *Beating the Street*

"Robert Hagstrom presents an in-depth examination of Warren Buffett's strategies, and the 'how and why' behind his selection of each of the major securities that have contributed to his remarkable record of success. His 'homespun' wisdom and philosophy are also part of this comprehensive, interesting, and readable book."

> John C. Bogle
> Chairman, The Vanguard Group

"Warren Buffett is surely the Greatest Investor of this century—not so much because he built a great fortune with a free market as because he shared his important thinking with us and has openly demonstrated the sagacity and courage so vital to success. Berkshire Hathaway has been my largest, longest investment. Warren has been my best teacher."

> Charles D. Ellis
> Managing Partner, Greenwich Associates

"Warren Buffett is often characterized simply as a 'value investor' or a 'Ben Graham disciple.' Hagstrom fills in the rest of the story with some immensely practical pointers on prospering in the market."

> Martin S. Fridson
> Managing Director, Merrill Lynch

"In simple language, this book tells the rules by which the most successful American stock investor of modern time got that way. It could be a godsend to the legion of unhappy investors who keep floundering because they ignore the basics of major investment success."

> Phil Fisher
> author, *Common Stocks and Uncommon Profits*

THE
WARREN
BUFFETT
WAY

THE
WARREN
BUFFETT
WAY

Second Edition

ROBERT G. HAGSTROM

WILEY

John Wiley & Sons, Inc.

Contents

Foreword to the Second Edition

When Robert Hagstrom first published *The Warren Buffett Way* in 1994, it quickly became a phenomenon. To date, more than 1.2 million copies have been sold. The book's popularity is a testimony to the accuracy of its analysis and the value of its advice.

Any time the subject is Warren Buffett, it is easy to become overwhelmed by the sheer size of the numbers. Whereas most investors think in terms of hundreds or perhaps thousands, Buffett moves in a world of millions and billions. But that does not mean he has nothing to teach us. Quite the opposite. If we look at what he does and has done, and are able to discern the underlying thinking, we can model our decisions on his.

That is the profound contribution of Robert's book. He closely studied Warren Buffett's actions, words, and decisions for a number of years, and then set about analyzing them for common threads. For this book, he distilled those common threads into twelve tenets, timeless principles that guide Buffett's investment philosophy through all circumstances and all markets. In just the same way, they can guide any investor.

The enduring value of Robert's work is due to this clear focus—although the book talks about investment techniques, it is fundamentally about investment principles. And principles do not change. I can almost hear Warren saying, with his wry smile, "That's why they call them principles."

The past ten years have given us a vivid demonstration of that basic truth. In those ten years, the trends of the stock market changed several times over. We witnessed a high-flying bubble that made many people rich, and then a steep crash into a protracted, painful bear market before the market finally hit bottom in the spring of 2003 and started to turn back up.

All along the way, Warren Buffett's investment approach never changed. He has continued to follow the same principles outlined in this book:

- Think of buying stocks as buying fractional interests in whole businesses.
- Construct a focused low-turnover portfolio
- Invest in only what you can understand and analyze
- Demand a margin of safety between the purchase price and the company's long-term value

Berkshire Hathaway investors, as usual, reap the benefits of that steady approach. Since the recovery began in 2003, Berkshire Hathaway stock is up about $20,000 per share, more than 30 percent, far surpassing the returns of the overall market over the comparable period.

There is a chain of thinking for value investors that begins with Benjamin Graham, through Warren Buffett and his contemporaries, to the next generation of practitioners such as Robert Hagstrom. Buffett, Graham's best-known disciple, frequently advises investors to study Graham's book *The Intelligent Investor*. I often make the same recommendation myself. And I am convinced that Robert's work shares with that classic book one critical quality: the advice may not make you rich, but it is highly unlikely to make you poor. If understood and intelligently implemented, the techniques and principles presented here should make you a better investor.

BILL MILLER
CEO, Legg Mason Capital Management

Foreword to the First Edition

One weekday evening early in 1989 I was home when the telephone rang. Our middle daughter, Annie, then eleven, was first to the phone. She told me that Warren Buffett was calling. I was convinced this had to be a prank. The caller started by saying, "This is Warren Buffett from Omaha [as if I might confuse him with some other Warren Buffett]. I just finished your book, I loved it, and I would like to quote one of your sentences in the Berkshire annual report. I have always wanted to do a book, but I never have gotten around to it." He spoke very rapidly with lots of enthusiasm and must have said forty words in fifteen or twenty seconds, including a couple of laughs and chuckles. I instantly agreed to his request and I think we talked for five or ten minutes. I remember he closed by saying, "If you ever visit Omaha and don't come by and see me, your name will be mud in Nebraska."

Clearly not wanting my name to be mud in Nebraska, I took him up on his offer about six months later. Warren Buffett gave me a personal tour of every square foot of the office (which did not take long, as the whole operation could fit inside less than half of a tennis court), and I said hello to all eleven employees. There was not a computer or a stock quotation machine to be found.

After about an hour we went to a local restaurant where I followed his lead and had a terrific steak and my first cherry Coke in thirty years. We talked about jobs we had as children, baseball, and bridge, and exchanged stories about companies in which we had held investments in the past. Warren discussed or answered questions about each stock and operation that Berkshire (he never called his company Berkshire Hathaway) owned.

Why has Warren Buffett been the best investor in history? What is he like as an individual, a shareholder, a manager, and an owner of entire companies? What is so unique about the Berkshire Hathaway annual report, why does he donate so much effort to it, and what can someone learn from it? To attempt to answer those questions, I talked with him directly, and reread the last five annual reports and his earliest reports as chairman (the 1971 and 1972 reports each had only two pages of text). In addition, I had discussions with nine individuals that have been actively involved with Warren Buffett in varied relationships and from different viewpoints during the past four to over thirty years: Jack Byrne, Robert Denham, Don Keough, Carol Loomis, Tom Murphy, Charlie Munger, Carl Reichardt, Frank Rooney, and Seth Schofield.

In terms of his personal qualities, the responses were quite consistent. Warren Buffett is, first of all, very content. He loves everything he does, dealing with people and reading mass quantities of annual and quarterly reports and numerous newspapers and periodicals. As an investor he has discipline, patience, flexibility, courage, confidence, and decisiveness. He is always searching for investments where risk is eliminated or minimized. In addition, he is very adept at probability and as an oddsmaker. I believe this ability comes from an inherent love of simple math computations, his devotion and active participation in the game of bridge, and his long experience in underwriting and accepting high levels of risk in insurance and in reinsurance. He is willing to take risks where the odds of total loss are low and upside rewards are substantial. He lists his failures and mistakes and does not apologize. He enjoys kidding himself and compliments his associates in objective terms.

Warren Buffett is a great student of business and a wonderful listener, and able to determine the key elements of a company or a complex issue with high speed and precision. He can make a decision not to invest in something in as little as two minutes and conclude that it is time to make a major purchase in just a few days of research. He is always prepared, for as he has said in an annual report, "Noah did not start building the Ark when it was raining."

As a manager he almost never calls a division head or the chief executive of a company but is delighted at any time of the day or night for them to call him to report something or seek counsel. After investing in a stock or purchasing an entire operation, he becomes a cheerleader and sounding board: "At Berkshire we don't tell 400% hitters how to swing," using an analogy to baseball management.

Two examples of Warren Buffett's willingness to learn and adapt himself are public speaking and computer usage. In the 1950s Warren invested $100 in a Dale Carnegie course "not to prevent my knees from knocking when public speaking but to do public speaking while my knees are knocking." At the Berkshire annual meeting in front of more than 2,000 people, Warren Buffett sits on a stage with Charlie Munger, and, without notes, lectures and responds to questions in a fashion that would please Will Rogers, Ben Graham, King Solomon, Phil Fisher, David Letterman, and Billy Crystal. To be able to play more bridge, early in 1994 Warren learned how to use a computer so he could join a network where you can play with other individuals from their locations all over the country. Perhaps in the near future he will begin to use some of the hundreds of data retrieval and information services on companies that are available on computers today for investment research.

Warren Buffett stresses that the critical investment factor is determining the intrinsic value of a business and paying a fair or bargain price. He doesn't care what the general stock market has done recently or will do in the future. He purchased over $1 billion of Coca-Cola in 1988 and 1989 after the stock had risen over fivefold the prior six years and over five-hundredfold the previous sixty years. He made four times his money in three years and plans to make a lot more the next five, ten, and twenty years with Coke. In 1976 he purchased a very major position in GEICO when the stock had declined from $61 to $2 and the general perception was that the stock was definitely going to zero.

How can the average investor employ Warren Buffett's methods? Warren Buffett never invests in businesses he cannot understand or that are outside his "Circle of Competence." All investors can, over time, obtain and intensify their "Circle of Competence" in an industry where they are professionally involved or in some sector of business they enjoy researching. One does not have to be correct very many times in a lifetime as Warren states that twelve investments decisions in his forty year career have made all the difference.

Risk can be reduced greatly by concentrating on only a few holdings if it forces investors to be more careful and thorough in their research. Normally more than 75 percent of Berkshire's common stock holdings are represented by only five different securities. One of the principles demonstrated clearly several times in this book is to buy great businesses when they are having a temporary problem or when the stock market declines and creates bargain prices for outstanding franchises. Stop trying to predict the direction of the stock market, the economy, interest rates, or elections, and stop wasting money on individuals that do this for a living. Study the facts and the financial condition, value the company's future outlook, and purchase when everything is in your favor. Many people invest in a way similar to playing poker all night without ever looking at their cards.

Very few investors would have had the knowledge and courage to purchase GEICO at $2.00 or Wells Fargo or General Dynamics when they were depressed as there were numerous learned people saying those companies were in substantial trouble. However, Warren Buffett's purchase of Capital Cities/ABC, Gillette, Washington Post, Affiliated Publications, Freddie Mac, or Coca-Cola (which have produced over $6 billion of profits for Berkshire Hathaway, or 60 percent of the $10 billion of shareholders' equity) were all well-run companies with strong histories of profitability, and were dominant business franchises.

In addition to his own shareholders, Warren Buffett uses the Berkshire annual report to help the general public become better investors. On both sides of his family he descended from newspaper editors, and his Aunt Alice was a public school teacher for more than thirty years. Warren Buffett enjoys both teaching and writing about business in general and investing in particular. He taught on a volunteer basis when he was twenty-one at the University of Nebraska in Omaha. In 1955, when he was working in New York City, he taught an adult education course on the stock market at Scarsdale High School. For ten years in the late 1960s and 1970s he gave a free lecture course at Creighton University. In 1977 he served on a committee headed by Al Sommer Jr., to advise the Securities and Exchange Commission on corporate disclosure. After that involvement, the scale of the Berkshire annual report changed dramatically with the 1977 report written in late 1977 and early 1978. The format became more similar to the partnership reports he produced from 1956 to 1969.

Since the early 1980s, the Berkshire annual reports have informed shareholders of the performance of the holdings of the company and new investments, updated the status of the insurance and the reinsurance industry, and (since 1982) have listed acquisition criteria about businesses Berkshire would like to purchase. The report is generously laced with examples, analogies, stories, and metaphors containing the do's and don'ts of proper investing in stocks.

Warren Buffett has established a high standard for the future performance of Berkshire by setting an objective of growing intrinsic value by 15 percent a year over the long term, something few people, and no one from 1956 to 1993 besides himself, have ever done. He has stated it will be a difficult standard to maintain due to the much larger size of the company, but there are always opportunities around and Berkshire keeps lots of cash ready to invest and it grows every year. His confidence is somewhat underlined by the final nine words of the June 1993 annual report on page 60: "Berkshire has not declared a cash dividend since 1967."

Warren Buffett has stated that he has always wanted to write a book on investing. Hopefully that will happen some day. However, until that event, his annual reports are filling that function in a fashion somewhat similar to the nineteenth-century authors who wrote in serial form: Edgar Allen Poe, William Makepeace Thackery, and Charles Dickens. The Berkshire Hathaway annual reports from 1977 through 1993 are seventeen chapters of that book. And also in the interim we now have *The Warren Buffett Way,* in which Robert Hagstrom outlines Buffett's career and presents examples of how his investment technique and methods evolved as well as the important individuals in that process. The book also details the key investment decisions that produced Buffett's unmatched record of performance. Finally, it contains the thinking and the philosophy of an investor that consistently made money using the tools available to every citizen no matter their level of wealth.

PETER S. LYNCH

Preface

Almost exactly twenty years ago, while training to become an investment broker with Legg Mason, I received a Berkshire Hathaway annual report as part of the training materials. It was my very first exposure to Warren Buffett.

Like most people who read Berkshire's annual reports, I was instantly impressed with the clarity of Buffett's writing. As a young professional during the 1980s, I found that my head was perpetually spinning as I tried to keep up with the stock market, the economy, and the constant buying and selling of securities. Yet, each time I read a story about Warren Buffett or an article written by him, his rational voice seemed to rise above the market's chaos. It was his calming influence that inspired me to write this book.

The principal challenge I faced writing *The Warren Buffett Way* was to prove or disprove Buffett's claim that "what [I] do is not beyond anybody else's competence." Some critics argue that, despite his success, Warren Buffett's idiosyncrasies mean his investment approach cannot be widely adopted. I disagree. Warren Buffett is idiosyncratic—it is a source of his success—but his methodology, once understood, is applicable to individuals and institutions alike. My goal in this book is to help investors employ the strategies that make Warren Buffett successful.

The Warren Buffett Way describes what is, at its core, a simple approach. There are no computer programs to learn, no two-inch-thick investment manuals to decipher. Whether you are financially able to purchase 10 percent of a company or merely a hundred shares, this book can help you achieve profitable investment returns.

But do not judge yourself against Warren Buffett. His five decades of simultaneously owning and investing in businesses make it improbable that you can imitate his historical investment returns. Instead, compare your ongoing results against your peer group, whether that group includes actively managed mutual funds, an index fund, or the broader market in general.

The original edition of this book enjoyed remarkable success, and I am deeply gratified that so many people found it useful. The success of *The Warren Buffett Way,* however, is first and foremost a testament to Warren Buffett. His wit and integrity have charmed millions of people worldwide; and his intellect and investment record have, for years, mesmerized the professional investment community, me included. This unparalleled combination makes Warren Buffett the single most popular role model in investing today.

I had never met Warren Buffett before writing this book, and I did not consult with him while developing it. Although consultation surely would have been a bonus, I was fortunate to be able to draw from his extensive writings on investing that date back more than four decades. Throughout the book, I have employed extensive quotes from Berkshire Hathaway's annual reports, especially the famous Chairman's Letters. Mr. Buffett granted permission to use this copyrighted material, but only after he had reviewed the book. This permission in no way implies that he cooperated on the book or that he made available to me secret documents or strategies that are not already available from his public writings.

Almost everything Buffett does is public, but it is loosely noted. What was needed, in my opinion, and what would be valuable to investors, was a thorough examination of his thoughts and strategies aligned with the purchases that Berkshire made over the years, all compiled in one source. And that was the starting point for the original edition of *The Warren Buffett Way.*

This revised edition, ten years later, retains that basic goal: to examine Buffett's more recent actions for the investment lessons they hold and to consider whether changes in the financial climate have triggered changes in his strategies.

Some things became clear quickly. Buffett's level of activity in the stock market has dropped off significantly in recent years; he has bought entire companies more often than he has bought shares. He has on occasion moved more strongly into bonds—investment-grade corporate, government, even high-yield—and then, when they became less attractive, moved out again.

Some of these newly acquired companies are profiled in the chapters that follow, along with a discussion of how the characteristics of those companies reflect the tenets of the Warren Buffett Way. However, since many of these companies were privately held before Buffett bought them, the specifics of their financial data were not publicly available. I cannot, therefore, discern with any confidence what Buffett might have thought of those companies' economic conditions, other than to say that he clearly liked what he saw.

For this updated edition, I also took the opportunity to incorporate some material that was not presented in the original book. I added a chapter on Buffett's style of portfolio management, a style he has labeled "focus investing." It is a cornerstone of his success, and I highly recommend it. I also included a chapter on the psychology of money, the many ways that emotion plays havoc with good decisions. To invest wisely, it is necessary to become aware of all the temptations to behave foolishly. It is necessary for two reasons: If you know how to recognize the emotional potholes, you can avoid tripping into them. And you will be able to recognize the missteps of others in time to profit from their mistakes.

Ten years is either a very long time, or not long at all, depending on your circumstances and your personal view of the world. For investors, what we can say is that during these ten years, context has changed but the basics have not. That's good, because in another ten years the context can change back again, or change in an entirely different direction. Those who remain grounded in basic principles can survive those upheavals far better than those who do not.

In the ten years since I wrote *The Warren Buffett Way*, the noise level in the stock market has continued to rise, sometimes to a deafening screech. Television commentators, financial writers, analysts, and market strategists are all overtalking each other to get investors' attention. At the same time, many investors are immersed in Internet chat rooms and message boards exchanging questionable information and misleading tips.

Yet, despite all this available information, investors find it increasingly difficult to earn a profit. Some are hard pressed even to continue. Stock prices skyrocket with little reason, then plummet just as quickly. People who have turned to investing for their children's education and their own retirement are constantly frightened. There appears to be neither rhyme nor reason to the market, only folly.

Far above the market madness stand the wisdom and counsel of Warren Buffett. In an environment that seems to favor the speculator over the investor, Buffett's investment advice has proven, time and again, to be a safe harbor for millions of lost investors. Occasionally, misaligned investors will yell out, "But it's different this time"; and occasionally they will be right. Politics spring surprises, markets react, then economics reverberate in a slightly different tone. New companies are constantly born while others mature. Industries evolve and adapt. Change is constant, but the investment principles outlined in this book have remained the same.

Here is a succinct and powerful lesson from the 1996 annual report: "Your goal as an investor should be simply to purchase, at a rational price, a part interest in an easily understood business whose earnings are virtually certain to be materially higher, five, ten, and twenty years from now. Over time, you will find only a few companies that meet those standards—so when you see one that qualifies, you should buy a meaningful amount of stock."

Whatever level of funds you have available for investing, whatever industry or company you are interested in, you cannot find a better touchstone than that.

ROBERT G. HAGSTROM

Villanova, Pennsylvania
September 2004

Introduction

My father, Philip A. Fisher, looked with great pride on Warren Buffett's adoption of some of his views and their long and friendly relationship. If my father had been alive to write this introduction, he would have jumped at the chance to share some of the good feelings he experienced over the decades from his acquaintance with one of the very few men whose investment star burned so brightly as to make his dim by comparison. My father genuinely liked Warren Buffett and was honored that Buffett embraced some of his ideas. My father died at 96—exactly three months before I received an unexpected letter asking if I would write about my father and Warren Buffett. This introduction has helped me to connect some dots and provide some closure regarding my father and Mr. Buffett. For readers of *The Warren Buffett Way,* I hope I can provide a very personal look into an important piece of investment history and some thoughts on how to best use this wonderful book.

There is little I will say about Mr. Buffett since that is the subject of this book and Robert Hagstrom covers that ground with grace and insight. It's well known that my father was an important influence on Warren Buffett and, as Mr. Hagstrom writes, my father's influence figured more prominently in Buffett's thinking in recent years. For his part, as my father became acquainted with Warren Buffett, he grew to admire qualities in him that he felt were essential to investing success but are rare among investment managers.

When he visited my father 40 years ago, in a world with relatively primitive information tools by today's standards, my father had his own ways of gathering information. He slowly built a circle of acquaintances over the decades—investment professionals he respected and who knew him well enough to understand what he was and wasn't interested in— and who might share good ideas with him. Toward that end, he concluded that he would meet any young investment professional once. If he was impressed, he might see him again and build a relationship. He rarely saw anyone twice. Very high standards! In his mind, if you didn't get an "A" you got an "F." And once he had judged against someone, he simply excluded that person, forever. One shot at building a relationship. Time was scarce.

Warren Buffett as a young man was among the very, very few who impressed my father sufficiently in his first meeting to merit a second meeting and many more meetings after that. My father was a shrewd judge of character and skill. Unusually so! He based his career on judging people. It was one of his best qualities and a major reason why he put so much emphasis on qualitative judgment of business management in his stock analysis. He was always very proud he picked Warren Buffett as an "A" before Buffett had won his much-deserved fame and acclaim.

The relationship between Warren Buffett and my father survived my father's occasional lapses when he would mistakenly call Mr. Buffett "Howard." This is an unusual story that has never been told and perhaps says much about both my father and Warren Buffett.

My father was a small man with a big mind that raced intensely. While kindly, he was nervous, often agitated, and personally insecure. He was also very, very much a creature of habit. He followed daily catechisms rigorously because they made him more secure. And he loved to sleep, because when he slept, he wasn't nervous or insecure. So when he couldn't stop his mind from racing at night, which was often, he played memory games instead of counting sheep. One sleep game he played was memorizing the names and districts of all the members of Congress until he drifted off.

Starting in 1942, he memorized the name of Howard Buffett and associated it with Omaha, over and over again, night after night, for more than a decade. His brain mechanically linked the words "Omaha," "Buffett," and "Howard" as a related series long before he met Warren Buffett. Later, as Warren's career began to build and his star rose, it was still fully two decades before my father could fully disentangle Buffett and Omaha, from "Howard." That annoyed my father because he couldn't control his mind and because he was fond of Warren Buffett and valued their relationship. Father knew exactly who Warren Buffett was but in casual conversation he often said something like, "That bright young Howard Buffett from Omaha." The more he said it, the harder it became to eliminate it from his phraseology. A man of habit habitually vexed.

Early one morning when they were to meet, my father was intent on sorting out "Howard" from "Warren." Still, at one point in the conversation, my father referred to Warren as "Howard." If Warren noticed, he gave no sign and certainly did not correct my father. This occurred sporadically throughout the 1970s. By the 1980s, my father finally had purged the word "Howard" from any sentence referencing Buffett. He was actually proud when he left "Howard" behind for good. Years later, I asked him if he ever explained this to Warren. He said he hadn't because it embarrassed him so much.

Their relationship survived because it was built on much stronger stuff. I think one of the kernels of their relationship was their shared philosophy in associating with people of integrity and skill. When Mr. Buffett says in regard to overseeing Berkshire Hathaway managers, "We don't tell .400 hitters how to swing," that is almost straight from Phil Fisher's playbook. Associate with the best, don't be wrong about that, and then don't tell them what to do.

Over the years, my father was very impressed with how Mr. Buffett evolved as investor without compromising any of his core principles. Every decade, Mr. Buffett has done things no one would have predicted from reading about his past, and done them well. Within professional investing, most people learn in craft-like form some particular style of investing and then never change. They buy low P/E stocks or leading tech names or whatever. They build that craft and then never change, or change only marginally. In contrast, Warren Buffett consistently took new approaches, decade-after-decade—so that it was impossible to predict what he might do next. You could not have predicted his 1970s franchise orientation from his original strict value bent. You could not have predicted his 1980s consumer products orientation at above market average P/Es from his previous approaches. His ability to change—and do it successfully—could be a book unto itself. When most people attempt to evolve as he has—they fail. Mr. Buffett didn't fail, my father believed, because he never lost sight of who he was. He always remained true to himself.

My father was never physically far for very long from Rudyard Kipling's famous poem, "If." In his desk, by his nightstand, in his den— always close. He read it over and over and quoted it often to me. I keep it by my desk as part of keeping him close to me. Being insecure but un- daunted, he would tell you in Kipling-like fashion to be very serious about your career and your investments, but do not take yourself too se- riously. He would urge you to contemplate others' criticisms of you, but never consider them your judge. He would urge you to challenge your- self, but not judge yourself too extremely either way and when in your eyes you've failed, force yourself to try again. And he would urge you to do the next thing, yet unfathomed.

It is that part about Mr. Buffett, his knack for evolving consistent with his values and past—doing the next thing unfathomed—that my father most admired. Moving forward unfettered by the past restraints, utterance, convention, or pride. Buffett, to my father's way of think- ing, embodied some of the qualities immortalized by Kipling.

Unfortunately, there will always be a small percent of society, but a large absolute number, of small-minded envious miscreants who can't create a life of their own. Instead they love to throw mud. The purpose of life for these misguided souls is to attempt to create pain where they can't otherwise create gain. By the time a successful career concludes, mud will have been thrown at almost everyone of any accomplishment. And if any can stick, it will. My insecure father always expected mud to be thrown at everyone, himself included, but for those he admired, he hoped it would not stick. And when mud was thrown, he would expect those he admired, in Kipling-like fashion, to contemplate the criticism or allegation without feeling judged by it. Always through Kipling's eyes!

Through a longer career than most, Warren Buffett has acquitted himself remarkably—little mud has been thrown at him and none has stuck. A testament indeed. Kipling would be pleased. As was my father. It goes back to Mr. Buffett's core values—he always knows exactly who he is and what he is about. He isn't tormented by conflicts of interest that can undermine his principles and lead to less-than-admirable be- haviors. There was no mud to throw so no mud stuck. And that is the prime part of Warren Buffett you should try to emulate. Know who you are.

I am writing this introduction in part to suggest to you how to use this book. Throughout my career, people have asked me why I don't do things more like my father did or why I don't do things more like Mr. Buffett. The answer is simple. I am I, not them. I have to use my own comparative advantages. I'm not as shrewd a judge of people as my father and I'm not the genius Buffett is.

It is important to use this book to learn, but don't use this book to be like Warren Buffett. You can't be Warren Buffett and, if you try, you will suffer. Use this book to understand Buffett's ideas and then take those ideas and integrate them into your own approach to investing. It is only from your own ideas that you create greatness. The insights in this book are only useful when you ingest them into your own persona rather than trying to twist your persona to fit the insights. (A twisted persona is a lousy investor unless you're twisted naturally.) Regardless, I guarantee that you cannot be Warren Buffett no matter what you read or how hard you try. You have to be yourself.

That is the greatest lesson I got from my father, a truly great teacher at many levels—not to be him or anyone else, but to be the best I could evolve into, never quitting the evolution. The greatest lesson you can glean from Warren Buffett? To learn from him without desiring to be like him. If you're a young reader, the greatest investment lesson is to find who you really are. If you're an old reader, the greatest lesson is that you really are much younger than you think you are and you should act that way—a rare gift. Were that not possible, then Mr. Buffett wouldn't still be ably evolving at what for most people is post-retirement age. Think of Warren Buffett as a teacher, not a role model, and think of this book as the single best explanation of his teachings, well stated and easily learned. You can learn an enormous amount from this book and that can be the foundation for developing your own successful investment philosophy.

KENNETH L. FISHER

1

The World's Greatest Investor

Every year, *Forbes* magazine publishes a list of the 400 richest Americans, the elite Forbes 400. Individuals on the list come and go from year to year, as their personal circumstances change and their industries rise and fall, but some names are constant. Among those leading the list year in and year out are certain megabillionaires who trace their wealth to a product (computer software or hardware), a service (retailing), or lucky parentage (inheritance). Of those perennially in the top five, only one made his fortune through investment savvy. That one person is Warren Buffett.

In the early 1990s, he was number one. Then for a few years, he see-sawed between number one and number two with a youngster named Bill Gates. Even for the dot-com-crazed year 2000, when so much of the wealth represented by the Forbes 400 came from the phenomenal growth in technology, Buffett, who smilingly eschews high-tech anything, was firmly in fourth position. He was still the only person in the top five for whom the "source of wealth" column read "stock market." In 2004, he was solidly back in the number two position.

In 1956, Buffett started his investment partnership with $100; after thirteen years, he cashed out with $25 million. At the time of this writing (mid-2004), his personal net worth has increased to $42.9 billion, the stock in his company is selling at $92,900 a share, and millions of investors around the world hang on his every word.

To fully appreciate Warren Buffett, however, we have to go beyond the dollars, the performance accolades, and the reputation.

INVESTMENT BEGINNINGS

Warren Edward Buffett was born August 30, 1930, in Omaha, Nebraska. His grandfather owned a grocery store (and once employed a young Charlie Munger); his father was a local stockbroker. As a boy, Warren Buffett was always fascinated with numbers and could easily do complex mathematical calculations in his head. At age eight, he began reading his father's books on the stock market; at age eleven, he marked the board at the brokerage house where his father worked. His early years were enlivened with entrepreneurial ventures, and he was so successful that he told his father he wanted to skip college and go directly into business. He was overruled.

Buffett attended the business school at the University of Nebraska, and while there, he read a new book on investing by a Columbia professor named Benjamin Graham. It was, of course, *The Intelligent Investor*. Buffett was so taken with Graham's ideas that he applied to Columbia Business School so that he could study directly with Graham. Bill Ruane, now chairman of the Sequoia Fund, was in the same class. He recalls that there was an instantaneous mental chemistry between Graham and Buffett, and that the rest of the class was primarily an audience.[1]

Not long after Buffett graduated from Columbia with a master's degree in economics, Graham invited his former student to join his company, the Graham-Newman Corporation. During his two-year tenure there, Buffett became fully immersed in his mentor's investment approach (see Chapter 2 for a full discussion of Graham's philosophy).

In 1956, Graham-Newman disbanded. Graham, then 61, decided to retire, and Buffett returned to Omaha. Armed with the knowledge he had acquired from Graham, the financial backing of family and friends, and $100 of his own money, Buffett began a limited investment partnership. He was twenty-five years old.

THE BUFFETT PARTNERSHIP, LTD.

The partnership began with seven limited partners who together contributed $105,000. The limited partners received 6 percent annually on their investment and 75 percent of the profits above this bogey; the remaining 25 percent went to Buffett, who as general partner had essentially free rein to invest the partnership's funds.

Over the next thirteen years, Buffett compounded money at an annual rate of 29.5 percent.[2] It was no easy task. Although the Dow Jones Industrial Average declined in price five different years during that thirteen-year period, Buffett's partnership never had a down year. Buffett, in fact, had begun the partnership with the ambitious goal of outperforming the Dow by ten points every year. And he did it—not by ten—but by twenty-two points!

As Buffett's reputation grew, more people asked him to manage their money. For the partnership, Buffett bought controlling interests in several public and private companies, and in 1962 he began buying shares in an ailing textile company called Berkshire Hathaway.

That same year, 1962, Buffett moved the partnership office from his home to Kiewit Plaza in Omaha, where his office remains today. The next year, he made a stunning purchase.

Tainted by a scandal involving one of its clients, American Express saw its shares drop from $65 to $35 almost overnight. Buffett had learned Ben Graham's lesson well: When stocks of a strong company are selling below their intrinsic value, act decisively. Buffett made the bold decision to put 40 percent of the partnership's total assets, $13 million, into American Express stock. Over the next two years, the shares tripled in price, and the partners netted a cool $20 million in profit. It was pure Graham—and pure Buffett.

By 1965, the partnership's assets had grown to $26 million. Four years later, explaining that he found the market highly speculative and worthwhile values increasingly scarce, Buffett decided to end the investment partnership.

When the partnership disbanded, investors received their proportional interests. Some of them, at Buffett's recommendation, sought out money manager Bill Ruane, his old classmate at Columbia. Ruane agreed to manage their money, and thus was born the Sequoia Fund. Others, including Buffett, invested their partnership revenues in Berkshire Hathaway. By that point, Buffett's share of the partnership had grown to $25 million, which was enough to give him control of Berkshire Hathaway.

What he did with it is well known in the investment world. Even those with only a passing interest in the stock market recognize Buffett's name and know something of his stunning success. In the following chapters, we trace the upward trajectory of Berkshire Hathaway in the forty years that Buffett has been in control. Perhaps more important, we also look beneath the surface to uncover the commonsense philosophy on which he founded his success.

THE MAN AND HIS COMPANY

Warren Buffett is not easy to describe. Physically, he is unremarkable, with looks often described as grandfatherly. Intellectually, he is considered a genius; yet his down-to-earth relationship with people is truly uncomplicated. He is simple, straightforward, forthright, and honest. He displays an engaging combination of sophisticated dry wit and cornball humor. He has a profound reverence for all things logical and a foul distaste for imbecility. He embraces the simple and avoids the complicated.

When reading Berkshire's annual reports, one is struck by how comfortable Buffett is quoting the Bible, John Maynard Keynes, or Mae West. The operable word here is *reading*. Each report is sixty to seventy pages of dense information: no pictures, no color graphics, no charts. Those who are disciplined enough to start on page one and continue uninterrupted are rewarded with a healthy dose of financial acumen, folksy humor, and unabashed honesty. Buffett is candid in his reporting. He emphasizes both the pluses and the minuses of Berkshire's businesses. He believes that people who own stock in Berkshire Hathaway are owners of the company, and he tells them as much as he would like to be told if he were in their shoes.

When Buffett took control of Berkshire, the corporate net worth was $22 million. Forty years later, it has grown to $69 billion. It has long been Buffett's goal to increase the book value of Berkshire Hathaway at a 15 percent annual rate—well above the return achieved by the average American company. Since he took control of Berkshire in 1964, the gain has been much greater: Book value per share has grown from $19 to $50,498, a rate of 22.2 percent compounded annually. This relative performance is all the more impressive when you consider that Berkshire is penalized by both income and capital gains taxes and the Standard & Poor's 500 returns are pretax.

Table 1.1 Berkshire's Corporate Performance versus the S&P 500

| Year | Annual Percentage Change | | |
	In Per-Share Book Value of Berkshire (1)	In S&P 500 with Dividends Included (2)	Relative Results (1)–(2)
1965	23.8	10.0	13.8
1966	20.3	(11.7)	32.0
1967	11.0	30.9	(19.9)
1968	19.0	11.0	8.0
1969	16.2	(8.4)	24.6
1970	12.0	3.9	8.1
1971	16.4	14.6	1.8
1972	21.7	18.9	2.8
1973	4.7	(14.8)	19.5
1974	5.5	(26.4)	31.9
1975	21.9	37.2	(15.3)
1976	59.3	23.6	35.7
1977	31.9	(7.4)	39.3
1978	24.0	6.4	17.6
1979	35.7	18.2	17.5
1980	19.3	32.3	(13.0)
1981	31.4	(5.0)	36.4

Source: Berkshire Hathaway 2003 Annual Report.

Notes: Data are for calendar years with these exceptions: 1965 and 1966, year ended 9/30; 1967, 15 months ended 12/31.

Starting in 1979, accounting rules required insurance companies to value the equity securities they hold at market rather than at the lower of cost or market, which was previuisly the requirement. In this table, Berkshire's results through 1978 have been restated to conform to the changed rules. In all other respects, the results are calculated using the numbers originally reported.

The S&P 500 numbers are *pre-tax* whereas the Berkshire numbers are *after-tax*. If a corporation such as Berkshire were simply to have owned the S&P 500 and accrued the appropriate taxes, its results would have lagged the S&P 500 in years when that index showed a positive return, but would have exceeded the S&P in years when the index showed a negative return. Over the years, the tax costs would have caused the aggregate lag to be substantial.

(continued)

Table 1.1 *Continued*

Year	Annual Percentage Change		
	In Per-Share Book Value of Berkshire (1)	In S&P 500 with Dividends Included (2)	Relative Results (1)–(2)
1982	40.0	21.4	18.6
1983	32.3	22.4	9.9
1984	13.6	6.1	7.5
1985	48.2	31.6	16.6
1986	26.1	18.6	7.5
1987	19.5	5.1	14.4
1988	20.1	16.6	3.5
1989	44.4	31.7	12.7
1990	7.4	(3.1)	10.5
1991	39.6	30.5	9.1
1992	20.3	7.6	12.7
1993	14.3	10.1	4.2
1994	13.9	1.3	12.6
1995	43.1	37.6	5.5
1996	31.8	23.0	8.8
1997	34.1	33.4	.7
1998	48.3	28.6	19.7
1999	.5	21.0	(20.5)
2000	6.5	(9.1)	15.6
2001	(6.2)	(11.9)	5.7
2002	10.0	(22.1)	32.1
2003	21.0	28.7	(7.7)
Average Annual Gain— 1965–2003	22.2	10.4	11.8
Overall Gain— 1964–2003	259,485	4,743	

On a year-by-year basis, Berkshire's returns have at times been volatile; changes in the stock market and thus the underlying stocks that Berkshire owns create wide swings in per share value (see Table 1.1).

To appreciate the volatility, compare the results for 1998 with 1999. In 1998, Berkshire's value increased more than 48 percent. Then, in 1999, Berkshire's increase dropped to a paltry 0.5 percent, yet the S&P 500 increased 21 percent. Two factors were involved: Berkshire's results can be traced to poor return on consumer nondurables (Coca-Cola and Gillette), while the S&P increase was fueled by the outstanding performance of technology stocks, which Berkshire does not own.

Speaking with the candor for which he is famous, Buffett admitted in the 1999 annual report that "truly large superiorities over the [S&P] index are a thing of the past."[3] He predicted, however, that over time Berkshire's performance would be "modestly" better than the S&P. And for the next three years, this turned out to be the case. Then in 2003, even though Berkshire had a terrific year—book value up 21 percent—the S&P did even better.

BUFFETT TODAY

Over the most recent years, starting in the late 1990s, Buffett has been less active in the stock market than he was in the 1980s and early 1990s. Many people have noticed this lack of activity and have wondered whether it signaled that the market had hit its top. Others have theorized that the lack of new major purchases of common stocks simply means that the type of stocks Buffett likes to purchase are no longer selling at attractive prices.

We know it is Buffett's preference to "buy certainties at a discount." "Certainties" are defined by the predictability of a company's economics. The more predicable a company's economics, the more certainty we might have about its valuation. When we look down the list of stocks that Buffett owns as well as the wholly owned companies inside Berkshire, we are struck by the high degree of predictability reflected there. The "discount" part of the statement obviously refers to the stock price.

Knowing that Buffett likes to buy highly predictable economics at prices below the intrinsic value of the business, we can conclude that his buyer's strike reflects the lack of choices in this arena. I am pretty sure that if Coca-Cola, Gillette, or other similar businesses were today selling at fifty cents on the dollar, Buffett would add more shares to Berkshire's portfolio.

We also know Buffett's discipline of operating only within his "circle of competence." Think of this circle of competence as the cumulative history of your experience. If someone had successfully operated a certain business within a certain industry for a decade or more, we would say that person had achieved a high level of competence for the task at hand. However, if someone else had only a few years' experience operating a new business, we could reasonably question that person's level of competence. Perhaps in Buffett's rational mind, the sum total of his business experience in studying and operating the businesses in Berkshire's portfolio sets the bar of competence so high that it would be difficult to achieve a similar level of insight into a new industry.

So perhaps Buffett faces a dilemma. Within his circle of competence, the types of stocks he likes to purchase are not currently selling at discounted prices. At the same time, outside his circle of competence, faster-growing businesses are being born in new industries that have yet to achieve the high level of economic certainty Buffett requires. If this analysis is correct, it explains why there have been no new large buys of common stocks in the past few years.

We would be foolish indeed to assume that because the menu of stocks available for purchase has been reduced, Warren Buffett is left without investment options. Certainly he has been active in the fixed-income market, including taking a significant position in high-yield bonds in 2002. He is alert for the periodic arbitrage opportunity as well, but considering the amount of capital Buffett needs to deploy to make meaningful returns, the arbitrage markets are perhaps not as fruitful as they once were.

But Berkshire Hathaway shareholders should not feel they are being deprived of opportunities. Too often, shareholders forget one of the most important owner-related business principles Buffett outlines each year in the annual report. The fourth principle states, "Our preference would be able to reach our goal [of maximizing Berkshire's average annual rate of gain in intrinsic value] by directly owning a diversified group of businesses that generate cash and consistently earn above-average returns on capital. Our second choice is to own parts of similar businesses attained primarily through the purchases of marketable common stocks."

In Berkshire's early years, owning common stocks made the most sense economically. Now, as common stock prices have risen dramatically and the purchasing power of Berkshire's retained earnings has mushroomed, the strategy of buying whole businesses, which is Buffett's stated preference, has come to the forefront.

There is a personal factor as well. We know that Buffett greatly enjoys his relationships with his operating managers and takes a great deal of pride in Berkshire's collection of operating businesses. Conversely, the angst he has endured by being a shareholder of publicly traded companies, with the issues of executive compensation and questionable capital reinvestment strategies that accompany ownership, may make being a shareholder less appealing for Buffett today than it used to be. If the economics are not compelling, why would Buffett choose to endure the corporate governance fiascos associated with being a major shareholder?

The only activity Buffett involves himself in with Berkshire's operating businesses is setting executive compensation and allocating the profits. Inside Berkshire's world, these decisions are highly rational. Outside in the stock market, management decisions on executive compensation and capital reallocation do not always reflect rationality.

What does this mean for individual investors? Because Buffett is not actively involved in the stock market, should they automatically pull back as well? Buffett's alternative strategy is to buy businesses outright, an option that is out of reach for most investors. So how should they proceed?

There appear to be two obvious choices. One is to make an investment in Berkshire Hathaway and so participate in the economics of these outstanding businesses. The second choice is to take the Buffett approach to investing, expand your circle of competence by studying intently the business models of the companies participating in the New Economy landscape, and march ahead.

I believe that the fundamental principles that have so long guided Buffett's decisions are uncompromised, and they still carry opportunities for careful investors to outperform the S&P 500. The purpose of this book is to present those principles in a way that thoughtful investors can understand and use.

2

The Education of
Warren Buffett

Very few people can come close to Warren Buffett's investment record, and no one can top it. Through four decades of market ups and downs, he has continued on a steady course with unmatched success. What he does is not flashy, even at times very much out of favor, and yet over and over, he has prevailed over others whose exploits gave them temporary, flash-in-the-pan stardom. He watches, smiles, and continues on his way.

How did Buffett come to his investment philosophy? Who influenced his thinking, and how has he integrated their teachings into action? To put the question another way, how is it that this particular genius turned out so differently?

Warren Buffett's approach to investing is uniquely his own, yet it rests on the bedrock of philosophies absorbed from four powerful figures: Benjamin Graham, Philip Fisher, John Burr Williams, and Charles Munger. Together, they are responsible for Buffett's financial education, both formal and informal. The first three are educators in the classic sense, and the last is Buffett's partner, alter ego, and pal. All have had a major influence on Buffett's thinking; they have much to offer modern-day investors as well.

BENJAMIN GRAHAM

Graham is considered the dean of financial analysis. He was awarded that distinction because "before him there was no [financial analysis] profession and after him they began to call it that."[1] Graham's two most celebrated works are *Security Analysis,* coauthored with David Dodd, and originally published in 1934; and *The Intelligent Investor,* originally published in 1949.

Security Analysis appeared just a few years after the 1929 stock market crash and in the depths of the nation's worst depression. While other academicians sought to explain this economic phenomenon, Graham helped people regain their financial footing and proceed with a profitable course of action.

Graham began his career on Wall Street as a messenger at the brokerage firm of Newburger, Henderson & Loeb, posting bond and stock prices on a blackboard for $12 a week. From messenger, he rose to writing research reports and soon was awarded a partnership in the firm. By 1919, he was earning an annual salary of $600,000; he was twenty-five years old.

In 1926, Graham formed an investment partnership with Jerome Newman. It was this partnership that hired Buffett some thirty years later. Graham-Newman survived the 1929 crash, the Great Depression, World War II, and the Korean War before it dissolved in 1956.

From 1928 through 1956, while at Graham-Newman, Graham taught night courses in finance at Columbia. Few people know that Graham was financially ruined by the 1929 crash. For the second time in his life—the first being when his father died, leaving the family financially unprotected—Graham set about rebuilding his fortune. The haven of academia allowed him the opportunity for reflection and reevaluation. With the counsel of David Dodd, also a professor at Columbia, Graham produced what became the classic treatise on conservative investing: *Security Analysis.* Between them, Graham and Dodd had over fifteen years of investment experience. It took them four years to complete the book.

The essence of *Security Analysis* is that a well-chosen diversified portfolio of common stocks, based on reasonable prices, can be a sound investment. Step by careful step, Graham helps the investor see the logic of his approach.

The first problem that Graham had to contend with was the lack of a universal definition for investment that would distinguish it from speculation. Considering the complexities of the issue, Graham proposed his own definition. "An investment operation is one which, upon thorough analysis, promises safety of principal and a satisfactory return. Operations not meeting these requirements are speculative."[2]

What did he mean by "thorough analysis"? Just this: "the careful study of available facts with the attempt to draw conclusions therefrom based on established principles and sound logic."[3]

The next part of Graham's definition is critical: A true investment must have two qualities—some degree of safety of principal and a satisfactory rate of return. Safety, he cautions, is not absolute; unusual or improbable occurrences can put even a safe bond into default. Rather, investors should look for something that would be considered safe from loss under reasonable conditions.

Satisfactory return—the second necessity—includes not only income but also price appreciation. Graham notes that "satisfactory" is a subjective term. Return can be any amount, however low, as long as the investor acts with intelligence and adheres to the full definition of investment.

Had it not been for the bond market's poor performance, Graham's definition of investing might have been overlooked. But when, between 1929 and 1932, the Dow Jones Bond Average declined from 97.70 to 65.78, bonds could no longer be mindlessly labeled pure investments. Like stocks, not only did bonds lose considerable value but many issuers went bankrupt. What was needed, therefore, was a process that could distinguish the investment characteristics of both stocks and bonds from their speculative counterparts.

Graham reduced the concept of sound investing to a motto he called the "margin of safety." With this motto, he sought to unite all securities, stocks, and bonds in a singular approach to investing.

In essence, a margin of safety exists when securities are selling—for whatever reason—at less than their real value. The notion of buying undervalued securities regardless of market levels was a novel idea in the 1930s and 1940s. Graham's goal was to outline such a strategy.

In Graham's view, establishing a margin-of-safety concept for bonds was not too difficult. It wasn't necessary, he said, to accurately determine the company's future income, but only to note the difference between earnings and fixed charges. If that margin was large enough, the investor would be protected from an unexpected decline in the company's income. If, for example, an analyst reviewed the operating history of a company and discovered that, on average, for the past five years the company was able to earn annually five times its fixed charges, then that company's bonds possessed a margin of safety.

The real test was Graham's ability to adapt the concept for common stocks. He reasoned that if the spread between the price of a stock and the intrinsic value of a company was large enough, the margin-of-safety concept could be used to select stocks.

For this strategy to work systematically, Graham admitted, investors needed a way to identify undervalued stocks. And that meant they needed a technique for determining a company's intrinsic value. Graham's definition of intrinsic value, as it appeared in *Security Analysis,* was "that value which is determined by the facts." These facts included a company's assets, its earnings and dividends, and any future definite prospects.

Graham acknowledged that the single most important factor in determining a company's value was its future earnings power, a calculation that is bound to be imprecise. Simply stated, a company's intrinsic value could be found by estimating the earnings of the company and multiplying the earnings by an appropriate capitalization factor. The company's stability of earnings, assets, dividend policy, and financial health influenced this capitalization factor, or multiplier.

Graham asked us to accept that intrinsic value is an elusive concept. It is distinct from the market's quotation price. Originally, intrinsic value was thought to be the same as a company's book value, or the sum of its real assets minus obligations. This notion led to the early belief that intrinsic value was definite. However, analysts came to know that the value of a company was not only its net real assets but also the value of the earnings that these assets produced. Graham proposed that it was not essential to determine a company's exact intrinsic value; instead, investors should accept an approximate measure or range of value. Even an approximate value, compared against the selling price, would be sufficient to gauge margin of safety.

There are two rules of investing, said Graham. The first rule is *don't lose.* The second rule is *don't forget rule number one.* This "don't lose" philosophy steered Graham toward two approaches for selecting common stocks that, when applied, adhered to the margin of safety. The first approach was buying a company for less than two-thirds of its net asset value, and the second was focusing on stocks with low price-to-earnings (P/E) ratios.

Buying a stock for a price that is less than two-thirds of its net assets fit neatly into Graham's sense of the present and satisfied his desire for some mathematical expectation. Graham gave no weight to a company's plant, property, and equipment. Furthermore, he deducted all the company's short- and long-term liabilities. What remained would be the net current assets. If the stock price was below this per share value, Graham reasoned that a margin of safety existed and a purchase was warranted.

Graham considered this to be a foolproof method of investing, but he acknowledged that waiting for a market correction before making an investment might be unreasonable. He set out to design a second approach to buying stocks. He focused on stocks that were down in price and that sold at a low P/E ratio. Additionally, the company must have some net asset value; it must owe less than its worth.

Over the years, many other investors have searched for similar shortcuts for determining intrinsic value. Low P/E ratios—Graham's first technique—was a general favorite. We have learned, however, that making decisions on P/E ratios alone is not enough to ensure profitable returns. Today, most investors rely on John Burr Williams's classic definition of value, described later in this chapter: The value of any investment is the discounted present value of its future cash flow.

> The basic ideas of investing are to look at stocks as businesses, use market fluctuations to your advantage, and seek a margin of safety. That's what Ben Graham taught us. A hundred years from now they will still be the cornerstones of investing.[4]
>
> WARREN BUFFETT, 1994

Both of Graham's approaches—buying a stock for less than two-thirds of net asset value and buying stocks with low P/E multiples—had a common characteristic. The stocks that Graham selected based on these methods were deeply out of favor with the market. Some macro- or microevent caused the market to price these stocks below their value. Graham felt strongly that these stocks, priced "unjustifiably low," were attractive purchases.

Graham's conviction rested on certain assumptions. First, he believed that the market frequently mispriced stocks, usually because of the human emotions of fear and greed. At the height of optimism, greed moved stocks beyond their intrinsic value, creating an overpriced market. At other times, fear moved prices below intrinsic value, creating an undervalued market. His second assumption was based on the statistical phenomenon known as "reversion to the mean," although he did not use that term. More eloquently, he quoted the poet Horace: "Many shall be restored that now are fallen, and many shall fall that now are in honor." However stated, by statistician or poet, Graham believed that an investor could profit from the corrective forces of an inefficient market.

PHILIP FISHER

While Graham was writing *Security Analysis,* Philip Fisher was beginning his career as an investment counselor. After graduating from Stanford's Graduate School of Business Administration, Fisher began work as an analyst at the Anglo London & Paris National Bank in San Francisco. In less than two years, he was made head of the bank's statistical department. It was from this perch that he witnessed the 1929 stock market crash. After a brief and unproductive career with a local brokerage house, Fisher decided to start his own investment counseling firm. On March 1, 1931, Fisher & Company began soliciting clients.

Starting an investment counseling firm in the early 1930s might have appeared foolhardy, but Fisher figured he had two advantages. First, any investors who had any money left after the crash were probably very unhappy with their existing broker. Second, in the midst of the Great Depression, businesspeople had plenty of time to sit and talk with Fisher.

At Stanford, one of Fisher's business classes had required him to accompany his professor on periodic visits to companies in the San Francisco area. The professor would get the business managers to talk about their operations, and often helped them solve an immediate problem. Driving back to Stanford, Fisher and his professor would recap what they observed about the companies and managers they visited. "That hour each week," Fisher said, "was the most useful training I ever received."[5]

From these experiences, Fisher came to believe that people could make superior profits by (1) investing in companies with above-average potential and (2) aligning themselves with the most capable management. To isolate these exceptional companies, Fisher developed a point system that qualified a company by the characteristics of its business and its management.

As to the first—companies with above-average potential—the characteristic that most impressed Fisher was a company's ability to grow sales over the years at rates greater than the industry average.[6] That growth, in turn, usually was a combination of two factors: a significant commitment to research and development, and an effective sales organization. A company could develop outstanding products and services but unless they were "expertly merchandised," the research and development effort would never translate into revenues.

In Fisher's view, however, market potential alone is only half the story; the other half is consistent profits. "All the sales growth in the world won't produce the right type of investment vehicle if, over the years, profits do not grow correspondingly," he said.[7] Accordingly, Fisher examined a company's profit margins, its dedication to maintaining and improving those margins and, finally, its cost analysis and accounting controls.

No company, said Fisher, will be able to sustain its profitability unless it is able to break down the costs of doing business while simultaneously understanding the cost of each step in the manufacturing process. To do so, he explained, a company must instill adequate accounting controls and cost analysis. This cost information, Fisher noted, enables a company to direct its resources to those products or services with the highest economic potential. Furthermore, accounting controls will help identify snags in a company's operations. These snags, or inefficiencies, act as an early warning device aimed at protecting the company's overall profitability.

Fisher's sensitivity about a company's profitability was linked with another concern: a company's ability to grow in the future without requiring equity financing. If a company is able to grow only by selling stocks, he said, the larger number of shares outstanding will cancel out any benefit that stockholders might realize from the company's growth.

A company with high profit margins, explained Fisher, is better able to generate funds internally and thus sustain growth without diluting existing shareholders' ownership.

Fisher's second touchstone for identifying outstanding companies was the quality of management. Superior managers, he believed, are determined to develop new products and services that will continue to spur sales growth long after current products or services are largely exploited. Management should be establishing policies to ensure consistent gains for ten to twenty years, even at the cost of subordinating immediate profits. Subordinate, he emphasized, not sacrifice. The above-average manager can implement the company's long-range plans while simultaneously focusing on daily operations.

Another trait that Fisher considered critical: Does the business have a management of unquestionable integrity and honesty? Do the managers behave as if they are trustees for the stockholders or are they concerned only with their own well-being?

One way to determine their intention, Fisher confided, is to observe how managers communicate with shareholders. All businesses, good and bad, will experience periods of unexpected difficulties. Commonly, when business is good, management talks freely; but when business declines, some managers clam up. How management responds to difficulties, Fisher noted, tells a lot about the company.

For a business to be successful, he argued, management must also develop good working relations with all its employees. Employees should genuinely feel that their company is a good place to work. Blue-collar employees should feel that they are treated with respect and decency. Executive employees should feel that promotion is based on ability, not favoritism.

Fisher also considered the depth of management. Has the chief executive officer a talented team, he asked, and is the CEO able to delegate authority to run parts of the business?

Finally, Fisher examined the specific business and management characteristics of a company and compared it with other businesses in the same industry. In this search, Fisher tried to uncover clues that might help him understand the superiority of a company in relation to its competitors.

He argued that reading only the financial reports of a company is not enough to justify an investment. The essential step in prudent investing, he explained, is to uncover as much about a company as possible from those individuals who are familiar with the company. Fisher admitted this was a catchall inquiry that he called "scuttlebutt." Today we might call it the business grapevine. If handled properly, Fisher claimed, scuttlebutt could provide the investor with substantial clues to identify outstanding investments.

Fisher's scuttlebutt investigation led him to interview as many sources as possible. He talked with customers and vendors. He sought out former employees as well as consultants who had worked for the company. He contacted research scientists in universities, government employees, and trade association executives. He also interviewed competitors. Although executives may sometimes hesitate to disclose too much about their own company, Fisher found that they never lack an opinion about their competitors.

Most investors are unwilling to commit the time and energy Fisher felt was necessary for understanding a company. Developing a scuttlebutt network and arranging interviews are time consuming; replicating the scuttlebutt process for each company under consideration can be exhausting. Fisher found a simple way to reduce his workload—he reduced the number of companies he owned. He always said he would rather own a few outstanding companies than a large number of average businesses. Generally, his portfolios included fewer than ten companies, and often three to four companies represented 75 percent of his entire equity portfolio.

Fisher believed that, to be successful, investors needed to do just a few things well. One was investing only in companies that were within their circle of competence. Fisher himself made that mistake in the beginning. "I began investing outside the industries which I believed I thoroughly understood, in completely different spheres of activity; situations where I did not have comparable background knowledge."[8]

JOHN BURR WILLIAMS

John Burr Williams graduated from Harvard University in 1923 and went on to Harvard Business School, where he got his first taste of economic forecasting and security analysis. After Harvard, he worked as a security analyst at two well-known Wall Street firms. He was there through the heady days of the 1920s and the disastrous crash of 1929 and its aftermath. That experience convinced him that to be a good investor, one also needs to be a good economist.[9]

So, in 1932 at the age of 30 and already a good investor, he enrolled in Harvard's Graduate School of Arts and Sciences. Working from a firm belief that what happened in the economy could affect the value of stocks, he had decided to earn an advanced degree in economics.

When it came time to choose a topic for his doctoral dissertation, Williams asked advice from Joseph Schumpeter, the noted Austrian economist best known for his theory of creative destruction, who was then a member of the economics faculty. Schumpeter suggested that Williams look at the "intrinsic value of a common stock," saying it would fit Williams's background and experience. Williams later commented that perhaps Schumpeter had a more cynical motive: The topic would keep Williams from "running afoul" of the rest of the faculty, "none of whom would want to challenge my own ideas on investments."[10] Nonetheless, Schumpeter's suggestion was the impetus for Williams's famous doctoral dissertation, which, as *The Theory of Investment Value,* has influenced financial analysts and investors ever since.

Williams finished writing his dissertation in 1937. Even though he had not yet defended it—and to the great indignation of several professors—he submitted the work to Macmillan for publication. Macmillan declined. So did McGraw-Hill. Both decided that the book had too many algebraic symbols. Finally, in 1938, Williams found a publisher in Harvard University Press, but only after he agreed to pay part of the printing cost. Two years later, Williams took his oral exam and, after some intense arguments over the causes of the Great Depression, passed.

The Theory of Investment Value is a genuine classic. For sixty years, it has served as the foundation on which many famous economists—Eugene Fama, Harry Markowitz, and Franco Modigliani, to name a few—have based their own work. Warren Buffett calls it one of the most important investment books ever written.

Williams's theory, known today as the *dividend discount model,* or discounted net cash-flow analysis, provides a way to put a value on a stock or a bond. Like many important ideas, it can be reduced to a very simple precept: To know what a security is worth today, estimate all the cash it will earn over its lifetime and then discount that total back to a present value. It is the underlying methodology that Warren Buffett uses to evaluate stocks and companies.

Buffett condensed Williams's theory as: "The value of a business is determined by the net cash flows expected to occur over the life of the business discounted at an appropriate interest rate." Williams described it this way: "A cow for her milk; a hen for her eggs; and a stock, by heck, for her dividends."[11]

Williams's model is a two-step process. First it measures cash flows to determine a company's current and future worth. How to estimate cash flows? One quick measure is dividends paid to shareholders. For companies that do not distribute dividends, Williams believed that in theory all retained earnings should eventually turn into dividends. Once a company reaches its mature stage, it would not need to reinvest its earnings for growth so the management could start distributing the earnings in the form of dividends. Williams wrote, "If earnings not paid out in dividends are all successfully reinvested, then these earnings should produce dividends later; if not, then they are money lost. In short, a stock is worth only what you can get out of it."[12]

The second step is to discount those estimated cash flows, to allow for some uncertainty. We can never be exactly sure what a company will do, how its products will sell, or what management will do or not do to improve the business. There is always an element of risk, particularly for stocks, even though Williams's theory applies equally well to bonds.

What, then, should we use as a discount rate? Williams himself is not explicit on this point, apparently believing his readers could determine for themselves what would be appropriate. Buffett's measuring stick is very straightforward: He uses either the interest rate for long-term (meaning ten-year) U.S. bonds, or when interest rates are very low, he uses the average cumulative rate of return of the overall stock market.

By using what amounts to a risk-free rate, Buffett has modified Williams's original thesis. Because he limits his purchases to those with Ben Graham's margin of safety, Buffett ensures that the risk is covered in the transaction itself, and therefore he believes that using a risk-free rate for discounting is appropriate.

Peter Bernstein, in his book *Capital Ideas,* writes that Graham's system is a set of rules, whereas Williams's dividend discount model is a theory; but "both approaches end up recommending the same kinds of stocks for purchase."[13]

Warren Buffett has used both, with stellar success.

CHARLES MUNGER

When Warren Buffett began his investment partnership in Omaha in 1956, he had just over $100,000 in capital to work with. One early task, therefore, was to persuade additional investors to sign on. He was making his usual careful, detailed pitch to neighbors Dr. and Mrs. Edwin Davis, when suddenly Dr. Davis interrupted him and abruptly announced they'd give him $100,000. When Buffett asked why, Davis replied, "Because you remind me of Charlie Munger."[14]

Charlie who?

Even though both men grew up in Omaha and had many acquaintances in common, they did not actually meet until 1959. By that time, Munger had moved to southern California, but he returned to Omaha for a visit when his father died. Dr. Davis decided it was time the two young men met and brought them together at a dinner in a local restaurant. It was the beginning of an extraordinary partnership.

Munger, the son of a lawyer and grandson of a federal judge, had established a successful law practice in the Los Angeles area, but his interest in the stock market was already strong. At that first dinner, the two young men found much to talk about, including securities. From then on, they communicated often, with Buffett frequently urging Munger to quit law and to concentrate on investing. For a while, he did both. In 1962, he formed an investment partnership much like Buffett's, while maintaining his law practice. Three very successful years later, he left the law altogether, although to this day he has an office in the firm that bears his name.

Munger's investment partnership in Los Angeles, and Buffett's in Omaha, were similar in approach; both sought to purchase some discount to underlying value. (They also enjoyed similar results, both of them outperforming the Dow Jones Industrial Average by impressive margins.) It is not surprising, then, that they bought some of the same stocks. Munger, like Buffett, began buying shares of Blue Chip Stamps in the late 1960s, and eventually he became chairman of its board. When

Berkshire and Blue Chip Stamps merged in 1978, he became Berkshire's vice chairman, a position he still holds.

The working relationship between Munger and Buffett was not formalized in an official partnership agreement, but it has evolved over the years into something perhaps even closer, more symbiotic. Even before Munger joined the Berkshire board, the two made many investment decisions together, often conferring daily; gradually their business affairs became more and more interlinked.

Today Munger continues as vice chairman of Berkshire Hathaway and also serves as chairman of Wesco Financial, which is 80 percent owned by Berkshire and holds many of the same investments. In every way, he functions as Buffett's acknowledged comanaging partner and alter ego. To get a sense of how closely the two are aligned, we have only to count the number of times Buffett reports "Charlie and I" did this, or decided that, or believe this, or looked into that, or think this—almost as if "Charlie-and-I" were the name of one person.

To their working relationship, Munger brought not only financial acumen but the foundation of business law. He also brought an intellectual perspective that is quite different from Buffett's. Munger is passionately interested in many areas of knowledge—science, history, philosophy, psychology, mathematics—and believes that each of those fields holds important concepts that thoughtful people can, and should, apply to all their endeavors, including investment decisions. He calls them "the big ideas," and they are the core of his well-known notion of "latticework of mental models" for investors.[15]

All these threads together—financial knowledge, background in the law, and appreciation of lessons from other disciplines—produced in Munger a somewhat different investment philosophy from that of Buffett. Whereas Buffett was still searching for opportunities at bargain prices, Munger believed in paying a fair price for quality companies. He can be very persuasive.

It's far better to buy a wonderful company at a fair price than a fair company at a wonderful price.[16]

WARREN BUFFETT

It was Munger who convinced Buffett that paying three times book value for See's Candy was actually a good deal (see Chapter 4 for the full story). That was the beginning of a plate-tectonic shift in Buffett's thinking, and he happily acknowledges that it was Charlie who pushed him in a new direction. Both would quickly add that when you find a quality company that also happens to be available at a discounted price, then you've struck oil—or, in Berkshire's case, the next best thing: Coca-Cola (see Chapter 4).

One reason Buffett and Munger fit so well is that both men possess an uncompromising attitude toward commonsense business principles. Like Buffett, who endured poor returns in the insurance industry and for a time refused to write policies, Charlie, in his function as CEO of Wesco, refused to make loans when confronted with an unruly savings and loan industry. Both exhibit managerial qualities necessary to run high-quality businesses. Berkshire Hathaway's shareholders are blessed in having managing partners who look after their interest and help them make money in all economic environments. With Buffett's policy on mandatory retirement—he does not believe in it—Berkshire's shareholders will continue to benefit not from one mind but two long into the future.

A BLENDING OF INFLUENCES

Shortly after Graham's death in 1976, Buffett became the designated steward of Graham's value approach to investing. Indeed, Buffett's name became synonymous with value investing. It is easy to see why. He was the most famous of Graham's dedicated students, and Buffett never missed an opportunity to acknowledge the intellectual debt he owed to Graham. Even today, Buffett considers Graham to be the one individual, after his father, who had the most influence on his investment life.[17]

How, then, does Buffett reconcile his intellectual indebtedness to Graham with stock purchases like the Washington Post Company (1973) and the Coca-Cola Company (1988)? Neither passed Graham's strict financial test for purchase, yet Buffett made significant investments in both.

As early as 1965, Buffett was becoming aware that Graham's strategy of buying cheap stocks was not ideal.[18] Following his mentor's approach of searching for companies that were selling for less than their net working capital, Buffett bought some genuine losers. Several companies that he had bought at a cheap price (hence they met Graham's test for purchase) were cheap because their underlying businesses were suffering.

From his earliest investment mistakes, Buffett began moving away from Graham's strict teachings. "I evolved," he admitted, "but I didn't go from ape to human or human to ape in a nice even manner."[19] He was beginning to appreciate the qualitative nature of certain companies, compared with the quantitative aspects of others. Despite that, however, he still found himself searching for bargains, sometimes with horrible results. "My punishment," he confessed, "was an education in the economics of short-line farm implementation manufacturers (Dempster Mill Manufacturing), third-place department stores (Hochschild-Kohn), and New England textile manufacturers (Berkshire Hathaway)."[20] Buffett's evolution was delayed, he admitted, because what Graham taught him was so valuable.

When evaluating stocks, Graham did not think about the specifics of the businesses. Nor did he ponder the capabilities of management. He limited his research investigation to corporate filings and annual reports. If there was a mathematical probability of making money because the share price was less than the assets of the company, Graham purchased the company, regardless of its business or its management. To increase the probability of success, he purchased as many of these statistical equations as possible.

If Graham's teachings were limited to these precepts, Buffett would have had little regard for him. But the margin-of-safety theory that Graham emphasized was so important to Buffett that he could overlook all other current weaknesses of Graham's methodology. Even today, Buffett continues to embrace Graham's primary idea, the theory of *margin of safety*. "Forty-two years after reading that," Buffett noted, "I still think those are the three right words."[21] The key lesson that Buffett took from Graham was that successful investing involved purchasing stocks when their market price was at a significant discount to the underlying business value.

In addition to the margin-of-safety theory, which became the intellectual framework of Buffett's thinking, Graham helped Buffett appreciate the folly of following stock market fluctuations. Stocks have an investment characteristic and a speculative characteristic, Graham taught, and the speculative characteristics are a consequence of people's fear and greed. These emotions, present in most investors, cause stock prices to gyrate far above and, more important, far below a company's intrinsic value, thus presenting a margin of safety. Graham taught Buffett that if he could insulate himself from the emotional whirlwinds of the stock market, he had an opportunity to exploit the irrational behavior of other investors, who purchased stocks based on emotion, not logic.

From Graham, Buffett learned how to think independently. If he reached a logical conclusion based on sound judgment, Graham counseled Buffett, he should not be dissuaded just because others disagree. "You are neither right or wrong because the crowd disagrees with you," he wrote. "You are right because your data and reasoning are right."[22]

Phil Fisher in many ways was the exact opposite of Ben Graham. Fisher believed that to make sound decisions, investors needed to become fully informed about a business. That meant they needed to investigate all aspects of the company. They needed to look beyond the numbers and learn about the business itself because that information mattered a great deal. They also needed to study the attributes of the company's management, for management's abilities could affect the value of the underlying business. They should learn as much as they could about the industry in which the company operated, and about its competitors. Every source of information should be exploited.

Appearing on the PBS show *Money World* in 1993, Buffett was asked what investment advice he would give a money manager just starting out. "I'd tell him to do exactly what I did 40-odd years ago, which is to learn about every company in the United States that has publicly traded securities."

Moderator Adam Smith protested, "But there's 27,000 public companies."

"Well," said Buffett, "start with the A's."[23]

From Fisher, Buffett learned the value of scuttlebutt. Throughout the years, Buffett has developed an extensive network of contacts who assist him in evaluating businesses.

Finally, Fisher taught Buffett the benefits of focusing on just a few investments. He believed that it was a mistake to teach investors that putting their eggs in several baskets reduces risk. The danger in purchasing too many stocks, he felt, is that it becomes impossible to watch all the eggs in all the baskets. In his view, buying shares in a company without taking the time to develop a thorough understanding of the business was far more risky than having limited diversification.

John Burr Williams provided Buffett with a methodology for calculating the intrinsic value of a business, which is a cornerstone of his investing approach.

The differences between Graham and Fisher are apparent. Graham, the quantitative analyst, emphasized only those factors that could be measured: fixed assets, current earnings, and dividends. His investigative research was limited to corporate filings and annual reports. He spent no time interviewing customers, competitors, or managers.

Fisher's approach was the antithesis of Graham. Fisher, the qualitative analyst, emphasized those factors that he believed increased the value of a company: principally, future prospects and management capability. Whereas Graham was interested in purchasing only cheap stocks, Fisher was interested in purchasing companies that had the potential to increase their intrinsic value over the long term. He would go to great lengths, including conducting extensive interviews, to uncover bits of information that might improve his selection process.

Although Graham's and Fisher's investment approach differ, notes Buffett, they "parallel in the investment world."[24] Taking the liberty of rephrasing, I would say that instead of paralleling, in Warren Buffett they dovetail: His investment approach combines qualitative understanding of the business and its management (as taught by Fisher) and a quantitative understanding of price and value (as taught by Graham).

Warren Buffett once said, "I'm 15 percent Fisher and 85 percent Benjamin Graham."[25] That remark has been widely quoted, but it is important to remember that it was made in 1969. In the intervening years, Buffett has made a gradual but definite shift toward Fisher's philosophy of buying a select few good businesses and owning those businesses for several years. My hunch is that if he were to make a similar statement today, the balance would come pretty close to 50/50.

Without question, it was Charlie Munger who was most responsible for moving Buffett toward Fisher's thinking.

In a real sense, Munger is the active embodiment of Fisher's qualitative theories. From the start, Charlie had a keen appreciation of the value of a better business, and the wisdom of paying a reasonable price for it. Through their years together, Charlie has continued to preach the wisdom of paying up for a good business.

In one important respect, however, Munger is also the present-day echo of Ben Graham. Years earlier, Graham had taught Buffett the twofold significance of emotion in investing—the mistakes it triggers for those who base irrational decisions on it, and the opportunities it thus creates for those who can avoid falling into the same traps. Munger, through his readings in psychology, has continued to develop that theme. He calls it the "psychology of misjudgment," a notion we look at more fully in Chapter 11; and through persistent emphasis, he keeps it an integral part of Berkshire's decision making. It is one of his most important contributions.

Buffett's dedication to Ben Graham, Phil Fisher, John Burr Williams, and Charlie Munger is understandable. Graham gave Buffett the intellectual basis for investing, the margin of safety, and helped Buffett learn how to master his emotions to take advantage of market fluctuations. Fisher gave Buffett an updated, workable methodology that enabled him to identify good long-term investments and manage a portfolio over the long term, and taught the value of focusing on just a few good companies. Williams gave him a mathematical model for calculating true value. Munger helped Buffett appreciate the economic returns that come from buying and owning great businesses. The frequent confusion surrounding Buffett's investment actions is easily understood when we acknowledge that Buffett is the synthesis of all four men.

"It is not enough to have good intelligence," Descartes wrote; "the principal thing is to apply it well." It is the application that separates Buffett from other investment managers. Many of his peers are highly intelligent, disciplined, and dedicated. Buffett stands above them all because of his formidable ability to integrate the strategies of the four wise men into a single cohesive approach.

3

"Our Main Business Is Insurance"

The Early Days of Berkshire Hathaway

When the Buffett Partnership took control of Berkshire Hathaway in 1965, stockholders' equity had dropped by half and loss from operations exceeded $10 million. Buffett and Ken Chace, who managed the textile group, labored intensely to turn the textile mills around. Results were disappointing; returns on equity struggled to reach double digits.

Amid the gloom, there was one bright spot, a sign of things to come: Buffett's deft handling of the company's common stock portfolio. When Buffett took over, the corporation had $2.9 million in marketable securities. By the end of the first year, Buffett had enlarged the securities account to $5.4 million. In 1967, the dollar return from investing was three times the return of the entire textile division, which had ten times the equity base.

Nonetheless, over the next decade Buffett had to come to grips with certain realities. First, the very nature of the textile business made high returns on equity improbable. Textiles are commodities and commodities by definition have a difficult time differentiating their products from those of competitors. Foreign competition, which employed a cheaper labor force, was squeezing profit margins. Second, to stay competitive, the textile mills would require significant capital improvements—a prospect that is frightening in an inflationary environment and disastrous if the business returns are anemic.

Buffett made no attempt to hide the difficulties, but on several occasions he explained his thinking: The textile mills were the largest employer in the area; the work force was an older age group with relatively nontransferable skills; management had shown a high degree of enthusiasm; the unions were being reasonable; and lastly, he believed that the textile business could attain some profits.

However, Buffett made it clear that he expected the textile group to earn positive returns on modest capital expenditures. "I won't close down a business of subnormal profitability merely to add a fraction of a point to our corporate returns," said Buffett. "I also feel it inappropriate for even an exceptionally profitable company to fund an operation once it appears to have unending losses in prospect. Adam Smith would disagree with my first proposition and Karl Marx would disagree with my second; the middle ground," he explained "is the only position that leaves me comfortable."[1]

In 1980, the annual report revealed ominous clues for the future of the textile group. That year, the group lost its prestigious lead-off position in the Chairman's Letter. By the next year, textiles were not discussed in the letter at all. Then, the inevitable: In July 1985, Buffett closed the books on the textile group, thus ending a business that had started some one hundred years earlier.

The experience was not a complete failure. First, Buffett learned a valuable lesson about corporate turnarounds: They seldom succeed. Second, the textile group generated enough capital in the earlier years to buy an insurance company and that is a much brighter story.

THE INSURANCE BUSINESS

In March 1967, Berkshire Hathaway purchased, for $8.6 million, the outstanding stock of two insurance companies headquartered in Omaha:

National Indemnity Company and National Fire & Marine Insurance Company. It was the beginning of a phenomenal success story. Berkshire Hathaway the textile company would not long survive, but Berkshire Hathaway the investment company that encompassed it was about to take off.

To appreciate the phenomenon, we must recognize the true value of owning an insurance company. Sometimes insurance companies are good investments, sometimes not. They are, however, always terrific investment *vehicles*. Policyholders, by paying their premiums, provide a constant stream of cash, known as the float. Insurance companies set aside some of this cash (called the reserve) to pay claims each year, based on their best estimates, and invest the rest. To give themselves a high degree of liquidity, since it is seldom possible to know exactly when claim payments will need to be paid, most opt to invest in marketable securities—primarily stocks and bonds. Thus Warren Buffett had acquired not only two modestly healthy companies, but a cast-iron vehicle for managing investments.

For a seasoned stock picker like Buffett, it was a perfect match. In just two years, he increased the combined stocks and bonds portfolio of the two companies from $31.9 million to nearly $42 million. At the same time, the insurance businesses themselves were doing quite well. In just one year, the net income of National Indemnity rose from $1.6 million to $2.2 million.

Buffett's early success in insurance led him to expand aggressively into this group. Over the next decade, he purchased three additional insurance companies and organized five more. And he has not slowed down. As of 2004, Berkshire owns 38 insurance companies, including two giants, the Government Employees Insurance Company (GEICO) and General Re, each of which has several subsidiaries.

Government Employees Insurance Company

Warren Buffett first became acquainted with GEICO while a student at Columbia because his mentor, Ben Graham, was a chairman of its board of directors. A favorite part of the Buffett lore is the now-familiar story of the young student visiting the company's offices on a Saturday morning and pounding on the door until a janitor let him in.

Buffett then spent five hours getting an education in the insurance business from the only person working that day: Lorimer Davidson, an investment officer who eventually became the company's CEO. What he learned intrigued him.

GEICO had been founded on a couple of simple but fairly revolutionary concepts: If you insure only people with good driving records, you'll have fewer claims; and if you sell direct to customers, without agents, you keep overhead costs down.

Back home in Omaha and working for his father's brokerage firm, a very young Warren Buffett wrote a report of GEICO for a financial journal in which he noted, in what may be the understatement of that decade, "There is reason to believe the major portion of growth lies ahead."[2] Buffett put $10,282 in the company, then sold it the next year at 50 percent profit. But he always kept track of the company.

Throughout the 1950s and 1960s, GEICO prospered. But then it began to stumble. For several years, the company had tried to expand its customer base by underpricing and relaxing its eligibility requirements, and two years in a row it seriously miscalculated the amount needed for reserves (out of which claims are paid). The combined effect of these mistakes was that, by the mid-1970s, the once-bright company was near bankruptcy.

When the stock price dropped from $61 to $2 a share in 1976, Warren Buffett started buying. Over a period of five years, with an unshakable belief that it was a strong company with its basic competitive advantages unchanged, he invested $45.7 million in GEICO.

The very next year, 1977, the company was profitable again. Over the next two decades, GEICO had positive underwriting ratios—meaning that it took in more in premiums than it paid out in claims—in every year but one. In the industry, where negative ratios are the rule rather than the exception, that kind of record is almost unheard of. And that excess float gives GEICO tremendous resources for investments, brilliantly managed by a remarkable man named Lou Simpson.

By 1991, Berkshire owned nearly half (48 percent) of GEICO. The insurance company's impressive performance, and Buffett's interest in the company, continued to climb. In 1994, serious discussions began about Berkshire's buying the entire company, and a year later the final deal was announced. At that point, Berkshire owned 51 percent of GEICO, and agreed to purchase the rest for $2.3 billion. This at a time when most of the insurance industry struggled with profitability and most investors stayed away in droves. By the time all the paperwork was done, it was early 1996. At that point, GEICO officially became a wholly owned unit of Berkshire Hathaway, managed independently from Berkshire's other insurance holdings.

Despite a rough spot or two, Buffett's trust in the basic concept of GEICO has been handsomely rewarded. From 1996 to 2003, the company increased its share of market from 2.7 to 5 percent. The biggest rough spot was the year 2000, when many policyholders switched to other insurers, and a very large, very expensive advertising campaign ($260 million) failed to produce as much new business as projected.

Things began to stabilize in 2001, and by 2002, GEICO was solidly back on track, with substantial growth in market share and in profits. That year, GEICO took in $6.9 billion in premiums, a huge jump from the $2.9 billion booked in 1996, the year Berkshire took full ownership. In April 2003, the company hit a major milestone when it added its five-millionth policyholder. By year-end 2003, those five million policyholders had sent in premiums totaling $8.1 billion.

Because its profit margins increase the longer policyholders stay with the company, GEICO focuses on building long-term relationships with customers. When Buffett took over the company in 1996, he put in a new incentive system that rewards this focus. Half the bonuses and profit sharing are based on policies that are at least one year old, the other half on policyholder growth.

The average GEICO customer has more than one vehicle insured, pays premiums of approximately $1,100 year after year, but maintains an excellent driving record. As Buffett once pointed out, the economics of that formula are simple: "Cash is pouring in rather than going out."[3]

From the early bargain days of $2 a share in 1976, Buffett paid close to $70 a share for the rest of the company in 1996. He makes no apologies. He considers GEICO a unique company with unlimited potential, something worth paying a hefty price for. In this perspective— if you want the very best companies, you have to be willing to pay up when they become available—Buffett's partner, Charlie Munger, has been a profound influence.

Knowing their close working relationship, it's a fair bet that Munger had a lot to say about Berkshire's other big insurance decision.

General Re Corporation

In 1996 Buffett paid $2.3 billion to buy the half of GEICO he didn't already own. Two years later, he paid *seven times* that amount—about $16 billion in Berkshire Hathaway stock—to acquire a reinsurance company called General Re.[4] It was his biggest acquisition by far; some have called it the single biggest event in Berkshire history.[5]

Reinsurance is a sector of the insurance industry not well known to the general public, for it doesn't deal in the familiar products of life, homeowner's, or auto insurance. In simplest terms, reinsurers insure other insurance companies. Through a contract that spells out how the premiums and the losses are to be apportioned, a reinsurer takes on some percentage of the original company's risk. This allows the primary insurer to assume a higher level of risk, reduces its needs for operating capital, and moderates loss ratios.

For its part, the reinsurer receives a share of premiums earned, to invest as it sees fit. At General Re, that investment had been primarily in bonds. This, in fact, was a key part of Buffett's strategy in buying the company.

When Buffett acquired it, General Re owned approximately $19 billion in bonds, $5 billion in stocks, and $15 billion in float. By using Berkshire stock to buy the company and its heavy bond portfolio, Buffett in one neat step shifted the balance of Berkshire's overall holdings from 80 percent stocks to 60 percent. When the IRS ruled late in 1998 that the merger involved no capital gains, that meant he had managed to "sell" almost 20 percent of Berkshire's equity holdings, thus deftly sidestepping the worst of price volatility, essentially tax free.

The only significant staff change that followed the merger was the elimination of General Re's investment unit. Some 150 people had been in charge of deciding where to invest the company's funds; they were replaced with just one individual—Warren Buffett.

Just after Berkshire bought General Re, the company had one of its worst years. In 1999, GenRe, as it is known, paid claims resulting from natural disasters (a major hailstorm in Australia, earthquakes in Turkey, and a devastating series of storms in Europe), from the largest house fire in history, and from high-profile movie flops (the company had insured box-office receipts). To make matters worse, GenRe was part of a grouping of several insurers and reinsurers that became ensnarled in a workers' compensation tangle that ended in multiple litigation and a loss exposure of approximately $275 million for two years running (1998 and 1999).

The problem, it later became apparent, was that GenRe was underpricing its product. Premiums coming in, remember, will ultimately be paid to policyholders who have claims. When more is paid out than comes in, the result is an underwriting loss. The ratio of that loss to the premiums received in any given year is known as the cost of float for that year. When the two parts of the formula are even, the cost of float is zero—which is a good thing. Even better is less than zero, or negative float cost, which is what happens when premiums outstrip loss payments, producing an underwriting profit. This is referred to as negative cost of float, but it is actually a positive: The insurer is literally being paid to hold the capital.

Float is a wonderful thing, Buffett has often commented, unless it comes at too high a cost. Premiums that are too low or losses that are unexpectedly high adversely affect the cost of float; when both occur simultaneously, the cost of float skyrockets.

And that is just what happened with GenRe, although it wasn't completely obvious at first. Buffett had realized as early as 1999 that the policies were underpriced, and he began working to correct it. The effects of such changes are not felt overnight, however, and in 2000, General Re experienced an underwriting loss of $1.6 billion, producing a float cost of 6 percent. Still, Buffett felt able to report in his 2000 letter to shareholders that the situation was improving and he expected the upward trend to continue. Then, in a moment of terrible, unintentional foreshadowing, he added, "Absent a mega-catastrophe, we expect our float cost to fall in 2001."[6] Some six months later, on September 11, the nation had an enormous hole torn in its soul by a mega-catastrophe we had never imagined possible.

In a letter to shareholders that was sent out with the third quarter 2001 report, Buffett wrote, "A mega-catastrophe is no surprise. One will occur from time to time, and this will not be our last. We did not, however, price for *manmade* mega-cats, and we were foolish in not doing so."[7]

Buffett estimated that Berkshire's underwriting losses from the terrorist attacks on September 11 totaled $2.275 billion, of which $1.7 billion fell to General Re. That level of loss galvanized a change at GenRe. More aggressive steps were taken to make sure the policies were priced correctly, and that sufficient reserves were in place to pay claims. These corrective maneuvers were successful. In 2002, after five years of losses, GenRe reported its first underwriting profit, prompting Buffett to announce at the 2002 annual meeting, "We're back."

Warren Buffett, as is well known, takes the long view. He is the first to admit, with his trademark candor, that he had not seen the problems at GenRe. That in itself is interesting, and oddly ironic, to Buffett's observers. That such an experienced hand as Buffett could miss the problems demonstrates the complexity of the insurance industry. Had those problems been apparent, I have no doubt Buffett would not have paid the price he did for GenRe. I'm also reasonably certain he would have proceeded, however, because his line of sight goes to the long term.

The reinsurance industry offers huge potential, and a well-run reinsurance business can create enormous value for shareholders. Buffett knows that better than most. So, even though GenRe's pricing errors created problems in the short run, and even though he bought those problems along with the company, this does not negate his basic conclusion that a well-managed reinsurance company could create great value for Berkshire. In a situation such as this, Buffett's instinct is to fix the problems, not unload the company.

As he usually does, Buffett credits the company's managers with restoring underwriting discipline by setting rational prices for the policies and setting up sufficient reserves. Under their leadership, he wrote in the 2003 letter to shareholders, General Re "will be a powerful engine driving Berkshire's future profitability."[8]

At this writing, General Re is one of only two major global reinsurers with a AAA rating. The other is also a Berkshire company: the National Indemnity reinsurance operation.

Berkshire Hathaway Reinsurance Group

The National Indemnity insurance operation inside Berkshire today is a far cry from the company that Buffett purchased in 1967. Different, that is, in operation and scope, but not in underlying philosophy.

One aspect of National Indemnity that did not exist under its founder, Jack Ringwalt, is the reinsurance division. Today, this division, run from National Indemnity's office in Stamford, Connecticut, contributes powerfully to Berkshire's revenues.

The reinsurance group is headed by Ajit Jain, born in India and educated at the Indian Institute of Technology and at Harvard. He recently joked that when he joined Berkshire in 1982, he didn't even know how to spell reinsurance, yet Jain has built a tremendously profitable operation that earns Buffett's highest praise year in and year out.[9]

Working on the foundation of Berkshire's financial strength, the reinsurance group is able to write policies that other companies, even other reinsurers, would shy away from. Some of them stand out because they are so unusual: a policy insuring against injury to superstar shortstop Alex Rodrigez for the Texas Rangers baseball team, or against a $1 billion payout by an Internet lottery. Commenting on the latter, a vice president in the reinsurance division noted, "As long as the premium is higher than the odds, we're comfortable."[10]

The bulk of underwriting at the reinsurance group is not quite so flashy. It is, however, extremely profitable. Significant revenue increases occurred in 2002 and 2003. In the aftermath of September 11, many companies and individuals increased their insurance coverage, often significantly, yet there were no catastrophic losses in the two following years. In 2003, the Berkshire Hathaway Reinsurance Group brought in $4.43 billion in premiums, bringing its total float to just under $14 billion.

Perhaps more significant, its cost of float that year was a negative 3 percent—meaning there was no cost, but rather a profit. (In this case, remember, "negative" is a positive.) That is because the reinsurance group in 2003 had an underwriting gain (more premiums than payouts) of more than $1 billion. For comparison, that same year the GEICO underwriting gain was $452 million, and General Re's was $145 million.

It is no wonder Buffett says of Jain, "If you see Ajit at our annual meeting, bow deeply."[11]

Warren Buffett understands the insurance business in a way that few others do. His success derives in large part from acknowledging the essential commodity nature of the industry and elevating his insurance companies to the level of a franchise.

Insurance companies sell a product that is indistinguishable from those of competitors. Policies are standardized and can be copied by anyone. There are no trademarks, no patents, no advantages in location or raw materials. It is easy to get licensed and insurance rates are an open book. Insurance, in other words, is a commodity product.

In a commodity business, a common way to gain market share is to cut prices. In periods of intense competition, other companies were willing to sell insurance policies below the cost of doing business rather than risk losing market share. Buffett held firm: Berkshire's insurance operations would not move into unprofitable territory. Only once—at General Re—did this happen, and it caught Buffett unaware.

> You can always write dumb insurance policies. There is an unlimited market for dumb insurance policies. And they're very troubling because the first day the premium comes in, that's the last time you see any new money. From then on, it's all going out. And that's not our aim in life.[12]
>
> WARREN BUFFETT, 2001

Unwilling to compete on price, Buffett instead seeks to distinguish Berkshire's insurance companies in two other ways. First, by financial strength. Today, in annual revenue and profit, Berkshire's insurance group ranks second, only to AIG, in the property casualty industry. Additionally, the ratio of Berkshire's investment portfolio ($35.2 billion) to its premium volume ($8.1 billion) is significantly higher than the industry average.

The second method of differentiation involves Buffett's underwriting philosophy. His goal is simple: to always write large volumes of insurance but only at prices that make sense. If prices are low, he is content to do very little business. This philosophy was instilled at National Indemnity by its founder, Jack Ringwalt. Since that time, says Buffett, Berkshire has never knowingly wavered from this underwriting discipline. The only exception is General Re, and its underpricing had a large impact on Berkshire's overall performance for several years. Today, that unpleasant state of affairs has been rectified.

Berkshire's superior financial strength has distinguished its insurance operations from the rest of the industry. When competitors vanish from the marketplace because they are frightened by recent losses, Berkshire stands by as a constant supplier of insurance. In a word, the financial integrity that Buffett has imposed on Berkshire's insurance companies has created a franchise in what is otherwise a commodity business. It's not surprising that Buffett notes, in his typical straightforward way, "Our main business is insurance."[13]

The stream of cash generated by Berkshire's insurance operations is mind-boggling: some $44.2 billion in 2003. What Buffett does with that cash defines him and his company. And that takes us to our next chapter.

4

Buying a Business

Berkshire Hathaway, Inc., is complex but not complicated. It owns (at the moment) just shy of 100 separate businesses—the insurance companies described in the previous chapter, and a wide variety of noninsurance businesses acquired through the income stream from the insurance operation. Using that same cash stream, it also purchases bonds and stocks of publicly traded companies. Running through it all is Warren Buffett's down-to-earth way of looking at a business: whether it's one he's considering buying in its entirety or one he's evaluating for stock purchase.

There is no fundamental difference, Buffett believes, between the two. Both make him an owner of the business, and therefore both decisions should, in his view, spring from this owner's point of view. This is the single most important thing to understand about Buffett's investment approach: Buying stocks means buying a business and requires the same discipline. In fact, it has always been Buffett's preference to directly own a company, for it permits him to influence what he considers the most critical issue in a business: capital allocation. But when stocks represent a better value, his choice is to own a portion of a company by purchasing its common stock.

In either case, Buffett follows the same strategy: He looks for companies he understands, with consistent earnings history and favorable long-term prospects, showing good return on equity with little debt, that are operated by honest and competent people, and, importantly, are available at attractive prices. This owner-oriented way of looking at potential investments is bedrock to Buffett's approach.

> All we want is to be in businesses that we understand, run by people whom we like, and priced attractively relative to their future prospects.[1]
>
> WARREN BUFFETT, 1994

Because he operates from this owner's perspective, wherein buying stock is the same as buying companies, it is also true that buying companies is the same as buying stock. The same principles apply in both cases, and therefore both hold important lessons for us.

Those principles are described in some detail in Chapters 5 through 8. Collectively, they make up what I have called the "Warren Buffett Way," and they are applied, almost subconsciously, every time he considers buying shares of a company, or acquiring the entire company. In this chapter, we take a brief background tour of some of these purchases, so that we may better understand the lessons they offer.

A MOSAIC OF MANY BUSINESSES

Berkshire Hathaway, Inc., as it exists today, is best understood as a holding company. In addition to the insurance companies, it also owns a newspaper, a candy company, an ice cream/hamburger chain, an encyclopedia publisher, several furniture stores, a maker of Western boots, jewelry stores, a supplier of custom picture framing material, a paint company, a company that manufactures and distributes uniforms, a vacuum cleaner business, a public utility, a couple of shoe companies, and a household name in underwear—among others.

Some of these companies, particularly the more recent acquisitions, are jewels that Buffett found in a typically Buffett-like way: He advertised for them in the Berkshire Hathaway annual reports.

His criteria are straightforward: a simple, understandable business with consistent earning power, good return on equity, little debt, and good management in place. He is interested in companies in the $5 billion to $20 billion range, the larger the better. He is not interested in turnarounds, hostile takeovers, or tentative situations where no asking price has been determined. He promises complete confidentiality and a quick response.

In Berkshire Hathaway's annual reports and in remarks to shareholders, he has often described his acquisition strategy this way: "It's very scientific. Charlie and I just sit around and wait for the phone to ring. Sometimes it's a wrong number."[1]

The strategy works. Through this public announcement, and also through referrals from managers of current Berkshire companies, Buffett has acquired an amazing string of successful businesses. Some of them have been Berkshire companies for decades, and their stories have become part of the Buffett lore.

See's Candy Shops, for example, has been a Berkshire subsidiary since 1972. It is noteworthy because it represents the first time Buffett moved away from Ben Graham's dictum to buy only undervalued companies. The net purchase price—$30 million—was three times book value. Without doubt, it was a good decision. In 2003 alone, See's pretax earnings were $59 million—almost exactly twice the original purchase price.

At Berkshire's annual meeting in 1997, 25 years after the See's purchase, Charlie Munger recalled, "It was the first time we paid for quality." To which Buffett added, "If we hadn't bought See's, we wouldn't have bought Coke."[3] Later on in this chapter, the full significance of that comment becomes apparent.

Another company well known to Berkshire followers is Nebraska Furniture Mart. This enormous retail operation began in Omaha, Buffett's hometown, in 1937 when a Russian immigrant named Rose Blumkin, who had been selling furniture from her basement, put up $500 to open a small store. In 1983, Buffett paid Mrs. B, as she was universally known, $55 million for 80 percent of her store.

Today the Nebraska Furniture Mart, which comprises three retail units totaling 1.2 million square feet on one large piece of real estate, sells more home furnishings than any other store in the country. Running a close second is the second Mart, opened in 2002 in Kansas City. In his 2003 letter to shareholders, Buffett linked the success of this 450,000-square-foot operation to the legendary Mrs. B., who was still at work until the year she died at the age of 104. "One piece of wisdom she imparted," Buffett wrote, "was 'if you have the lowest price, customers will find you at the bottom of a river.' Our store serving greater Kansas City, which is located in one of the area's more sparsely populated parts, has proved Mrs. B's point. Though we have more than 25 acres of parking, the lot has at times overflowed."[4]

In January 1986, Buffett paid $315 million in cash for the Scott & Fetzer Company, a conglomerate of twenty-one separate companies, including the makers of Kirby vacuum cleaners and *World Book* encyclopedia. It was one of Berkshire's largest business acquisitions up to that point, and has since exceeded Buffett's own optimistic expectations. It is a model of an organization that creates a large return on equity with very little debt—and that is one of Buffett's favorite traits. In fact, he calculates that Scott Fetzer's return on equity would easily place it among the top 1 percent of the Fortune 500.

Scott Fetzer's various companies make a range of rather specialized (some would say boring) industrial products, but what they really make is money for Berkshire Hathaway. Since Buffett bought it, Scott Fetzer has distributed over 100 percent of its earnings back to Berkshire while simultaneously increasing its own earnings.

In recent years, Warren Buffett has turned more and more of his attention to buying companies instead of shares. The story of how Buffett came to acquire these diverse businesses is interesting in itself. Perhaps more to the point, the stories collectively give us valuable insight into Buffett's way of looking at companies. In this chapter, we have space for an abbreviated visit to just three of these acquisitions, but that is by no means all. To illustrate the wide range of industries within Berkshire, here are a few examples of recent acquisitions:

- Fruit of the Loom, which produces one-third of the men's and boys' underwear sold in the United States. Purchased in 2002 for $835 million, which, after accounting for the earned interest on assumed debt, was a net of $730 million.
- Garan, which makes children's clothing, including the popular Garanimals line. Purchased in 2002 for $270 million.
- MiTek, which produces structural hardware for the building industry. Purchased in 2001 for $400 million. An interesting aspect of this deal is that Berkshire now owns only 90 percent of

the company. The other 10 percent is owned by 55 managers who love their company and wanted to be part owners; this entrepreneurial spirit among management is one of the qualities Buffett looks for.

- Larson-Juhl, the leading supplier of framing materials to custom framing shops. Purchased in 2001 for $225 million.
- CORT Business Services, which leases quality furniture to offices and corporate-owned apartments. Purchased in 2000 for $467 million, including $83 million of debt.
- Ben Bridge Jeweler, a West Coast chain owned and operated by the same family for four generations. A requirement of the purchase was that the Bridge family remain to manage the company. Purchased in 2000 for a price not disclosed publicly.
- Justin Industries, which makes Western boots (Justin, Tony Lama, and other brands) and, under the Acme brand name, bricks. Purchased in 2000 for $600 million.
- Benjamin Moore, which has been making paint for 121 years. Purchased in 2000 for $1 billion.
- Shaw Industries, the largest manufacturer of carpeting in the world. Purchased 87 percent of the company in 2000 and the remainder in early 2002, for a total of $2 billion. Currently, Shaw is, except for insurance, Berkshire's largest business, with 2003 earnings of $436 million.

CLAYTON HOMES

In 1966, James Clayton, the son of a Tennessee sharecropper, started a mobile home business with $25,000 of borrowed money. Within four years, Clayton Homes was selling 700 units annually. Clayton is now one of the largest makers of manufactured homes in the United States, with about $1.2 billion in sales in 2003. Home models range from modest (500 square feet, priced at $10,000) to luxury ($100,000 for 1,500 square feet, with hardwood floors, stainless steel appliances, and island kitchens).

Clayton has about 976 retailers in the United States, including 302 company-owned stores, 86 company-owned community sales offices, and 588 manufactured housing communities in 33 states. It also owns and operates financing, loan-servicing, and insurance subsidiaries. The company went public in 1983, and Berkshire Hathaway acquired it in August 2003 for $1.7 billion.

James Clayton gained his experience and education the hard way. Determined to pull himself out of the backbreaking work his parents endured (his father picked cotton and his mother worked in a shirt factory), Clayton financed his education at the University of Tennessee by playing guitar on the radio. He eventually became a part-time host on *Startime,* a weekly variety program on Knoxville TV and sang along with people like Dolly Parton. Then, while in college, he started a used car business with his fraternity brothers but the business went bankrupt in 1961 when the bank called his loan. "My parents thought for sure that we were going to jail and I made a pact with myself that I haven't violated: I was never going to be vulnerable to a bank again."[5]

The acquisition of Clayton Homes is a typical Buffett story— meaning that it is atypical compared with the rest of the business world.

The first aspect of the story is that Buffett had some hands-on experience with the industry. In 2002, Berkshire had purchased junk bonds from Oakwood Homes, another mobile home manufacturer. As Buffett has freely admitted, at the time he was not fully aware of the "atrocious consumer financing practices" that were common in the industry. "But I learned," he added. "Oakwood rather promptly went bankrupt."[6]

Fast forward to February 2003. Al Auxier, a professor of finance at the University of Tennessee, brought a group of MBA students to Omaha to meet with Buffett for what Buffett describes as "two hours of give-and-take." It was the fifth time Auxier had made the trip, and it had become traditional for the visiting students to bring a thank-you gift for Buffett. This time, the gift was the autobiography of James Clayton, who had located his company in Knoxville, home of his alma mater.

After he finished reading the book, Buffett phoned James Clayton's son Kevin, who is now CEO. "As I talked with Kevin, it became clear that he was both able and a straight-shooter. Soon thereafter, I made an offer for the business based solely on Jim's book, my evaluation of Kevin, the public financials of Clayton and what I had learned from the Oakwood experience."[7] Two weeks later, Berkshire announced its acquisition of Clayton Homes. "I made the deal over the phone," Buffett said, "without ever seeing it."[8]

In the fall of 2003, Buffett was invited to attend the University of Tennessee's MBA Symposium. He recounted the Clayton story, and then presented all the students who had started the ball rolling with honorary PhDs (for Phenomenal, hard-working Dealmaker) from the University of Berkshire Hathaway. Each student was also given one class B share of Berkshire, and their teacher, Al Auxier, was presented with an A share.

McLANE COMPANY

In 1894, Robert McLane, escaping the post-Civil War poverty of South Carolina, moved to Cameron, Texas, and started a small grocery store. Over the years, he developed it into a wholesale grocery and distribution business. His son, Robert D. McLane, known by his middle name of Drayton, joined the company in 1921. Drayton's son, Drayton Jr., began working in the family business at the age of nine, and spent many teenage Saturdays sweeping floors in the warehouse. After college, he joined the company full time.

Eventually Drayton Jr. convinced his father to move the company close to an interstate highway and then in 1962 to automate the business with computers. In 1990, he sold the company to his tennis pal Sam Walton, and McLane became a Wal-Mart subsidiary, supplying Wal-Mart and Sam's Club stores, as well as convenience stores and fast-food restaurants across the nation with everything from peanuts to pepperoni.

By 2003, McLane had become the largest distributor in the United States to corner and convenience stores. McLane's innovative software systems for pricing, freight, delivery, and point-of-sales processing and its excellent delivery service had made the company a lean and efficient full-service delivery company.

An efficient, well-run company built on strong principles and showing consistent profitability is just what Warren Buffett likes to see. In May 2003, Berkshire announced it had acquired McLane for $1.45 billion in cash, and assumed an additional $1.2 billion in liabilities.

The acquisition positioned McLane for even greater growth, as it freed the company to pursue distribution contracts with supermarket chains and with Wal-Mart competitors, such as Target and Dollar General. "In the past some retailers had shunned McLane," wrote Buffett in his 2003 shareholder letter, "because it was owned by their major competitor. But Grady Rosier, McLane's superb CEO, has already landed some of these accounts—he was in full stride the day the deal closed—and more will come."[9]

THE PAMPERED CHEF

In 1980, Doris Christopher, a former teacher of home economics and a stay-at-home mom, was looking for part-time work with flexible hours that would add to the family income but still allow her time with her two young daughters. She decided to leverage what she knew—cooking and teaching—and that led her to the idea of selling kitchenware with in-home demonstrations. So she borrowed $3,000 against her life insurance policy, went shopping at the wholesale mart and bought $175 worth of products she admired, then asked a friend to host a demonstration party.

Christopher was a nervous wreck before the first party, but it was a resounding success. Not only did everyone have a great time, several guests suggested they'd like to host a party themselves. That was the beginning of the Pampered Chef, a company that markets gourmet kitchenware through direct sales and in-home parties.

The 34-year-old Christopher, who had no business background, started the company in the basement of her Chicago home with the $3,000 loan. The first year, working with her husband, she had sales of $50,000 and never looked back. In 1994, the Pampered Chef was among *Inc.* magazine's 500 fastest-growing privately held companies in the United States, and Christopher has been recognized by *Working Woman* magazine as one of the top 500 women business owners.

Doris Christopher started her business with a passionate belief that sitting down together at mealtime brings families together in a way that few other experiences can match. That philosophy has shaped and guided the Pampered Chef from the beginning, and it is at the core of the sales approach: a friendly, hands-on pitch to housewives that links the quality of family life to the quality of kitchen products.

Many of the company's "kitchen consultants," as they are called, are stay-at-home moms, and most of the sales are conducted in their homes at "kitchen shows." These are cooking demonstrations where guests see products and recipes in action, learn quick and easy food preparation techniques, and receive tips on how to entertain with style and ease. The products are professional-quality kitchen tools and pantry food items; some 80 percent of the products are exclusive to the company or can only be bought from TPC representatives.

Today, the Pampered Chef has 950 employees in the United States, Germany, the United Kingdom, and Canada, and its products are sold by over 71,000 independent consultants during in-home demonstrations. Over one million kitchen shows were held throughout the United States in 2002, producing sales of $730 million. And the only debt the company has ever incurred is the original $3,000 seed money.

In 2002, Doris Christopher realized that in case she either keeled over or decided to slow down, the Pampered Chef needed a backup plan. So, on the advice of her bankers at Goldman Sachs, she approached Warren Buffett. That August, Christopher and her then CEO, Sheila O'Connell Cooper, met with Buffett at his headquarters in Omaha. A month later, Berkshire announced it had bought the company, for a price thought to be approximately $900 million.

Recalling that August meeting, Buffett wrote to Berkshire shareholders, "It took me about ten seconds to decide that these were two managers with whom I wished to partner, and we promptly made a deal. I've been to a TPC party and it's easy to see why this business is a success. The company's products, in large part proprietary, are well-styled and highly useful, and the consultants are knowledgeable and enthusiastic. Everyone has a good time."[10]

Buffett is often asked what types of companies he will purchase in the future. First, he says, I will avoid commodity businesses and managers that I have little confidence in. He has three touchstones: It must be the type of company that he understands, possessing good economics, and run by trustworthy managers. That's also what he looks for in stocks—and for the same reasons.

INVESTING IN STOCKS

It is patently obvious that few of us are in a position to buy whole companies, as Buffett does. Their stories are included in this chapter because they give us such crisp insight into Buffett's way of thinking.

That same chain of thinking also applies to his decisions about buying stocks, and that does present some examples that ordinary mortals might follow. We may not be able to buy shares on the same scale as Warren Buffett, but we can profit from watching what he does.

At the end of 2003, Berkshire Hathaway's common stock portfolio had a total market value of more than $35 billion (see Table A.27 in the Appendix)—an increase of almost $27 billion from the original purchase prices. In that portfolio, Berkshire Hathaway owns, among others, 200 million shares of Coca-Cola, 96 million shares of the Gillette Company, and 56-plus million shares of Wells Fargo & Company. Soft drinks, razor blades, neighborhood banks—products and services that are familiar to us all. Nothing esoteric, nothing high-tech, nothing hard to understand. It is one of Buffett's most strongly held beliefs: It makes no sense to invest in a company or an industry you don't understand, because you won't be able to figure out what it's worth or to track what it's doing.

The Coca-Cola Company

Coca-Cola is the world's largest manufacturer, marketer, and distributor of carbonated soft drink concentrates and syrups. The company's soft drink product, first sold in the United States in 1886, is now sold in more than 195 countries worldwide.

Buffett's relationship with Coca-Cola dates back to his childhood. He had his first Coca-Cola when he was five years old. Soon afterward, he started buying six Cokes for 25 cents from his grandfather's grocery store and reselling them in his neighborhood for 5 cents each. For the next fifty years, Buffett admits, he observed the phenomenal growth of Coca-Cola, but he purchased textile mills, department stores, and windmill and farming equipment manufacturers. Even in 1986, when he formally announced that Cherry Coke would become the official soft drink of Berkshire Hathaway's annual meetings, Buffett had still not purchased a share of Coca-Cola. It was not until two years later, in the summer of 1988, that Buffett purchased his first shares of Coca-Cola.

The strength of Coca-Cola is not only its brand-name products, but also its unmatched worldwide distribution system. Today, international sales of Coca-Cola products account for 69 percent of the company's total sales and 80 percent of its profits. In addition to Coca-Cola Amatil, the company has equity interests in bottlers located in Mexico, South America, Southeast Asia, Taiwan, Hong Kong, and China. In 2003, the company sold more than 19 billion cases of beverage products.

The best business to own, says Buffett, is one that over time can employ large amounts of capital at very high rates of return. This description fits Coca-Cola perfectly. It is easy to understand why Buffett considers Coca-Cola, the most widely recognized brand name around the world, to be the world's most valuable franchise.

Because of this financial strength, and also because the product is so well known, I use Coca-Cola as the primary example in Chapters 5 through 8, which detail the tenets of the Warren Buffett Way.

> I buy businesses, not stocks, businesses I would be willing to own forever.[11]
>
> WARREN BUFFETT, 1998

The Gillette Company

Gillette is an international consumer products company that manufactures and distributes blades and razors, toiletries and cosmetics, stationery products, electric shavers, small household appliances, and oral care appliances and products. It has manufacturing operations in 14 countries and distributes its products in over 200 countries and territories. Foreign operations account for over 63 percent of Gillette's sales and earnings.

King C. Gillette founded the company at the turn of the twentieth century. As a young man, Gillette spent time strategizing how he would make his fortune. A friend suggested that he should invent a product that consumers would use once, throw away, and replace with another. While working as a salesperson for Crown Cork & Seal, Gillette hit on the idea of a disposable razor blade. In 1903, his fledgling company began selling the Gillette safety razor with 25 disposable blades for $5.

Today, Gillette is the world's leading manufacturer and distributor of blades and razors. Razor blades account for approximately one-third of the company's sales but two-thirds of its profits. Its global share of market is 72.5 percent, almost six times greater than the nearest competitor. The company has a 70 percent market share in Europe, 80 percent in Latin America. Sales are just beginning to grow in Eastern Europe, India, and China. For every one blade that Gillette sells in the United States, it sells five overseas. In fact, Gillette is so dominant worldwide that in many languages its name has become the word for "razor blade."

Buffett became interested in Gillette in the 1980s. Wall Street observers had begun to see the company as a mature, slow-growing consumer company ripe for a takeover. Profit margins hovered between 9 percent and 11 percent, return on equity flattened out with no sign of improvement, and income growth and market value were anemic (see Figures 4.1 and 4.2). In short, the company appeared stagnant.

CEO Colman Mockler fought off four takeover attempts during this time, culminating in a hotly contested battle against Coniston Partners in 1988. Gillette won—barely—but in so doing obligated itself to buy back 19 million shares of Gillette stock at $45 per share. Between 1986 and 1988, the company replaced $1.5 billion in equity with debt, and for a short period Gillette had a negative net worth.

At this point Buffett called his friend Joseph Sisco, a member of Gillette's board, and proposed that Berkshire invest in the company. "Gillette's business is very much the kind we like," Buffett said.

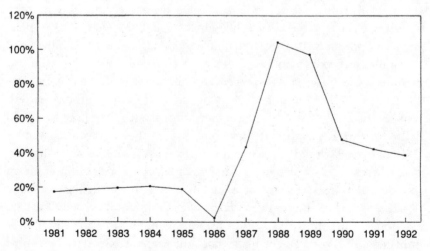

Figure 4.1 The Gillette Company return on equity.

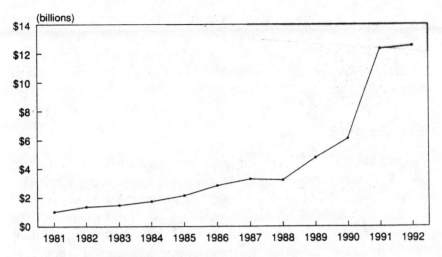

Figure 4.2 The Gillette Company market value.

"Charlie and I think we understand the company's economics and therefore believe we can make a reasonably intelligent guess about its future."[12] Gillette issued $600 million in convertible preferred stock to Berkshire in July 1989 and used the funds to pay down debt. Buffett received a 8.75 percent convertible preferred security with a mandatory redemption in ten years and the option to convert into Gillette common at $50 per share, 20 percent higher than the then-current price.

In 1989, Buffett joined Gillette's board of directors. That same year, the company introduced a highly successful new product, the Sensor. It was the beginning of a turnaround. With Sensor sales, Gillette's prosperity magnified. Earnings per share began growing at a 20 percent annual rate. Pretax margins increased from 12 to 15 percent and return on equity reached 40 percent, twice its return in the early 1980s.

In February 1991, the company announced a 2-for-1 stock split. Berkshire converted its preferred stock and received 12 million common shares or 11 percent of Gillette's shares outstanding. In less than two years, Berkshire's $600 million investment in Gillette had grown to $875 million. Buffett's next step was to calculate the value of those 12 million shares; in Chapter 8, we'll see how he went about it.

Gillette's razor blade business is a prime beneficiary of globalization. Typically, Gillette begins with low-end blades that have lower margins and over time introduces improved shaving systems with higher margins. The company stands to benefit not only from increasing unit sales but from steadily improving profit margins as well. Gillette's future appears bright. "It's pleasant to go to bed every night," says Buffett, "knowing there are 2.5 billion males in the world who will have to shave in the morning."[13]

The Washington Post Company

The Washington Post Company today is a media conglomerate with operations in newspaper publishing, television broadcasting, cable television systems, magazine publishing, and the provision of educational services. The newspaper division publishes the *Washington Post,* the *Everett* (Washington) *Herald,* and the Gazette Newspapers, a group of 39 weekly papers. The television broadcasting division owns six television stations located in Detroit, Miami, Orlando, Houston, San Antonio, and Jacksonville, Florida. The cable television systems division provides cable and digital video services to more than 1.3 billion subscribers. The magazine division publishes *Newsweek,* with domestic circulation of over 3 million and over 600,000 internationally.

In addition to the four major divisions, the Washington Post Company owns the Stanley H. Kaplan Educational Centers, a large network of schools that prepare students for college admission tests and professional licensing exams. Best known for its original program that helps high school students do well on Scholastic Aptitude Tests, Kaplan has aggressively expanded its operations in recent years. It now includes after-school classes for grades K-12, the world's only accredited online law school, test-prep materials for engineers and CFAs, and campus-based schools with programs in business, finance, technology, health, and other professions. In 2003, Kaplan's sales totaled $838 million, making it a significant element in the Post Company.

The company owns 28 percent of Cowles Media, which publishes the *Minneapolis Star Tribune,* several military newspapers, and 50 percent of the Los Angeles-Washington News Service.

Today, the Washington Post Company is an $8 billion company generating $3.2 billion in annual sales. Its accomplishments are especially impressive when you consider that seventy years ago, the company was in one business—publishing a newspaper.

In 1931, the *Washington Post* was one of five dailies competing for readers. Two years later, the *Post,* unable to pay for its newsprint, was placed in receivership. That summer, the company was sold at auction to satisfy creditors. Eugene Meyer, a millionaire financier, bought the paper for $825,000. For the next two decades, he supported the operation until it turned a profit.

Management of the paper passed to Philip Graham, a brilliant Harvard-educated lawyer who had married Meyer's daughter Katherine. In 1954, Phil Graham convinced Eugene Meyer to purchase a rival newspaper, the *Times-Herald*. Later, Graham purchased *Newsweek* magazine and two television stations before his tragic death in 1963. It is Phil Graham who is credited with transforming the *Washington Post* from a single newspaper into a media and communications company.

After Phil Graham's death, control of the *Washington Post* passed to his wife, Katherine. Although she had no experience managing a major corporation, she quickly distinguished herself by confronting difficult business issues.

Katherine Graham realized that to be successful the company would need a decision maker not a caretaker. "I quickly learned that things don't stand still," she said. "You have to make decisions."[14] Two decisions that had a pronounced impact on the *Washington Post* were hiring Ben Bradlee as managing editor of the newspaper and then inviting Warren Buffett to become a director of the company. Bradlee encouraged Katherine Graham to publish the Pentagon Papers and to pursue the Watergate investigation, which earned the *Washington Post* a reputation for prizewinning journalism. Buffett taught Katherine Graham how to run a successful business.

Buffett first met Katherine Graham in 1971. At that time, Buffett owned stock in the *New Yorker*. Hearing that the magazine might be for sale, he asked Katherine Graham whether the *Washington Post* would be interested in purchasing it. Although the sale never materialized, Buffett came away very much impressed with the publisher of the *Washington Post*.

That same year, Katherine Graham decided to take the *Washington Post* public. Two classes of stock were created. Class A common stock elected a majority of the board of directors, thus effectively controlling the company. Class A stock was, and still is, held by the Graham family. Class B stock elected a minority of the board of directors. In June 1971, the *Washington Post* issued 1,354,000 shares of class B stock. Remarkably, two days later, despite threats from the federal government, Katherine Graham gave Ben Bradlee permission to publish the Pentagon Papers.

For the next two years, while business at the paper was improving, the mood on Wall Street was turning gloomy. In early 1973, the Dow Jones Industrial Average began to slide. The *Washington Post* share price was slipping as well; by May, it was down 14 points to $23. That same month, IBM stock declined over 69 points, gold broke through $100 an ounce, the Federal Reserve boosted the discount rate to 6 percent, and the Dow fell 18 points—its biggest loss in three years. And all the while, Warren Buffett was quietly buying shares in the *Washington Post* (see Figure 4.3). By June, he had purchased 467,150 shares at an average price of $22.75, worth $10,628,000.

Katherine Graham was initially unnerved at the idea of a nonfamily member owning so much Post stock, even though the stock was non-controlling. Buffett assured her that Berkshire's purchase was for investment purposes only. To further reassure her, he offered to give her son Don, slated to take over the company someday, a proxy to vote Berkshire's shares. That clinched it. Katherine Graham responded by inviting Buffett to join the board of directors in 1974 and soon made him chairman of the finance committee.

Katherine Graham died in July 2001, after a fall in which she sustained severe head injuries. Warren Buffett was one of the ushers at her funeral services at Washington's National Cathedral.

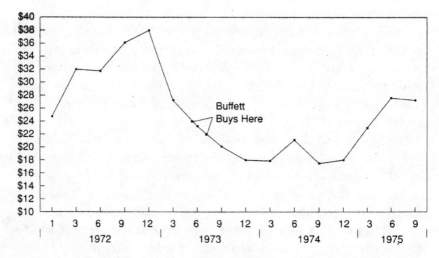

Figure 4.3 The Washington Post Company price per share, 1972–1975.

Donald E. Graham, son of Phil and Katherine, is chairman of the board of the Washington Post Company. Don Graham graduated magna cum laude from Harvard in 1966, having majored in English history and literature. After graduation, he served two years in the army. Knowing that he would eventually lead the *Washington Post,* Graham decided to get better acquainted with the city. He took the unusual path of joining the metropolitan police force of Washington, DC, and spent fourteen months as a patrolman walking the beat in the ninth precinct. In 1971, Graham went to work at the *Washington Post* as a Metro reporter. Later, he spent ten months as a reporter for *Newsweek* at the Los Angeles bureau. Graham returned to the *Post* in 1974 and became the assistant managing sports editor. That year, he was added to the company's board of directors.

Buffett's role at the *Washington Post* is widely documented. He helped Katherine Graham persevere during the labor strikes of the 1970s, and he also tutored Don Graham in business, helping him understand the role of management and its responsibility to its owners. "In finance," Don Graham says, "he's the smartest guy I know. I don't know who is second."[15]

Looking at the story from the reverse side, it's also clear that the *Post* has played a major role for Buffett as well. Finance journalist Andrew Kilpatrick, who has followed Buffett's career for years, believes that the Washington Post Company investment "locked up Buffett's reputation as a master investor."[16] Berkshire has not sold any of its *Washington Post* stock since the original purchase in 1973. In 2004, the Class B stock was selling for more than $900 a share, making it the second most expensive stock on the New York Stock Exchange. Berkshire's holdings are now worth more than $1 billion, and Buffett's original investment has increased in value more than fiftyfold.[17]

Wells Fargo & Company

In October 1990, Berkshire Hathaway announced it had purchased 5 million shares of Wells Fargo & Company at an average price of $57.88 per share, a total investment of $289 million. With this purchase, Berkshire became the largest shareholder of the bank, owning 10 percent of the shares outstanding.

It was a controversial move. Earlier in the year, the share price traded as high as $86, then dropped sharply as investors abandoned

California banks in droves. At the time, the West Coast was in the throes of a severe recession and some speculated that banks, with their loan portfolios stocked full of commercial and residential mortgages, were in trouble. Wells Fargo, with the most commercial real estate of any California bank, was thought to be particularly vulnerable.

In the months following Berkshire's announcement, the battle for Wells Fargo resembled a heavyweight fight. Buffett, in one corner, was the bull, betting $289 million that Wells Fargo would increase in value. In the other corner, short sellers were the bears, betting that Wells Fargo, already down 49 percent for the year, was destined to fall further. The rest of the investment world decided to sit back and watch.

Twice in 1992, Berkshire acquired more shares, bringing the total to 63 million by year-end. The price crept over $100 per share, but short sellers were still betting the stock would lose half its value. Buffett has continued to add to his position, and by year-end 2003, Berkshire owned more than 56 million shares, with a market value of $4.6 billion and a total accumulated purchase cost of $2.8 billion. In 2003, Moody's gave Wells Fargo a AAA credit rating, the only bank in the country with that distinction.

THE INTELLIGENT INVESTOR

The most distinguishing trait of Buffett's investment philosophy is the clear understanding that by owning shares of stocks he owns businesses, not pieces of paper. The idea of buying stocks without understanding the company's operating functions—its products and services, labor relations, raw material expenses, plant and equipment, capital reinvestment requirements, inventories, receivables, and needs for working capital—is unconscionable, says Buffett. This mentality reflects the attitude of a business owner as opposed to a stock owner, and is the only mentality an investor should have. In the summation of *The Intelligent Investor,* Benjamin Graham wrote, "Investing is most intelligent when it is most businesslike." Those are, says Buffett, "the nine most important words ever written about investing."

A person who holds stocks has the choice to become the owner of a business or the bearer of tradable securities. Owners of common stocks who perceive that they merely own a piece of paper are far removed from the company's financial statements. They behave as if the market's ever-changing price is a more accurate reflection of their stock's value than the business's balance sheet and income statement. They draw or discard stocks like playing cards. For Buffett, the activities of a common stock holder and a business owner are intimately connected. Both should look at ownership of a business in the same way. "I am a better investor because I am a businessman," Buffett says, "and a better businessman because I am an investor."[18]

THE WARREN BUFFETT WAY

Business Tenets

1. Is the business simple and understandable?
2. Does the business have a consistent operating history?
3. Does the business have favorable long-term prospects?

Management Tenets

4. Is management rational?
5. Is management candid with its shareholders?
6. Does management resist the institutional imperative?

Financial Tenets

7. What is the return on equity?
8. What are the company's "owner earnings"?
9. What are the profit margins?
10. Has the company created at least one dollar of market value for every dollar retained?

Value Tenets

11. What is the value of the company?
12. Can it be purchased at a significant discount to its value?

5

Investing Guidelines

Business Tenets

We come now to the heart of the matter—the essence of Warren Buffett's way of thinking about investing. Warren Buffett is so thoroughly identified with the stock market that even people who have no interest in the market know his name and reputation. Others, those who read the financial pages of the newspaper only casually, may know him as the head of an unusual company whose stock sells for upward of $90,000 per share. And even the many new investors who enthusiastically devote careful attention to market news think of him primarily as a brilliant stock picker.

Few would deny that the world's most famous and most successful investor is indeed a brilliant stock picker. But that seriously understates the case. His real gift is picking *companies*. I mean this in two senses: First, Berkshire Hathaway, in addition to its famous stock portfolio, owns many companies directly. Second, when considering new stock purchases, Buffett looks at the underlying business as thoroughly as he would if he were buying the whole company, using a set of basic principles developed over many years. "When investing," he says, "we view ourselves as business analysts—not as market analysts, not as macroeconomic analysts, and not even as security analysts."[1]

If we go back through time and review all of Buffett's purchases, looking for the commonalities, we find a set of basic principles, or tenets, that have guided his decisions. If we extract these tenets and spread them out for a closer look, we see that they naturally group themselves into four categories:

1. *Business tenets.* Three basic characteristics of the business itself
2. *Management tenets.* Three important qualities that senior managers must display
3. *Financial tenets.* Four critical financial decisions that the company must maintain
4. *Value tenets.* Two interrelated guidelines about purchase price

Not all of Buffett's acquisitions will display all the tenets, but taken as a group, these tenets constitute the core of his investment approach. They can also serve as guideposts for all investors. In this chapter, we look at the first group—the characteristics of the business—and study how some of Buffett's investment decisions reflect those tenets.

> I want to be in businesses so good even a dummy can make money.[2]
>
> WARREN BUFFETT, 1988

For Buffett, stocks are an abstraction.[3] He does not think in terms of market theories, macroeconomic concepts, or sector trends. Rather, he makes investment decisions based only on how a business operates. He believes that if people choose an investment for superficial reasons instead of business fundamentals, they are more likely to be scared away at the first sign of trouble, in all likelihood losing money in the process. Buffett concentrates on learning all he can about the business under consideration, focusing on three main areas:

1. Is the business simple and understandable?
2. Does the business have a consistent operating history?
3. Does the business have favorable long-term prospects?

A SIMPLE AND UNDERSTANDABLE BUSINESS

In Buffett's view, investors' financial success is correlated to the degree in which they understand their investment. This understanding is a distinguishing trait that separates investors with a business orientation from most hit-and-run investors, people who merely buy shares of stock. It is critical to the buy-or-don't-buy decision for this reason: In the final analysis, after all their research, investors must feel convinced that the business they are buying into will perform well over time. They must have some confidence in their estimate of its future earnings, and that has a great deal to do with how well they understand its business fundamentals. Predicting the future is always tricky; it becomes enormously more difficult in an arena you know nothing about.

Over the years, Buffett has owned a vast array of businesses: a gas station; a farm implementation business; textile companies; a major retailer; banks; insurance companies; advertising agencies; aluminum and cement companies; newspapers; oil, mineral, and mining companies; food, beverage, and tobacco companies; television and cable companies. Some of these companies he controlled, and in others he was or is a minority shareholder. But in all cases, he was or is acutely aware of how these businesses operate. He understands the revenues, expenses, cash flow, labor relations, pricing flexibility, and capital allocation needs of every single one of Berkshire's holdings.

Buffett is able to maintain a high level of knowledge about Berkshire's businesses because he purposely limits his selections to companies that are within his area of financial and intellectual understanding. He calls it his "circle of competence." His logic is compelling: If you own a company (either fully or some of its shares) in an industry you do not understand, it is impossible to accurately interpret developments and therefore impossible to make wise decisions. "Invest within your circle of competence," he counsels. "It's not how big the circle is that counts, it's how well you define the parameters."[4]

Critics have argued that Buffett's self-imposed restrictions exclude him from industries that offer the greatest investment potential, such as technology. His response: Investment success is not a matter of how much you know but how realistically you define what you don't know. "An investor needs to do very few things right as long as he or she avoids big mistakes."[5] Producing above-average results, Buffett has learned, often comes from doing ordinary things. The key is to do those things exceptionally well.

Coca-Cola Company

The business of Coca-Cola is relatively simple. The company purchases commodity inputs and combines them to manufacture a concentrate that is sold to bottlers. The bottlers then combine the concentrate with other ingredients and sell the finished product to retail outlets including minimarts, supermarkets, and vending machines. The company also provides soft drink syrups to fountain retailers, who sell soft drinks to consumers in cups and glasses.

The company's name brand products include Coca-Cola, Diet Coke, Sprite, PiBB Xtra, Mello Yello, Fanta soft drinks, Tab, Dasani, and Fresca. The company's beverages also include Hi-C brand fruit drinks, Minute Maid orange juice, Powerade, and Nestea. The company owns 45 percent of Coca-Cola Enterprises, the largest bottler in the United States, and 35 percent of Coca-Cola Amatil, an Australian bottler that has interests not only in Australia but also in New Zealand and Eastern Europe.

The strength of Coca-Cola is not only its name-brand products but also its unmatched worldwide distribution system. Today, international sales of Coca-Cola products account for 69 percent of the company's net sales and 80 percent of its profits. In addition to Coca-Cola Amatil, the company has equity interests in bottlers located in Mexico, South America, Southeast Asia, Taiwan, Hong Kong, and China.

The Washington Post Company

Buffett's grandfather once owned and edited the *Cuming County Democrat,* a weekly newspaper in West Point, Nebraska. His grandmother helped out at the paper and also set the type at the family's printing shop. His father, while attending the University of Nebraska, edited the *Daily Nebraskan.* Buffett himself was once the circulation manager for the *Lincoln Journal.* It has often been said that if Buffett had not embarked on a business career, he most surely would have pursued journalism.

(Text continues on page 67.)

CASE IN POINT
BENJAMIN MOORE, 2000

In November 2000, Warren Buffett and Berkshire Hathaway paid about $1 billion for Benjamin Moore & Co., the Mercedes of paint companies. Founded in 1883 by the Moore brothers in their Brooklyn basement, Benjamin Moore today is fifth largest paint manufacturer in the United States and has an unmatched reputation for quality.

It was reported that Buffett paid a 25 percent premium over the stock's then current price. On the surface, that might seem to contradict one of Buffett's iron-clad rules: that he will act only when the price is low enough to constitute a margin of safety. However, we also know that Buffett is not afraid to pay for quality. Even more revealing, the stock price jumped 50 percent to $37.62 per share after the deal was announced. This tells us that either Buffett found yet another company that was undervalued or else that the rest of the investing world was betting on Buffett's acumen and traded the price up even higher— or both.

Benjamin Moore is just the sort of company Buffett likes. The paint business is nothing if not simple and easy to understand. One of the largest paint manufacturers in the United States and the tenth largest specialty paint producer, Benjamin Moore makes one of the finest, if not *the* finest, architectural paint in the United States. The company is not just famous for the quality of its paint, however; architects, designers, and builders regard Benjamin Moore colors as the gold standard for their industry. In fact, the company developed the first computerized color matching system, and it is still recognized as the industry standard. With roughly 3,200 colors, Benjamin Moore can match almost any shade.

Buffett also tends to buy companies that have a consistent operating history and as a result, upon buying a company, he

(Continued)

does not expect to have to change much. His modus operandi is to buy companies that are already successful and still have potential for growth. Benjamin Moore's current success and status in the marketplace over the decades speak to the company's consistent product quality, production, brand strength, and service. Now, 121 years after its founding, the company brings in about $80 million of profit on $900 million in sales.

Looking at Benjamin Moore, Buffett also saw a well-run company. Although there were questions a few years ago about Moore's retail strategy, the company has undertaken a brand rejuvenation program in the United States and Canada. Benjamin Moore increased its retail presence in independent stores with its Signature Store Program and bought certain retail stores, such as Manhattan-based Janovic, outright. Just before the Berkshire acquisition in 2000, the company underwent a cost-cutting and streamlining program to improve its operations.

All that adds up to favorable long-term prospects. Benjamin Moore is a classic example of a company that has turned a commodity into a franchise. Buffett's definition of a franchise is one where the product is needed or desired, has no close substitute, and is unregulated. Most people in the building industry would agree that Moore is a master in all three categories. Considering the company's arsenal of over 100 chemists, chemical engineers, technicians, and support staff that maintain the company's strict product standards and develop new products, the risk of Benjamin Moore paints becoming a perishable commodity is slight. The on-going and rigorous testing to which all the Moore products are subjected is a sign that Benjamin Moore will continue to set industry standards. Finally, although Benjamin Moore products are not cheap, their quality commands pricing power that defeats any notion of inflation.

In 1969, Buffett bought his first major newspaper, the *Omaha Sun,* along with a group of weekly papers; from them he learned the business dynamics of a newspaper. He had four years of hands-on experience running a newspaper before he bought his first share of the *Washington Post.*

Wells Fargo

Buffett understands the banking business very well. In 1969, Berkshire bought 98 percent of the Illinois National Bank and Trust Company and held it until 1979, when the Bank Holding Act required Berkshire to divest its interest. During that ten-year period, the bank took its place beside Berkshire's other controlled holdings and Buffett reported its sales and earnings each year in Berkshire's annual reports.

Just as Jack Ringwalt helped Buffett understand the intricacy of the insurance business (see Chapter 3), Gene Abegg, who was chairman of Illinois National Bank, taught Buffett about the banking business. He learned that banks are profitable businesses as long as loans are issued responsibly and costs are curtailed. A well-managed bank could not only grow its earnings but also earn a handsome return on equity.

The key is "well managed." The long-term value of a bank, as Buffett learned, is determined by the actions of its managers, because they control the two critical variables: costs and loans. Bad managers have a way of running up the costs of operations while making foolish loans; good managers are always looking for ways to cut costs and rarely make risky loans. Carl Reichardt, then chairman of Wells Fargo, had run the bank since 1983, with impressive results. Under his leadership, growth in earnings and return on equity were both above average and operating efficiencies were among the highest in the country. Reichardt had also built a solid loan portfolio.

CONSISTENCY

Warren Buffett cares very little for stocks that are "hot" at any given moment. He is far more interested in buying into companies that he believes will be successful and profitable for the long term. And while predicting future success is certainly not foolproof, a steady track record is a relatively reliable indicator. When a company has demonstrated consistent results with the same type of products year after year, it is not unreasonable to assume that those results will continue.

As long, that is, as nothing major changes. Buffett avoids purchasing companies that are fundamentally changing direction because their previous plans were unsuccessful. It has been his experience that undergoing major business changes increases the likelihood of committing major business errors.

"Severe change and exceptional returns usually don't mix," Buffett observes.[6] Most individuals, unfortunately, invest as if the opposite were true. Too often, they scramble to purchase stocks of companies that are in the midst of a corporate reorganization. For some unexplained reason, says Buffett, these investors are so infatuated with the notion of what tomorrow may bring that they ignore today's business reality. In contrast, Buffett says, his approach is "very much profiting from lack of change. That's the kind of business I like."[7]

Buffett also tends to avoid businesses that are solving difficult problems. Experience has taught him that turnarounds seldom turn. It can be more profitable to expend energy purchasing good businesses at reasonable prices than difficult businesses at cheaper prices. "Charlie and I have not learned how to solve difficult business problems," Buffett admits. "What we have learned is to avoid them. To the extent that we have been successful, it is because we concentrated on identifying one-foot hurdles that we could step over rather than because we acquired any ability to clear seven-footers."[8]

The Coca-Cola Company

No other company today can match Coca-Cola's consistent operating history. This is a business that was started in the 1880s selling a beverage product. Today, 120 years later, Coca-Cola is selling the same beverage. Even though the company has periodically invested in unrelated businesses, its core beverage business has remained largely unchanged.

The only significant difference today is the company's size and its geographic reach. One hundred years ago, the company employed ten traveling salesmen to cover the entire United States. At that point, the company was selling 116,492 gallons of syrup a year, for annual sales of $148,000.[9] Fifty years later, in 1938, the company was selling 207 million cases of soft drinks annually (having converted sales from gallons to cases). That year, an article in *Fortune* noted, "It would be hard to name any company comparable to Coca-Cola and selling, as Coca-Cola does, an unchanged product that can point to a ten year record anything like Coca-Cola's."[10]

Today, nearly seventy years after that article was published, Coca-Cola is still selling syrup. The only difference is the increase in quantity. By the year 2003, the company was selling over 19 billion cases of soft drink in more than 200 countries, generating $22 billion a year in sales.

The Washington Post Company

Buffett tells Berkshire's shareholders that his first financial connection with the *Washington Post* was at age 13. He delivered both the *Washington Post* and the *Times-Herald* on his paper route while his father served in Congress. Buffett likes to remind others that with this dual delivery route he merged the two papers long before Phil Graham bought the *Times-Herald*.

Obviously, Buffett was aware of the newspaper's rich history. And he considered *Newsweek* magazine a predictable business. He quickly learned the value of the company's television stations. The *Washington Post* had been reporting for years the stellar performance of its broadcast division. Buffett's personal experience with the company and its own successful history led him to believe that the *Washington Post* was a consistent and dependable business performer.

Gillette

Few companies have dominated their industry as long as Gillette. It was the lead brand of razors and blades in 1923 and the lead brand in 2003. Maintaining that position for so many years has required the company to spend hundreds of millions of dollars inventing new, improved products. Even though Wilkinson, in 1962, developed the first coated stainless steel blade, Gillette bounced back quickly and has since worked hard to remain the world's leading innovator of shaving products. In 1972, Gillette developed the popular twin-blade Trac II; in 1977, the Atra razor with its pivoting head. Then, in 1989, the company developed the popular Sensor, a razor with independently suspended blades. Gillette's consistent success is a result of its innovation and patent protection of its new products.

Clayton Homes

In fiscal year 2002, Clayton reported its twenty-eighth consecutive year of profits, $126 million, up 16 percent from the year before, on revenue of $1.2 billion.[11] This performance is all the more extraordinary when we consider the fearsome problems that others in the industry experienced. In the late 1990s, over 80 factories and 4,000 retailers went out of business, a victim of two colliding forces: Many manufacturers had expanded too quickly and at the same time had made too many weak loans, which inevitably led to widespread repossessions, followed by diminished demand for new housing.

Clayton had a different way of doing business (more about their policies in Chapter 6). Its sound management and skillful handling of rough times enabled the company to maintain profitability even as competitors were going bankrupt.

FAVORABLE LONG-TERM PROSPECTS

"We like stocks that generate high returns on invested capital," Buffett told those in attendance at Berkshire's 1995 annual meeting, "where there is a strong likelihood that it will continue to do so."[12] "I look at long-term competitive advantage," he later added, "and [whether] that's something that's enduring."[13] That means he looks for what he terms *franchises*.

According to Buffett, the economic world is divided into a small group of franchises and a much larger group of commodity businesses, most of which are not worth purchasing. He defines a franchise as a company whose product or service (1) is needed or desired, (2) has no close substitute, and (3) is not regulated.

Individually and collectively, these create what Buffett calls a *moat*—something that gives the company a clear advantage over others and protects it against incursions from the competition. The bigger the moat, the more sustainable, the better he likes it. "The key to investing," he says, "is determining the competitive advantage of any given company and, above all, the durability of that advantage. The products or services that have wide, sustainable moats around them are the ones that deliver rewards to investors."[14] (To see what a moat looks like, read the story of Larson-Juhl in Chapter 8.)

A franchise that is the only source of a product people want can regularly increase prices without fear of losing market share or unit volume. Often a franchise can raise its prices even when demand is flat and capacity is not fully utilized. This pricing flexibility is one of the defining characteristics of a franchise; it allows franchises to earn above-average returns on invested capital.

> Look for the durability of the franchise. The most important thing to me is figuring out how big a moat there is around the business. What I love, of course, is a big castle and a big moat with piranhas and crocodiles.[15]
>
> WARREN BUFFETT, 1994

Another defining characteristic is that franchises possess a greater amount of economic goodwill, which enables them to better withstand the effects of inflation. Another is the ability to survive economic mishaps and still endure. In Buffett's succinct phrase, "The definition of a great company is one that will be great for 25 to 30 years."[16]

Conversely, a commodity business offers a product that is virtually indistinguishable from the products of its competitors. Years ago, basic commodities included oil, gas, chemicals, wheat, copper, lumber, and orange juice. Today, computers, automobiles, airline service, banking, and insurance have become commodity-type products. Despite mammoth advertising budgets, they are unable to achieve meaningful product differentiation.

Commodity businesses, generally, are low-returning businesses and "prime candidates for profit trouble."[17] Since their product is basically no different from anyone else's, they can compete only on the basis of price, which severely undercuts profit margins. The most dependable

(Text continues on page 77.)

CASE IN POINT

JUSTIN INDUSTRIES, 2000

In July 2000, Berkshire Hathaway bought 100 percent of Texas-based Justin Industries for $600 million. The company has two divisions: Justin Brands, which comprises four brands of Western boots, and Acme Building Brands, with companies that make bricks and other building products.

Cowboy boots and bricks. It is one of Berkshire's most interesting, and most colorful, acquisitions. And it says a great deal about Warren Buffett.

In many ways, Justin epitomizes all the business strengths that Buffett looks for. Clearly, it is simple and understandable; there's nothing particularly complex about boots or bricks. It represents a remarkably consistent operating history, as a look at the separate companies will show; all have been at the same business for many decades, and most are at least a century old. Finally, and most especially, Buffett recognized favorable long-term prospects, because of one aspect that he highly admires: in what are essentially commodity industries, the products have achieved franchise status.

Justin Brands

The company that is now Justin began in 1879 when H. J. (Joe) Justin, who was then 20 years old, started making boots for cowboys and ranchers from his small shop in Spanish Fort, Texas, near the Chisholm Trail. When Joe died in 1918, his sons John and Earl took over and in 1925 moved the company to Fort Worth. In 1948, Joe's grandson John Jr. bought out his relatives (except Aunt Enid), and guided the business for the next fifty years.

John Justin Jr. was a legendary figure in Fort Worth. He built an empire of Western boots by acquiring three rival companies, worked out the deal to buy Acme Bricks in 1968, and served a term as Fort Worth mayor. He retired in 1999, but stayed on as chairman emeritus, and that's why, at the age of 83, it was he who welcomed Warren Buffett to town in April 2000.

Justin Boots, known for rugged, long-lasting boots for working cowboys, remains the flagship brand. But Justin Brands includes other names.

- **Nocona,** founded in 1925 by Enid Justin. One of Joe Justin's seven children, Enid started working in her father's company when she was twelve. After her nephews moved the family business from the small town of Nocona, Texas, to Fort Worth in 1925, Enid set up a rival company in the original locale. Against all odds, she built a success. Fierce competitors for years, the two companies were joined under the Justin name in 1981. Enid, who was then 85, reluctantly agreed to the merger because of her declining health.

- **Chippewa,** founded in 1901 as a maker of boots for loggers, today makes sturdy hiking boots and quality outdoor work boots. It was acquired by Justin in 1985.

- **Tony Lama,** which dates back to 1911, when Tony Lama, who had been a cobbler in the U.S. Army, opened a shoe-repair and boot-making shop in El Paso. The boots quickly became a favorite of local ranchers and cowboys who valued the good fit and long-lasting quality. In recent years, for many the Tony Lama name has become synonymous with high-end boots handcrafted from exotic leathers such as boa, alligator, turtle, and ostrich, many with prices near $500. In 1990, Tony Lama Jr., chairman and CEO, agreed to merge with archrival Justin.

Two groups of people buy Western-style boots: those who wear them day in and day out, because they can't imagine wearing anything else; and those who wear them as fashion. The first group is the heart of Justin's customer base, but the second group, while smaller, does have an impact on sales volume as fashion trends twist and turn.

When big-name designers like Ralph Lauren and Calvin Klein show Western styles in their catalogs, boot sales climb. But fashion is notoriously fickle, and the company struggled in the late 1990s. After a peak in 1994, the sales of Western boots began to decline. In 1999, Justin's stock price dipped below $13.

(Continued)

John Justin Jr. retired in April 1999, and John Roach, former head of the Tandy Corp., came in to lead a restructuring. In just over a year, the new management engineered an impressive turnaround—adding new footwear products, consolidating the existing lines to eliminate duplicate designs, and instituting efficiencies in manufacturing and distribution. In April 2000, the streamlined company announced first quarter results: footwear sales rose 17 percent to $41.1 million, and both net earnings and gross margins increased significantly.

Two months later, Berkshire Hathaway announced it had reached an agreement to buy the company, prompting Bear Stearns analyst Gary Schneider to comment, "This is good news for employees. Management made all the changes last year. They've already taken the tough measures necessary to lower costs."[18]

Today the boot division of Justin has 4,000 vendors and about 35 percent of the Western footwear market; in stores that specialize in Western apparel, some 70 percent of the boots on the shelves are Justin brands. Most prices start at around $100. In the higher price brackets (several hundred dollars and up), Justin has about 65 percent of market share.

Acme Building Brands

The other division of Justin Industries is also a pioneer Texas company that is more than a century old. Founded in 1891 in Milsap, Texas, Acme became a Justin company in 1968, when John Justin Jr. bought it. Today, Acme is the largest and most profitable brick manufacturer in the country.

Because long-distance shipping costs are prohibitive, bricks tend to be a regional product. Acme dominates its region (Texas and five surrounding states) with more than 50 percent of market share. In its six-state area, Acme has 31 production facilities, including 22 brick plants, its own sales offices, and its own fleet of trucks. Builders, contractors, and homeowners can order bricks direct from the company, and they will be delivered on Acme trucks. Acme sells more than one billion bricks a year, each one stamped with the Acme logo, and each one guaranteed for 100 years.

Demand for bricks is tied to housing starts and, therefore, subject to changes in interest rates and in the overall economy. Even a run of bad weather can affect sales. Nonetheless, Acme fared better during the techno-crazed 1990s than the boot companies, and today is still the chief Justin money-maker. In addition to its bricks, Acme Building Brands includes Featherlite Building Products Corporation (concrete masonry) and the American Tile Supply Company, maker of ceramic and marble tiles.

The Berkshire Deal

For years Justin was largely ignored by Wall Street. With just two divisions, it was not large enough to be a conglomerate. Yet, operating in two different categories made it something of a puzzlement. As John Justin noted in 1999, just before he retired, "The analysts who understand the footwear business don't understand the building materials business, and the other way around."[19]

Warren Buffett understands both. For one thing, Berkshire already owned several footwear companies, so he had years to learn the industry. More to the point, he understands stable, steady businesses that make products people never stop needing.

And the timing was right. The company with a reputation for more than 100 years of quality was facing rocky times; its stock price had dropped 37 percent over the prior five years, and there was pressure to split the company into two parts. Buffett's well-known preference for simple, low-tech businesses made this a perfect fit.

When Buffett first met with John Justin in Fort Worth, he remarked that the city reminded him of Omaha; he meant it as a great compliment. When he looked into the two components of the company, he saw something else he admires: franchise

(Continued)

quality. Both divisions of Justin have managed to turn themselves into a franchise, through a combination of top quality, good marketing, and shrewd positioning.

Acme sells a product that most people consider a commodity. Who, after all, can name the brand of bricks they prefer? Acme customers, that's who. With a skillful marketing campaign featuring football legend Troy Aikman, Acme has made itself so well known that when Texans were recently asked to name their favorite brand of brick, 75 percent of respondents said Acme. That brand consciousness is reinforced every time a consumer picks up a brick and sees the Acme logo stamped into it.

The boots, too, have established themselves as franchises. Spend a few minutes in any Western-apparel retail outlet, and you'll hear customers say things like "My son is ready for some new Justins" or "Show me what you've got in Tony Lamas" more often than you hear "I'm looking for some cowboy boots." When they mention the boots by name, and when they're willing to pay top price for top quality, that's a franchise.

After the improvements of its new management team in 1999 and 2000, Justin began attracting attention. According to Bear Stearns analyst Gary Schneider, there was widespread interest from many buyers, including Europeans, but Buffett's was the first offer the company seriously contemplated.[20]

Berkshire's offer was for $22 per share in cash. That represented a 23 percent premium over closing stock price, but Buffett was not fazed. "It was a chance to get not only one good business but two good businesses at one time," he remarked. "A double dip, in effect. First-class businesses with first-class managements, and that's just what we look for." Nor, he added, did he have plans to change anything. "We buy business that are running well to start with. If they needed me in Fort Worth, we wouldn't be buying it."[21] The day after the deal was announced, Justin's stock price jumped 22 percent, and Warren Buffett returned to Omaha with a brand-new pair of ostrich-skin Tony Lamas.

way to make a commodity business profitable, then, is to be the low-cost provider.

The only other time commodity businesses turn a profit is during periods of tight supply—a factor that can be extremely difficult to predict. In fact, a key to determining the long-term profitability of a commodity business, Buffett notes, is the ratio of "supply-tight to supply-ample years." This ratio, however, is often fractional. The most recent supply-tight period in Berkshire's textile division, Buffett quips, lasted the "better part of a morning."

The Coca-Cola Company

Shortly after Berkshire's 1989 public announcement that it owned 6.3 percent of the Coca-Cola Company, Buffett was interviewed by Mellisa Turner, a business writer for the Atlanta *Constitution*. She asked Buffett a question he has been asked often: Why hadn't he purchased shares in the company sooner? By way of answer, Buffett related what he was thinking at the time he finally made the decision.

"Let's say you were going away for ten years," he explained, "and you wanted to make one investment and you know everything that you know now, and you couldn't change it while you're gone. What would you think about?" Of course, the business would have to be simple and understandable. Of course, the company would have to have demonstrated a great deal of business consistency over the years. And of course, the long-term prospects would have to be favorable. "If I came up with anything in terms of certainty, where I knew the market was going to continue to grow, where I knew the leader was going to continue to be the leader—I mean worldwide—and where I knew there would be big unit growth, I just don't know anything like Coke. I'd be relatively sure that when I came back they would be doing a hell of a lot more business than they do now."[22]

But why purchase at that particular time? Coca-Cola's business attributes, as described by Buffett, have existed for several decades. What caught his eye, he confesses, were the changes occurring at Coca-Cola, during the 1980s, under the leadership of Roberto Goizueta.

Goizueta, raised in Cuba, was Coca-Cola's first foreign chief executive officer. In 1980, Robert Woodruff, the company's 91-year-old patriarch, brought him in to correct the problems that had plagued the company during the 1970s. It was a dismal period for Coca-Cola—disputes with bottlers, accusations of mistreatment of migrant workers at the company's Minute Maid groves, environmentalists' claim that Coke's "one way" containers contributed to the country's growing pollution problem, and the Federal Trade Commission charge that the company's exclusive franchise system violated the Sherman Anti-Trust Act. Coca-Cola's international business was reeling as well.

One of Goizueta's first acts was to bring together Coca-Cola's top fifty managers for a meeting in Palm Springs, California. "Tell me what we're doing wrong," he said. "I want to know it all and once it's settled, I want 100 percent loyalty. If anyone is not happy, we will make you a good settlement and say goodbye."[23]

Goizueta encouraged his managers to take intelligent risks. He wanted Coca-Cola to initiate action rather than to be reactive. He began cutting costs. And he demanded that any business that Coca-Cola owned must optimize its return on assets. These actions immediately translated into increasing profit margins. And captured the attention of Warren Buffett.

The Washington Post Company

"The economics of a dominant newspaper," Buffett once wrote, "are excellent, among the very best in the world."[24] The vast majority of U.S. newspapers operate without any direct competition. The owners of those newspapers like to believe that the exceptional profits they earn each year are a result of their paper's journalistic quality. The truth, said Buffett, is that even a third-rate newspaper can generate adequate profits if it is the only paper in town. That makes it a classic franchise, with all the benefits thereof.

It is true that a high-quality paper will achieve a greater penetration rate, but even a mediocre paper, he explains, is essential to a community for its "bulletin board" appeal. Every business in town, every home seller, every individual who wants to get a message out to the community needs the circulation of a newspaper to do so. The paper's owner receives, in effect, a royalty on every business in town that wants to advertise.

In addition to their franchise quality, newspapers possess valuable economic goodwill. As Buffett points out, newspapers have low capital needs, so they can easily translate sales into profits. Even expensive computer-assisted printing presses and newsroom electronic systems are quickly paid for by lower fixed wage costs. Newspapers also are able to increase prices relatively easily, thereby generating above-average returns on invested capital and reducing the harmful effects of inflation. Buffett figures that a typical newspaper could double its price and still retain 90 percent of its readership.

The McLane Company

McLane is perched on the edge of great growth potential. Now that it is no longer part of Wal-Mart, it is free to pursue arrangements with Wal-Mart's competitors, such as Target and other large stores in the United States. This, combined with the company's focus on efficiency and investment in enterprise-wide software systems, freight management, and point-of-sales systems among other automated processes, will enable McLane to maintain price efficiency and service quality.

At the time Buffett bought McLane, some of the industry players, such as Fleming and U.S. Food Service, a division of Royal Ahold, were going through difficult times for various reasons. Although it is doubtful that this influenced Buffett's decision, it was said at the time that if Fleming did indeed go under, an extra $7 billion worth of business would be up for grabs.

The Pampered Chef

The Pampered Chef has demonstrated a consistency that many older businesses might well envy, with a growth rate of 22 percent each year from 1995 to 2001. And the long-term outlook is strong. According to the Direct Selling Association, party plan businesses raked in more than $7 billion nationwide in 2000, an increase of $2.7 billion since 1996.

Christopher herself is not slowing down. She believes that American cupboards have plenty of room for more products and points out that Mary Kay, a direct-sell cosmetics company, has a sales force of 600,000—giving her plenty of room to grow. Christopher is developing new products, such as ceramic serving ware, and is expanding into Canada, the United Kingdom, and Germany. Finally, the company is structured in such a way that it does not need a lot of capital to expand and it has no sizable competition in its category.

6

Investing Guidelines

Management Tenets

When considering a new investment or a business acquisition, Buffett looks very hard at the quality of management. He tells us that the companies or stocks Berkshire purchases must be operated by honest and competent managers whom he can admire and trust. "We do not wish to join with managers who lack admirable qualities," he says, "no matter how attractive the prospects of their business. We've never succeeded in making a good deal with a bad person."[1]

When he finds managers he admires, Buffett is generous with his praise. Year after year, readers of the Chairman's Letter in Berkshire's annual reports find Buffett's warm words about those who manage the various Berkshire companies.

He is just as thorough when it comes to the management of companies whose stock he has under consideration. In particular, he looks for three traits:

1. Is management rational?
2. Is management candid with the shareholders?
3. Does management resist the institutional imperative?

The highest compliment Buffett can pay a manager is that he or she unfailingly behaves and thinks like an owner of the company. Managers who behave like owners tend not to lose sight of the company's prime objective—increasing shareholder value—and they tend to make rational decisions that further that goal. Buffett also greatly admires managers who take seriously their responsibility to report fully and genuinely to shareholders and who have the courage to resist what he has termed the *institutional imperative*—blindly following industry peers.

> When you have able managers of high character running businesses about which they are passionate, you can have a dozen or more reporting to you and still have time for an afternoon nap.[2]
>
> WARREN BUFFETT, 1986

All this has taken on a new level of urgency, as shocking discoveries of corporate wrongdoings have come to light. Buffett has always insisted on doing business only with people of the highest integrity. Sometimes that stance has put him at odds with other well-known names in the corporate world. It has not always been fashionable in business circles to speak of integrity, honesty, and trustworthiness as qualities to be admired. In fact, at times such talk might have been disparaged as naive and out of touch with business reality. It is a particularly sweet bit of poetic justice that Buffett's stand on corporate integrity now seems to be a brilliant strategy. But his motivation is not strategic: It comes from his own unshakable value system. And no one has ever seriously accused Warren Buffett of being naive.

Later in this chapter, we look more deeply into Buffett's responses to these issues of ethical corporate behavior, particularly excessive executive compensation, stock options, director independence and accountability, and accounting trickery. He tells us what he thinks must be changed to protect shareholder interests and gives us ideas on how investors can evaluate managers to determine whether they are trustworthy.

RATIONALITY

The most important management act, Buffett believes, is allocation of the company's capital. It is the most important because allocation of

(Text continues on page 85.)

CASE IN POINT

SHAW INDUSTRIES, 2000–2002

In late 2000, Warren Buffett's Berkshire Hathaway group agreed to acquire 87 percent of Shaw Industries, the world's largest carpet manufacturer, for $19 per share, or approximately $2 billion. Although the price was a 56 percent premium over the trading price of $12.19, Shaw's share price had been a good deal higher a year earlier. Buffett paid the premium because the company had so many of the qualities he likes to see: The business was simple and understandable, had a consistent operating history, and exhibited favorable long-term prospects.

Carpet manufacturing is not simplistic, given the gargantuan and complicated machines that spin, dye, tuft, and weave, but the basic premise is simple and understandable: to make the best carpets possible and sell them profitably. Shaw now produces about 27,000 styles and colors of tufted and woven carpet for homes and commercial use. It also sells flooring and project management services. It has more than 100 manufacturing plants and distribution centers and makes more than 600 million square yards of carpet a year and employs about 30,000 workers.

Buffett clearly believed that people would need carpets and flooring for a long time to come and that Shaw would be there to provide them. That translates to excellent long-term prospects, one of Buffett's requirements.

What really attracted Buffett, however, was the company's senior management. In his 2000 annual report to shareholders, he commented about the Shaw transaction. "A key feature of the deal was that Julian Saul, president, and Bob Shaw, CEO, were to continue to own at least 5 percent of Shaw. This leaves us associated with the best in the business as shown by Bob and Julian's record: Each built a large, successful carpet business before joining forces in 1998."[3]

From 1960 to 1980, the company delivered a 27 percent average annual return on investment. In 1980, Bob Shaw predicted

(Continued)

that his company would quadruple its $214 million in sales in ten years; he did it in eight years.

Clearly, Bob Shaw managed his company well, and in a way that fits neatly with Buffett's approach. "You have to grow from earnings," Shaw said. "If you use that as your philosophy—that you grow out of earnings rather than by borrowing—and you manage your balance sheet, then you never get into serious trouble."[4]

This type of thinking is right up Buffett Alley. He believes that management's most important act is the allocation of capital and that this allocation, over time, will determine shareholder value. In Buffett's mind, the issue is simple: If extra cash can be reinvested internally and produce a return higher than the cost of capital, then the company should retain its earnings and reinvest them, which is exactly what Shaw did.

It was not just that Bob Shaw made good financial decisions, he also made strong product and business decisions by adapting to changing market conditions. For example, Shaw retrofitted all of its machines in 1986 when DuPont came out with new stain-resistant fibers. "Selling is just meeting people, figuring out what they need, and supplying their needs," Shaw said. "But those needs are ever changing. So if you're doing business the same way you did it five years ago, or even two years ago—you're doing it wrong."[5]

Shaw's strong management is reflected in the company's consistent operating history. It has grown to the number one carpet seller in the world, overcoming changing marketplace conditions, changes in technology, and even the loss of major outlets. In 2002, Sears, one of Shaw's largest vendors at the time, closed its carpet business. But the management appeared to see those difficulties more as challenges to overcome rather than barriers to success.

In 2002, Berkshire bought the remaining portion of Shaw that it did not already own. By 2003, Shaw was bringing in $4.6 billion in sales. Except for the insurance segment, it is Berkshire's largest company.

capital, over time, determines shareholder value. Deciding what to do with the company's earnings—reinvest in the business, or return money to shareholders—is, in Buffett's mind, an exercise in logic and rationality. "Rationality is the quality that Buffett thinks distinguishes his style with which he runs Berkshire—and the quality he often finds lacking in other corporations," writes Carol Loomis of *Fortune*.[6]

The issue usually becomes important when a company reaches a certain level of maturity, where its growth rate slows and it begins to generate more cash than it needs for development and operating costs. At that point, the question arises: How should those earnings be allocated?

If the extra cash, reinvested internally, can produce an above-average return on equity—a return that is higher than the cost of capital—then the company should retain all its earnings and reinvest them. That is the only logical course. Retaining earnings to reinvest in the company at *less* than the average cost of capital is completely irrational. It is also quite common.

A company that provides average or below-average investment returns but generates cash in excess of its needs has three options: (1) It can ignore the problem and continue to reinvest at below-average rates, (2) it can buy growth, or (3) it can return the money to shareholders. It is at this crossroad that Buffett keenly focuses on management. It is here that managers will behave rationally or irrationally.

Generally, managers who continue to reinvest despite below-average returns do so in the belief that the situation is temporary. They are convinced that, with managerial prowess, they can improve their company's profitability. Shareholders become mesmerized with management's forecast of improvements.

If a company continually ignores this problem, cash will become an increasingly idle resource and the stock price will decline. A company with poor economic returns, a lot of cash, and a low stock price will attract corporate raiders, which often is the beginning of the end of current management tenure. To protect themselves, executives frequently choose the second option instead: purchasing growth by acquiring another company.

Announcing acquisition plans excites shareholders and dissuades corporate raiders. However, Buffett is skeptical of companies that need to buy growth. For one thing, it often comes at an overvalued price. For

(*Text continues on page 89.*)

CASE IN POINT
Fruit of the Loom, 2002

In 2002, Warren Buffett bought the core business (apparel) of bankrupt Fruit of the Loom for $835 million in cash. With the purchase, Berkshire acquired two strong assets: an outstanding manager and one of the country's best-known and best-loved brand names. It also acquired some $1.6 billion in debt, and a bitter history of ill will among shareholders, suppliers, retailers, and consumers.

The company that sells one-third of all men's and boys' underwear in the United States started as a small Rhode Island mill in 1851. Over the next century, it grew into the nation's leading maker of underwear and T-shirts. It could not, however, escape the economic struggles that increasingly threatened the apparel industry, and in 1985 was snapped up by financier William Farley, known for acquiring financially troubled companies.

Farley, often described as "flashy" and "flamboyant," guided the company through a few years of growth and then into a disastrous decline. Everything seemed to go wrong. An aggressive $900 million acquisitions program left the company over-leveraged—long-term debt was 128 percent of common shareholders' equity in 1996—without providing the expected rise in revenues. Suppliers went unpaid and stopped shipping raw materials. Farley moved 95 percent of manufacturing operations offshore, closing more than a dozen U.S. plants and displacing some 16,000 workers, only to find that the net result was serious problems of quality control and on-time delivery. To counteract the delivery snafus, he parceled out the manufacturing to contract firms, adding enormous layers of overtime costs. He created a holding company for Fruit of the Loom and moved its headquarters to the Cayman Islands, avoiding U.S. taxes on foreign sales but triggering a massive public relations headache.

The headache got worse when Farley, in a maneuver that is now illegal, convinced his hand-picked board to guarantee a personal bank loan of $65 million in case he defaulted—which he did. The board, which earlier had set his compensation at nearly $20 million and repriced stock options to significantly favor key executives, then forgave $10 million of the loan.

In spite of the cost-cutting attempts, the company was sinking deeper into the red. In 1999, Fruit of the Loom posted losses of $576 million, seven times larger than analysts' expectations; and gross margins sagged to a paltry 2 percent, not enough to cover the $100 million interest expense needed to service its $1.4 billion debt. That same year the Council of Institutional Investors listed Fruit of the Loom as one of the nation's twenty most underperforming companies. Shareholders cringed as the stock price plunged: From $44 a share in early 1997 to just over $1 by the end of 1999; in that one year, 1999, the shares lost more than 90 percent of their value.

Few were surprised, therefore, when the company filed for Chapter 11 bankruptcy protection in December 1999. The company's shares sank even lower, and by October 2001 were down to $0.23.

So why would Warren Buffett be interested? Two reasons: a very strong brand that offered growth potential under the right management, and the arrival of a man on a white horse.

John B. Holland had been a highly respected executive with Fruit of the Loom for more than twenty years, including several years as president and CEO, when he retired in 1996. In 2000, he was brought back as executive vice-president charged with revamping operations.

Holland represents a perfect example of the management qualities Buffett insists upon. Although publicly he remained largely silent about Farley, beyond a brief reference to "poor management," Buffett has made no secret of his disdain for executives who bully their boards into sweet compensation deals, and boards that allow it. In contrast, he is enthusiastically vocal about his admiration for Holland.

(Continued)

He explained his thinking to Berkshire shareholders: "John Holland was responsible for Fruit's operations in its most bountiful years. . . . [After the bankruptcy] John was rehired, and he undertook a major reworking of operations. Before John's return, deliveries were chaotic, costs soared, and relations with key customers deteriorated. . . . He's been restoring the old Fruit of the Loom, albeit in a much more competitive environment. [In our purchase offer] we insisted on a very unusual proviso: John had to be available to continue serving as CEO after we took over. To us, John and the brand are Fruit's key assets."[7]

Since Holland took the reins, Fruit of the Loom has undergone a massive restructuring to lower its costs. It slashed its freight costs, reduced overtime, and trimmed inventory levels. It disposed of sideline businesses, eliminated unprofitable product lines, found new efficiencies in manufacturing process, and worked to restore customer satisfaction by filling orders on time.

Almost immediately, improvement was apparent. Earnings increased, operating expenses decreased. In 2000, gross earnings rose by $160.3 million—a 222 percent increase—compared to 1999, and gross margin increased 11 percentage points. The company reported an operating loss in 2000 of $44.2 million, compared to the 1999 loss of $292.3 million. Even more revealing of improvement are the fourth-quarter results—an operating loss of $13.5 million (which included one-time consolidation costs related to the closure of four U.S. plants) in 2000, compared to $218.6 million—more than sixteen times greater—just one year earlier.

In 2001, the positive trend continued. Gross earnings grew another $72.5 million, a 31 percent increase over 2000, and gross margin increased 7.7 percentage points to 22.7 percent for the year. That means the company ended 2001 with operating earnings of $70.1 million, compared to 2000's $44.2 million loss.

Of course monumental problems such as the company faced are not fully corrected overnight, and Fruit of the Loom must still operate in a ferociously competitive industry environment, but so far Buffett is pleased with the company's performance.

Lest anyone still consider buying a debt-ridden bankrupt company a surprising move, there was also a third reason for Buffett's decision, which should come as no surprise whatsoever: He was able to acquire the company on very favorable financial terms. For details, see Chapter 8.

Buying an underwear maker creates lots of opportunities for corny jokes, and Buffett, an accomplished punster, made the most of it. At the 2002 shareholders meeting, when asked the obvious question, he teased the audience with a half answer: "When I wear underwear at all, which I rarely do . . ." Leaving the crowd to decide for themselves whether it's boxers or briefs for Buffett. He pointed out why there's "a favorable bottom line" in underwear: "It's an elastic market." Finally, he deadpanned, Charlie Munger had given him an additional reason to buy the company: "For years Charlie has been telling me, 'Warren, we have to get into women's underwear.' Charlie is 78. It's now or never."[8]

another, a company that must integrate and manage a new business is apt to make mistakes that could be costly to shareholders.

In Buffett's mind, the only reasonable and responsible course for companies that have a growing pile of cash that cannot be reinvested at above-average rates is to return that money to the shareholders. For that, two methods are available: raising the dividend or buying back shares.

With cash in hand from their dividends, shareholders have the opportunity to look elsewhere for higher returns. On the surface, this seems to be a good deal, and therefore many people view increased dividends as a sign of companies that are doing well. Buffett believes that this is so only if investors can get more for their cash than the company could generate if it retained the earnings and reinvested in the company.

Over the years, Berkshire Hathaway has earned very high returns from its capital and has retained all its earnings. With such high returns, shareholders would have been ill served if they were paid a dividend. Not surprisingly, Berkshire does not pay a dividend. And that's just fine with the shareholders. The ultimate test of owners' faith is allowing management to reinvest 100 percent of earnings; Berkshire's owners' faith in Buffett is high.

If the real value of dividends is sometimes misunderstood, the second mechanism for returning earnings to the shareholders—stock repurchase—is even more so. The benefit to the owners is in many respects less direct, less tangible, and less immediate.

When management repurchases stock, Buffett feels that the reward is twofold. If the stock is selling below its intrinsic value, then purchasing shares makes good business sense. If a company's stock price is $50 and its intrinsic value is $100, then each time management buys its stock, they are acquiring $2 of intrinsic value for every $1 spent. Such transactions can be highly profitable for the remaining shareholders.

Furthermore, says Buffett, when executives actively buy the company's stock in the market, they are demonstrating that they have the best interests of their owners at hand rather than a careless need to expand the corporate structure. That kind of stance sends good signals to the market, attracting other investors looking for a well-managed company that increases shareholders' wealth. Frequently, shareholders are rewarded twice; first from the initial open market purchase and then subsequently from the positive effect of investor interest on price.

Coca-Cola

Growth in net cash flow has allowed Coca-Cola to increase its dividend to shareholders and also repurchase its shares in the open market. In 1984, the company authorized its first-ever buyback, announcing it would repurchase 6 million shares of stock. Since then, the company has repurchased more than 1 billion shares. This represented 32 percent of the shares outstanding as of January 1, 1984, at an average price per share of $12.46. In other words, the company spent approximately $12.4 billion to buy in shares that only ten years later would have a market value of approximately $60 billion.

In July 1992, the company announced that through the year 2000, it would buy back 100 million shares of its stock, representing 7.6 percent of the company's outstanding shares. Remarkably, because of its strong cash-generating abilities, the company was able to accomplish this while it continued its aggressive investment in overseas markets.

American Express

Buffett's association with American Express dates back some forty years, to his bold purchase of its distressed stock in 1963, and the astronomical profits he quickly earned for his investment partners (see Chapter 1 for the full story). Buffett's faith in the company has not diminished, and he has continued to purchase its stock. A big buy in 1994 can be traced to management decisions, both good and bad, about the use of excess cash.

The division of the company that issues the charge card and travelers' checks, American Express Travel Related Services, contributes the lion's share of profits. It has always generated substantial owner earnings and has easily funded its own growth. In the early 1990s, it was generating more cash than it needed for operations—the very point at which management actions collide with Buffett's acid test. In this case, American Express management did not do well.

Then-CEO James Robinson decided to use excess cash to build the company into a financial services powerhouse by buying other related businesses. His first acquisition, IDS Financial Services, proved profitable. But then he bought Shearson Lehman, which did not. Over time, Shearson needed more and more cash to carry its operations. When Shearson had swallowed up $4 billion, Robinson contacted Buffett, who agreed to buy $300 million worth of preferred shares. Until the company got back on track, he was not at all interested in buying common stock.

In 1992, Robinson abruptly resigned and was replaced by Harvey Golub. He set himself the immediate task of strengthening brand awareness. Striking a familiar tone with Buffett, he began using terms such as *franchise* and *brand value* to describe the American Express Card. Over the next two years, Golub began to liquidate the company's underperforming assets and to restore profitability and high returns on equity. One of his first actions was to get rid of Shearson Lehman, with its massive capital needs.

Soon American Express was showing signs of its old profitable self. The resources of the company were solidly behind Golub's goal of building the American Express Card into "the world's most respected service brand," and every communication from the company emphasized the franchise value of the name "American Express."

Next, Golub set financial targets for the company: to increase earnings per share by 12 to 15 percent a year and 18 to 20 percent return on equity. Before long, the company was again generating excess cash and had more capital and more shares than it needed. Then, in September 1994 the company announced that, subject to market conditions, it planned to repurchase 20 million shares of its common stock. That was music to Buffett's ears.

That summer, Buffett had converted Berkshire's holdings in preferred stock to common, and soon thereafter, he began to acquire even more. By the end of the year, Berkshire owned 27 million shares. In March 1995, Buffett added another 20 million shares; in 1997, another 49.5 million; and 50.5 million more in 1998. At the end of 2003, Berkshire owned more than 151 million shares of American Express stock, nearly 12 percent of the company, with a market value of more than $7 billion—seven times what Buffett paid for it.

The Washington Post Company

The *Washington Post* generates substantial cash flow for its owners, more than can be reinvested in its primary businesses. So its management is confronted with two rational choices: Return the money to shareholders and/or profitably invest the cash in new investment opportunities. As we know, Buffett prefers to have companies return excess earnings to shareholders. The Washington Post Company, while Katherine Graham was president, was the first newspaper company in its industry to repurchase shares in large quantities. Between 1975 and 1991, the company bought an unbelievable 43 percent of its shares at an average price of $60 per share.

A company can also choose to return money to shareholders by increasing the dividend. In 1990, confronted with substantial cash reserves, the *Washington Post* voted to increase the annual dividend to its shareholders from $1.84 to $4.00, a 117 percent increase (see Figure 6.1).

In addition to returning excess cash to its owners, the *Washington Post* has made several profitable business purchases: cable properties from Capital Cities, cellular telephone companies, and television stations. Don Graham, who now runs the company, is continually beset with offers. To further his goal of developing substantial cash flows at favorable investment costs, he has developed specific guidelines for evaluating those

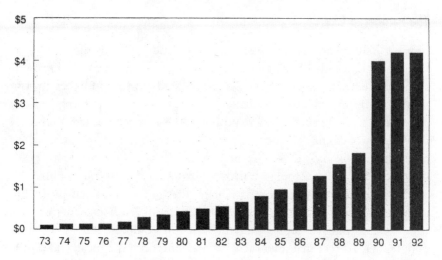

Figure 6.1 The Washington Post Company dividend per share.

offers. He looks for a business that "has competitive barriers, does not require extensive capital expenditures, and has reasonable pricing power."
Furthermore, he notes, "we have a strong preference for businesses we
know" and given the choice, "we're more likely to invest in a handful
of big bets rather than spread our investment dollars around thinly."[9]
Graham's acquisition approach mimics Buffett's strategy at Berkshire
Hathaway.

The dynamics of the newspaper business have changed in recent
years. Earlier, when the economy slowed and advertisers cut spending,
newspapers could maintain profitability by raising lineage rates. But
today's advertisers have found cheaper ways to reach their customers:
cable television, direct mail, and newspaper inserts. Newspapers are no
longer monopolies; they have lost their pricing flexibility.

Even so, Buffett is convinced that the Post is in better shape than
other media companies. There are two reasons for his optimism. First,
the Post's long-term debt was more than offset by its cash holdings.
The *Washington Post* is the only public newspaper that is essentially
free of debt. "As a result," explains Buffett, "the shrinkage in the value
of their assets has not been accentuated by the effects of leverage."[10]
Second, he notes, the Washington Post Company has been exceptionally well managed.

The Pampered Chef

Doris Christopher, the founder, chairman and CEO of the Pampered Chef, has allocated her capital well—financing all expansion and growth through internal earnings. She has reinvested virtually all her profits in the company and the resulting expansion has brought tremendous growth in sales. Between 1995 and 2001, the Pampered Chef's business grew an astonishing 232 percent, with pretax profit margins above 25 percent. And the only debt the company ever had was the original $3,000 seed money that Christopher borrowed from her life insurance policy.

From all appearances, Doris Christopher is a careful and profitable manager, and she runs a tight ship. She displays keen management intuition by treating her representatives well but competitively. The Pampered Chef's direct marketers across the country are the bread and butter of the business and the company's only direct contact with its over 12 million customers. The sales force earns commissions of 18 to 20 percent on goods they sell, and 1 to 4 percent on the sales of kitchen consultants whom they bring into the company.

CANDOR

Buffett holds in high regard managers who report their companies' financial performance fully and genuinely, who admit mistakes as well as share successes, and who are in all ways candid with shareholders. In particular, he respects managers who are able to communicate the performance of their company without hiding behind Generally Accepted Accounting Principles (GAAP).

Financial accounting standards only require disclosure of business information classified by industry segment. Some managers exploit this minimum requirement and lump together all the company's businesses into one industry segment, making it difficult for owners to understand the dynamics of their separate business interests.

"What needs to be reported," Buffett insists, "is data—whether GAAP, non-GAAP, or extra GAAP—that helps the financially literate readers answer three key questions: (1) Approximately how much is this company worth? (2) what is the likelihood that it can meet its future obligations? and (3) how good a job are its managers doing, given the hand they have been dealt?"[11]

Berkshire Hathaway's own annual reports are a good example. They meet GAAP obligations, but they go much further. Buffett includes the separate earnings of each of Berkshire's businesses and any other additional information that he feels owners would deem valuable when judging a company's economic performance. Buffett admires CEOs who are able to report to their shareholders in the same candid fashion.

He also admires those with the courage to discuss failure openly. He believes that managers who confess mistakes publicly are more likely to correct them. According to Buffett, most annual reports are a sham. Over time, every company makes mistakes, both large and inconsequential. Too many managers, he believes, report with excess optimism instead of honest explanation, serving perhaps their own interests in the short term but no one's interests in the long run.

Buffett credits Charlie Munger with helping him understand the value of studying one's mistakes instead of concentrating only on success. In his annual reports to Berkshire Hathaway shareholders, Buffett is open about Berkshire's economic and management performance, both good and bad. Through the years, he has admitted the difficulties that Berkshire encountered in both the textile and insurance businesses and his own management failures with these businesses.

His self-criticism is blunt, and unstinting. The merger with General Re reinsurance company in 1998 brought significant trouble, a good deal of which remained undiagnosed for several years, and came to light only in the wake of the World Trade Center bombing in 2001. At the time of the merger, Buffett said later, he thought the reinsurance company operated with the same discipline he demanded of other Berkshire insurance companies. "I was dead wrong," he admitted in 2002. "There was much to do at that company to get it up to snuff."[12]

The General Re problem was not limited to its insurance practices. The company also had a division that dealt in trading and derivatives, a business Buffett considered unattractive at the time of the merger (although, as part of the package, unavoidable) and financially disastrous several years later. In 2003, he wrote this straightforward apology to shareholders: "I'm sure I could have saved you $100 million or so, if I had acted more promptly to shut down Gen Re Securities. Charlie would have moved swiftly to close [it] down—no question about that. I, however, dithered. As a consequence, our shareholders are paying a far higher price than was necessary to exit this business."[13]

Critics have argued that Buffett's practice of publicly admitting his mistakes is made easier because, since he owns such a large share of Berkshire's common stock, he never has to worry about being fired. This is true. But it does not diminish the fundamental value of Buffett's belief that candor benefits the manager at least as much as it benefits the shareholder. "The CEO who misleads others in public," he says, "may eventually mislead himself in private."[14]

Coca-Cola

Roberto Goizueta's strategy for strengthening Coca-Cola when he took over as CEO pointedly included shareholders. "We shall, during the next decade, remain totally committed to our shareholders and to the protection and enhancement of their investment," he wrote. "In order to give our shareholders an above-average total return on their investment, we must choose businesses that generate returns in excess of inflation."[15]

Goizueta not only had to grow the business, which required capital investment, he was also obliged to increase shareholder value. By increasing profit margins and return on equity, Coca-Cola was able to increase dividends while simultaneously reducing the dividend payout ratio. Dividends to shareholders, in the 1980s, were increasing 10 percent per year while the payout ratio was declining from 65 percent to 40 percent. This enabled Coca-Cola to reinvest a greater percentage of the company's earnings to help sustain its growth rate without shortchanging shareholders.

Coca-Cola is undeniably a superior company with an outstanding historical economic performance record. In the most recent years, however, that level of growth has moderated. Where some shareholders might have panicked, Buffett did not. He did not, in fact, do anything; he didn't sell even one share. It is a clear testament to his belief in the company, and a clear illustration of staying true to his principles.

THE INSTITUTIONAL IMPERATIVE

If management stands to gain wisdom and credibility by facing mistakes, why do so many annual reports trumpet only successes? If allocation of capital is so simple and logical, why is capital so poorly allocated? The answer, Buffett has learned, is an unseen force he calls "the institutional imperative"—the lemminglike tendency of corporate management to imitate the behavior of other managers, no matter how silly or irrational that behavior may be.

He says it was the most surprising discovery of his business career. At school, he was taught that experienced managers were honest, intelligent, and automatically made rational business decisions. Once out in the business world, he learned instead that "rationality frequently wilts when the institutional imperative comes into play."[16]

Buffett believes that the institutional imperative is responsible for several serious, but distressingly common, conditions: "(1) [The organization] resists any change in its current direction; (2) just as work expands to fill available time, corporate projects or acquisitions will materialize to soak up available funds; (3) any business craving of the leader, however foolish, will quickly be supported by detailed rate-of-return and strategic studies prepared by his troops; and (4) the behavior of peer companies, whether they are expanding, acquiring, setting executive compensation or whatever, will be mindlessly imitated."[17]

Buffett learned this lesson early. Jack Ringwalt, head of National Indemnity, which Berkshire acquired in 1967, helped Buffett discover the destructive power of the imperative. While the majority of insurance companies were writing insurance policies on terms guaranteed to produce inadequate returns or worse, a loss, Ringwalt stepped away from the market and refused to write new policies. (For the full story, refer to Chapter 3.) Buffett recognized the wisdom of Ringwalt's decisions and followed suit. Today, Berkshire's insurance companies still operate on this principle.

What is behind the institutional imperative that drives so many businesses? Human nature. Most managers are unwilling to look foolish and expose their company to an embarrassing quarterly loss when other "lemming" companies are still able to produce quarterly gains, even though they assuredly are heading into the sea. Shifting direction is never easy. It is often easier to follow other companies down the same path toward failure than to alter the direction of the company.

Admittedly, Buffett and Munger enjoy the same protected position here as in their freedom to be candid about bad news: They don't have to worry about getting fired, and this frees them to make unconventional decisions. Still, a manager with strong communication skills should be able to convince owners to accept a short-term loss in earnings and a change in the direction of their company if it means superior results over time. Inability to resist the institutional imperative, Buffett has learned, often has less to do with the owners of the company than the willingness of its managers to accept fundamental change.

Even when managers accept the notion that their company must radically change or face the possibility of shutting down, carrying out this plan is too difficult for most managers. Many succumb to the temptation to buy a new company instead of facing the financial facts of the current problem.

Why would they do this? Buffett isolates three factors he feels most influence management's behavior. First, most managers cannot control their lust for activity. Such hyperactivity often finds its outlet in business takeovers. Second, most managers are constantly comparing the sales, earnings, and executive compensation of their business with other companies in and beyond their industry. These comparisons invariably invite corporate hyperactivity. Lastly, Buffett believes that most managers have an exaggerated sense of their own management capabilities.

Another common problem is poor allocation skills. As Buffett points out, CEOs often rise to their position by excelling in other areas of the company, including administration, engineering, marketing, or production. Because they have little experience in allocating capital, most CEOs instead turn to their staff members, consultants, or investment bankers. Here the institutional imperative begins to enter the decision-making process. Buffett points out that if the CEO craves a potential acquisition requiring a 15 percent return on investment to justify the purchase, it is amazing how smoothly his troops report back to him that the business can actually achieve 15.1 percent.

The final justification for the institutional imperative is mindless imitation. If companies A, B, and C are all doing the same thing, well then, reasons the CEO of company D, it must be all right for our company to behave the same way.

It is not venality or stupidity, Buffett believes, that positions these companies to fail. Rather, it is the institutional dynamics of the imperative that make it difficult to resist doomed behavior. Speaking before a group of Notre Dame students, Buffett displayed a list of thirty-seven failed investment banking firms. All of them, he explained, failed even though the volume of the New York Stock Exchange had multiplied fifteenfold. These firms were headed by hard-working individuals with very high IQs, all of whom had an intense desire to succeed. Buffett paused; his eyes scanned the room. "You think about that," he said sternly. "How could they get a result like that? I'll tell you how," he said, "mindless imitation of their peers."[18]

Coca-Cola

When Goizueta took over Coca-Cola, one of his first moves was to jettison the unrelated businesses that the previous CEO had developed and return the company to its core business, selling syrup. It was a clear demonstration of Coca-Cola's ability to resist the institutional imperative.

Reducing the company to a single-product business was undeniably a bold move. What made Goizueta's strategy even more remarkable was his willingness to take this action at a time when others in the industry were doing the exact opposite. Several leading beverage companies were investing their profits in other unrelated businesses. Anheuser-Busch used the profits from its beer business to invest in theme parks. Brown-Forman, a producer and distributor of wine and spirits, invested its profits in china, crystal, silver, and luggage businesses, all of them with much lower returns. Seagram Company, Ltd., a global spirits and wine business, bought Universal Studios. Pepsi, Coca-Cola's chief beverage rival, bought snack businesses (Frito-Lay) and restaurants including Taco Bell, Kentucky Fried Chicken, and Pizza Hut.

Not only did Goizueta's action focus the company's attention on its largest and most important product, but it worked to reallocate the company's resources into its most profitable business. Since the economic returns of selling syrup far outweighed the economic returns of the other businesses, the company was now reinvesting its profits in its highest-returning business.

Clayton Homes

In an industry that is strangled by problems of its own making, Clayton stands out for its strong management and smart business model.

Manufactured homes now constitute 15 percent of the total housing units in the United States. In many respects, their historically negative image is disappearing. The homes are becoming more like site-built homes in size and scope; construction quality has consistently improved; they are competitive with rentals; they have tax advantages in that owners do not have to own the underlying property; and mortgages are now supported by other large mortgage companies and government agencies, such as Fannie Mae.

Still, since they are considerably less expensive than site-built homes (2002 average prices: $48,800 compared with $164,217), the primary market remains consumers toward the lower end of the economic range. In 2002, over 22 million Americans lived in manufactured homes, with a median family income of $26,900.[19]

Many manufacturers were caught in a self-inflicted double bind in the 1990s, and many of them failed. One arm of this double bind was the increasing acceptance and popularity of these homes, which rushed many in the industry toward overexpansion. The other squeeze factor was simple greed.

The homes are sold through retailers that are either independent dealers representing several manufacturers or company-owned outlets. Right there, on the same lot, shoppers usually find a financing operation, often a subsidiary of the manufacturer/retailer. In and of itself, there is nothing wrong with this; it sounds like, and in fact operates like, a car dealership. The problem is that it has become endemic in the industry to push sales to anybody who can sign their name to a sales agreement, regardless of credit history, based on loans that are destined to default.

Selling scads of units creates immediate profits for the retailers and huge commissions for the salespeople. It also creates enormous economic problems longer range. It is an unfortunate reality that many homes are sold to people with fragile economic circumstances, and repossession rates are high, which reduces the demand for new homes. As unemployment rates rose in the past few years, so did loan delinquencies. Factor in the oversupply of inventory from the 1990s, and the tight economic times that diminished spending across the board, and it adds up to a sorry state of affairs for the industry as a whole.

Much of the problem can be traced to the very weak loans that are so common in the manufactured home business. Why do they all do it? Because they all do it, and each company fears losing market share if it does otherwise. That, in a nutshell, is the curse of the institutional imperative. Clayton has not been completely immune, but it has avoided the most egregious faults.

Most importantly, Clayton compensates its salespeople in a different way. The commissions of sellers and managers are based not only on the number of homes sold but also on the quality and performance of the loans made. Sales staff share the financial burden when loan payments are missed, and share the revenue when the loan performs well. Take, for example, a sales manager who handles the sale and financing of a $24,000 mobile home. If the customer cannot make the payments, Clayton would typically lose $2,500, and the manager is responsible for up to half the loss.[20] But if the loan performs, the manager shares up to half of that, too. That puts the burden to avoid weak loans on the sales personnel.

The methodology paid off: In 2002, "only 2.3 percent of the home-owners with a Clayton mortgage are 30 days delinquent."[21] That is roughly half the industry delinquency rate. In the late 1990s, when more than 80 factories and 4,000 retailers went out of business, Clayton closed only 31 retailers and did not shut any factories. By 2003, when Buffett entered the picture, Clayton had emerged from the downturn in the economy in general and the mobile home industry in particular stronger and better positioned than any of its competitors.

Warren Buffett bought Clayton Homes because he saw in Jim Clayton a hardworking self-starter with strong management skills and a lot of smarts. Clayton showed not once but twice that he could weather a downturn in the industry by structuring his business model in a way that avoided an especially damaging institutional imperative.

The Washington Post Company

Buffett has told us that even third-rate newspapers can earn substantial profits. Since the market does not require high standards of a paper, it is up to management to impose its own. And it is management's high standards and abilities that can differentiate the business's returns when compared with its peer group. In 1973, if Buffett had invested in Gannett, Knight-Ridder, the *New York Times,* or *Times Mirror* the same $10 million he did in the Post, his investment returns would have been above average, reflecting the exceptional economics of the news-paper business during this period. But the extra $200–$300 million in market value that the *Washington Post* gained over its peer group,

Buffett says, "came, in very large part, from the superior nature of the managerial decisions made by Kay [Katherine Graham] as compared to those made by managers of most other media companies."[22]

Katherine Graham had the brains to purchase large quantities of the Post's stock at bargain prices. She also had the courage, he said, to confront the labor unions, reduce expenses, and increase the business value of the paper. *Washington Post* shareholders are fortunate that Katherine Graham positioned the company so favorably.

> In evaluating people, you look for three qualities: integrity, intelligence, and energy. If you don't have the first, the other two will kill you.[23]
>
> WARREN BUFFETT, 1993

WARREN BUFFETT ON MANAGEMENT, ETHICS, AND RATIONALITY

In all his communications with Berkshire shareholders, and indeed with the world at large, Buffett has consistently emphasized his search for honest and straightforward managers. He believes that not only are these binding corporate values in today's world, they are also pivotal issues that determine a company's ultimate success and profitability in the long term. Executive compensation, stock options, director independence, accounting trickery—these issues strike a very personal chord with Buffett, and he does not hesitate to let us know how he feels.

CEO Avarice and the Institutional Imperative

In his 2001 letter to shareholders, Buffett wrote, "Charlie and I are disgusted by the situation, so common in the last few years, in which shareholders have suffered billions in losses while the CEOs, promoters and other higher-ups who fathered these disasters have walked away with extraordinary wealth. Indeed, many of these people were urging investors to buy shares while concurrently dumping their own, sometimes using methods that hid their actions. To their shame, these business leaders view shareholders as patsies, not partners. . . . There is no shortage of egregious conduct in corporate America."[24]

The accounting scandals set off alarm bells across the United States, especially for anyone who held stock in a company 401(k) plan. Shareholders started asking questions and wondering if their companies were managing their affairs honestly and transparently. We all became increasingly aware that there were major problems in the system: CEOs were getting huge paychecks while using company money for private jets and ostentatious parties, and directors were often rubber-stamping whatever decisions management decided to take. It seemed as if not one CEO could resist the temptation to get in on the enormous salaries and extravagant lifestyles enjoyed by others. That is the institutional imperative at its most destructive.

Things have not improved much, according to Buffett. In his 2003 letter to shareholders, he lambasted the seemingly unabated "epidemic of greed." He wrote, "Overreaching by CEOs greatly accelerated in the 1990s as compensation packages gained by the most avaricious—a title for which there was vigorous competition—were promptly replicated elsewhere. In judging whether Corporate America is serious about reforming itself, CEO pay remains the acid test. To date, the results aren't encouraging."[25] This from a man who has no stock options and still pays himself $100,000 a year.

Stock Options

In addition to these lofty salaries, executives of publicly traded companies are customarily rewarded with fixed-price stock options, often tied to corporate earnings but very seldom tied to the executive's actual job performance.

This goes against the grain for Buffett. When stock options are passed out indiscriminately, he says, managers with below-average performance are rewarded just as generously as the managers who have had excellent performance. In Buffett's mind, even if your team wins the pennant, you don't pay a .350 hitter the same as a .150 hitter.

At Berkshire, Buffett uses a compensation system that rewards managers for performance. The reward is not tied to the size of the enterprise, the individual's age, or Berkshire's overall profits. Buffett believes that good unit performance should be rewarded whether Berkshire's stock price rises or falls. Instead, executives are compensated based on their success at meeting performance goals keyed to their area of responsibility. Some managers are rewarded for increasing sales, others for reducing expenses or curtailing capital expenditures. At the end of the year, Buffett does not hand out stock options—he writes checks. Some are quite large. Managers can use the cash as they please. Many use it to purchase Berkshire stock.

Even when stock options are treated as a legitimate aspect of executive compensation, Buffett cautions us to watch how they are accounted for on a company's balance sheet. He believes they should be considered an expense so that their effect on reported earnings is clear. This seems so obvious as to be unarguable; sadly, not all companies see it this way.

In Buffett's mind, this is another facet of the ready acceptance of excessive pay. In his 2003 letter to shareholders, he wrote, "When CEOs or their representatives meet with compensation committees, too often one side—the CEO's—has cared far more than the other about what bargain is struck. A CEO, for example, will always regard the difference between receiving options for 100,000 shares or for 500,000 as monumental. To a comp committee, however, the difference may seem unimportant—particularly if, as has been the case at most companies, neither grant will have any effect on reported earnings. Under these conditions, the negotiation often has a 'play money' quality."[26]

Buffett's strong feelings about this subject can be seen in his response to Amazon's announcement in April 2003 that it would start expensing stock options. Buffett wrote to CEO Jeff Bezos that it took "particular courage" and his decision would be "recognized and remembered."[27] A week later, Buffett bought $98.3 million of Amazon's high-yield bonds.

Malfeasant Accounting and Shady Financing Issues

Anyone who was reading a daily newspaper in the second half of 2001 could not help but be aware of the growing tide of corporate wrongdoing. For months, we all watched with something amounting to horror as one scandal followed another, involving some of the best-known names in American industry. All came to be lumped under the umbrella term "accounting scandal" because the misdeeds centered on accounting trickery and because the outside auditors who were supposed to verify the accounting reports were themselves named as parties to the actions.

> In the long run, of course, trouble awaits managements that paper over operating problems with accounting maneuvers.[28]
>
> WARREN BUFFETT, 1991 [NOTE THE DATE OF THIS REMARK.]

It's far broader than accounting, of course; it's about greed, lies, and criminal acts. But accounting reports are a good place to look for signs of trouble. In his 2002 letter to shareholders, Buffett warned investors to be careful in reading annual reports. "If you've been a reader of financial reports in recent years," he wrote, "you've seen a flood of 'pro-forma' earnings statements—tabulations in which managers invariably show 'earnings' far in excess of those allowed by their auditors. In these presentations, the CEO tells his owners 'don't count this, don't count that—just count what makes earnings fat.' Often, a forget-all-this-bad-stuff message is delivered year after year without management so much as blushing."[29]

Buffett is plainly disgusted by the scandals. "The blatant wrongdoing that has occurred has betrayed the trust of so many millions of shareholders." He blames the heady days of the 1990s, the get-rich-quick period he calls the Great Bubble, for the deterioration of corporate ethics. "As stock prices went up," he says, "the behavioral norms of managers went down. By the late 90s, CEOs who traveled the high road did not encounter heavy traffic. Too many have behaved badly, fudging numbers and drawing obscene pay for mediocre business achievements."[30] And in too many cases, their companies' directors, charged with upholding shareholder interests, failed miserably.

Director Negligence and Corporate Governance

Part of the problem, Buffett suggests, is the shameful tendency of boards of directors to blithely rubber-stamp whatever senior management asks for. It is a question of independence and guts—the degree to which directors are willing to honor their fiduciary responsibility at the risk of displeasing the senior executives. That willingness, or lack of it, is on display in boardrooms across the country.

"True independence—meaning the willingness to challenge a forceful CEO when something is wrong or foolish—is an enormously valuable trait in a director," Buffett writes. "It is also rare. The place to look for it is among high-grade people whose interests are in line with those of rank and file shareholders." Buffett illuminates his position by describing what he looks for in members of the Berkshire Hathaway board—"very high integrity, business savvy, shareholder orientation and a genuine interest in the company."[31]

CAN WE REALLY PUT A VALUE ON MANAGEMENT?

Buffett would be the first to admit that evaluating managers along his three dimensions—rationality, candor, and independent thinking—is more difficult than measuring financial performance, for the simple reason that human beings are more complex than numbers.

Indeed, many analysts believe that because measuring human activity is vague and imprecise, we simply cannot value management with any degree of confidence, and therefore the exercise is futile. Without a decimal point, they seem to suggest, there is nothing to measure. Others hold the view that the value of management is fully reflected in the company's performance statistics, including sales, profit margins, and return on equity, and no other measuring stick is necessary.

Both opinions have some validity, but neither is strong enough to outweigh the original premise. The reason for taking the time to evaluate management is that it gives you early warning signs of eventual financial performance. If you look closely at the words and actions of a management team, you will find clues that can help you measure the value of their work long before it shows up in the company's financial reports or in the stock pages of your daily newspaper. Doing so will take some digging on your part, and that may be enough to discourage the weak of heart or the lazy. That is their loss, and your gain.

How to go about gathering the necessary information? Buffett offers a few tips. He suggests reviewing annual reports from a few years back, paying special attention to what management said then about strategies for the future. Then compare those plans to today's results: How fully were they realized? Also compare strategies of a few years ago to this year's strategies and ideas: How has the thinking changed? Buffett also suggests that it can be very valuable to compare annual reports of the company you are interested in with reports from similar companies in the same industry. It is not always easy to find exact duplicates, but even relative performance comparison can yield insights.

> I read annual reports of the company I'm looking at and I read the annual reports of the competitors. That's the main source material.
>
> WARREN BUFFETT, 1993
>
> We like to keep things simple, so the chairman can sit around and read annual reports.[32]
>
> CHARLIE MUNGER, 1993

Expand your reading horizons. Be alert for articles in newspapers and financial magazines about the company you are interested in and about its industry in general. Read what the company's executives have to say and what others say about them. If you notice that the chairman recently made a speech or presentation, get a copy from the investor relations department and study it carefully. Make use of the company's web pages for up-to-the-minute information. In every way you can think of, raise your antennae. The more you develop the habit of staying alert for information, the easier the process will become.

It must be said here, with sadness, that it is possible that the documents you study are filled with inflated numbers, half-truths, and deliberate obfuscations. We all know the names of the companies charged with doing this; they are a rogue's gallery of American businesses, and some of their leaders are finding themselves with lots of time in prison to rethink their actions. Sometimes the manipulations are so skillful that even forensic accountants are fooled; how then can you, an investor without any special knowledge, fully understand what you are seeing?

The regrettable answer is, you cannot. You can learn how to read annual reports and balance sheets—and you should—but if they are based on flagrant deception and lies, you might not be able to detect it.

I do not mean to say that you should simply give up. Keep doing your research, and strive to be alert for signs of trouble. It should not surprise us that Warren Buffett gives us some valuable tips:[33]

- "Beware of companies displaying weak accounting." In particular, he cautions us to watch out for companies that do not expense stock options. It's an obvious red flag that other less obvious maneuvers are also present.
- Another red flag: "unintelligible footnotes." If you can't understand them, he says, don't assume it's your shortcoming; it's a favored tool for hiding something management doesn't want you to know.
- "Be suspicious of companies that trumpet earnings projections and growth expectations." No one can know the future, and any CEO who claims to do so is not worthy of your trust.

In conclusion, Buffett wants to work with managers who are straight shooters, who are candid with their shareholders and their employees. His unshakable insistence on ethical behavior as a condition of doing business has taken on added significance since the outbreak of corporate scandals. However, he would be the first to acknowledge that taking such a stand will not, in and of itself, insulate investors from losses triggered by fraud.

I must add my own caution: I cannot promise that following the tenets of the Warren Buffett Way described in this book will protect you 100 percent. If company officials are flat-out lying to investors through fraudulent accounting or other illegal maneuvers and if they're good at it, it can be difficult, often impossible, to detect in time. Eventually the perpetrators end up in jail, but by then the damage to shareholders is done; the money is gone. What I can say is this: If you adopt the careful, thoughtful way of looking at investments that Buffett teaches us and take the time to do your homework, you will be right more often than you are wrong, and certainly more often than those who allow themselves to be pushed and pulled willy-nilly by headlines and rumor.

7

Investing Guidelines

Financial Tenets

The financial tenets by which Buffett values both managerial excellence and economic performance are all grounded in some typically Buffett-like principles. For one thing, he does not take yearly results too seriously. Instead, he focuses on four- or five-year averages. Often, he notes, profitable business returns might not coincide with the time it takes for the planet to circle the sun.

He also has little patience with accounting sleight-of-hand that produces impressive year-end numbers but little real value. Instead, he relies on a few timeless financial principles:

- Focus on return on equity, not earnings per share.
- Calculate "owner earnings" to get a true reflection of value.
- Look for companies with high profit margins.
- For every dollar retained, has the company created at least a dollar of market value?

RETURN ON EQUITY

Customarily, analysts measure annual company performance by looking at earnings per share. Did they increase over the preceding year? Are they high enough to brag about? For his part, Buffett considers earnings per share a smoke screen. Since most companies retain a portion of their previous year's earnings to increase their equity base, he sees no reason to get excited about record earnings per share. There is nothing spectacular about a company that increases earnings per share by 10 percent if at the same time it is growing its equity base by 10 percent. That's no different, he explains, from putting money in a savings account and letting the interest accumulate and compound.

The test of economic performance, Buffett believes, is whether a company achieves a high earnings rate on equity capital ("without undue leverage, accounting gimmickry, etc."), not whether it has consistent gains in earnings per share.[1] To measure a company's annual performance, Buffett prefers return on equity—the ratio of operating earnings to shareholders' equity.

To use this ratio, though, we need to make several adjustments. First, all marketable securities should be valued at cost and not at market value, because values in the stock market as a whole can greatly influence the returns on shareholders' equity in a particular company. For example, if the stock market rose dramatically in one year, thereby increasing the net worth of a company, a truly outstanding operating performance would be diminished when compared with a larger denominator. Conversely, falling prices reduce shareholders' equity, which means that mediocre operating results appear much better than they really are.

Second, we must also control the effects that unusual items may have on the numerator of this ratio. Buffett excludes all capital gains and losses as well as any extraordinary items that may increase or decrease operating earnings. He is seeking to isolate the specific annual performance of a business. He wants to know how well management accomplishes its task of generating a return on the operations of the business given the capital it employs. That, he says, is the single best measure of management's economic performance.

Furthermore, Buffett believes that a business should achieve good returns on equity while employing little or no debt. We know that companies can increase their return on equity by increasing their debt-to-equity ratio. Buffett is aware of this, but the idea of adding a couple of points to Berkshire Hathaway's return on equity simply by taking on more debt does not impress him. "Good business or investment decisions," he says, "will produce quite satisfactory economic results with no aid from leverage."[2] Furthermore, highly leveraged companies are vulnerable during economic slowdowns.

Buffett does not give us any suggestions as to what debt levels are appropriate or inappropriate for a business. Different companies, depending on their cash flows, can manage different levels of debt. What Buffett does tell us is that a good business should be able to earn a good return on equity without the aid of leverage. Investors should be wary of companies that can earn good returns on equity only by employing significant debt.

Coca-Cola

In "Strategy for the 1980s," his plan for revitalizing the company, Goizueta pointed out that Coca-Cola would divest any business that no longer generated acceptable returns on equity. Any new business venture must have sufficient real growth potential to justify an investment. Coca-Cola was no longer interested in battling for share in a stagnant market. "Increasing earnings per share and effecting increased return on equity are still the name of the game," Goizueta announced.[3] His words were followed by actions. Coca-Cola's wine business was sold to Seagram's in 1983.

Although the company earned a respectable 20 percent return on equity during the 1970s, Goizueta was not impressed. He demanded better returns and the company obliged. By 1988, Coca-Cola's return on equity had increased to 31.8 percent (see Figure 7.1).

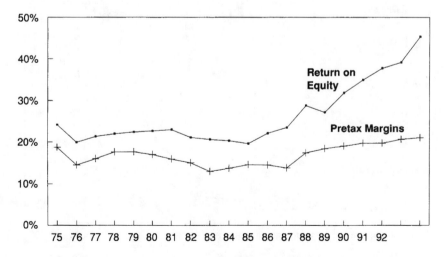

Figure 7.1 The Coca-Cola Company return on equity and pretax margins.

By any measurement, Goizueta's Coca-Cola was doubling and tripling the financial accomplishments of the previous CEO. The results could be seen in the market value of the company. In 1980, Coca-Cola had a market value of $4.1 billion. By the end of 1987, even after the stock market crash in October, the market value had risen to $14.1 billion (see Figure 7.2). In seven years, Coca-Cola's market value rose at an average annual rate of 19.3 percent.

The Washington Post Company

When Buffett purchased stock in the *Washington Post* in 1973, its return on equity was 15.7 percent. This was an average return for most newspapers and only slightly better than the Standard & Poor's Industrial Index. But within five years, the Post's return on equity doubled. By then, it was twice as high as the S&P Industrials and 50 percent higher than the average newspaper. Over the next ten years, the Post Company maintained its supremacy, reaching a high of 36.3 percent return on equity in 1988.

These above-average returns are more impressive when you observe that the company has, over time, purposely reduced its debt. In 1973, long-term debt to shareholder's equity stood at 37.2 percent, the second highest ratio in the newspaper group. Astonishingly, by 1978, Katherine

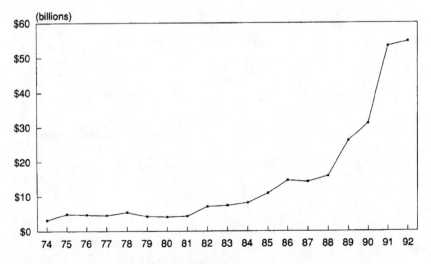

Figure 7.2 The Coca-Cola Company market value.

Graham had reduced the company's debt by 70 percent. In 1983, long-term debt to equity was a low 2.7 percent—one-tenth the newspaper group average—yet the Post generated a return on equity 10 percent higher than these same companies.

"OWNER EARNINGS"

Investors, Buffett warns, should be aware that accounting earnings per share represent the starting point for determining the economic value of a business, not the ending point. "The first point to understand," he says, "is that not all earnings are created equal."[4] Companies with high assets to profits, he points out, tend to report ersatz earnings. Because inflation extracts a toll on asset-heavy businesses, the earnings of these businesses take on a miragelike quality. Hence, accounting earnings are useful to the analyst only if they approximate the expected cash flow of the company.

But even cash flow, Buffett warns, is not a perfect tool for measuring value; often it misleads investors. Cash flow is an appropriate way to measure businesses that have large investments in the beginning and smaller outlays later on, such as real estate, gas fields, and cable companies. On the other hand, companies that require ongoing capital expenditures, such as manufacturers, are not accurately valued using only cash flow.

A company's cash flow is customarily defined as net income after taxes plus depreciation, depletion, amortization, and other noncash charges. The problem with this definition, Buffett explains, is that it leaves out a critical economic fact: capital expenditures. How much of the year's earnings must the company use for new equipment, plant upgrades, and other improvements to maintain its economic position and unit volume? According to Buffett, approximately 95 percent of U.S. businesses require capital expenditures that are roughly equal to their depreciation rates. You can defer capital expenditures for a year or so, he says, but if over a long period, you don't make the necessary improvements, your business will surely decline. These capital expenditures are as much an expense to a company as are labor and utility costs.

Popularity of cash-flow numbers heightened during the leveraged buyout period of the 1980s because the exorbitant prices paid for businesses were justified by a company's cash flow. Buffett believes that cash-flow numbers "are frequently used by marketers of business and securities to justify the unjustifiable and thereby sell what should be un-salable. When earnings look inadequate to service debt of a junk bond or justify a foolish stock price, how convenient it becomes to focus on cash flow."[5] But you cannot focus on cash flow, Buffett cautions, un-less you are willing to subtract the necessary capital expenditures.

Instead of cash flow, Buffett prefers to use what he calls "owner earnings"—a company's net income plus depreciation, depletion, and amortization, less the amount of capital expenditures and any addi-tional working capital that might be needed. It is not a mathematically precise measure, Buffett admits, for the simple reason that calculating future capital expenditures often requires rough estimates. Still, quot-ing Keynes, he says, "I would rather be vaguely right than precisely wrong."

Coca-Cola

In 1973, "owner earnings" (net income plus depreciation minus capital expenditures) were $152 million. By 1980, owner earnings were $262 million, an 8 percent annual compounded growth rate. Then from 1981 through 1988, owner earnings grew from $262 million to $828 million, a 17.8 percent average annual compounded growth rate (see Figure 7.3).

The growth in owner earnings is reflected in the share price of Coca-Cola. In the ten-year period from 1973 to 1982, the total return of Coca-Cola grew at a 6.3 percent average annual rate. Over the next ten years, from 1983 to 1992, the total return grew at an average an-nual rate of 31.1 percent.

PROFIT MARGINS

Like Philip Fisher, Buffett is aware that great businesses make lousy in-vestments if management cannot convert sales into profits. In his expe-rience, managers of high-cost operations tend to find ways that continually add to overhead, whereas managers of low-cost operations are always finding ways to cut expenses.

Buffett has little patience for managers who allow costs to esca-late. Frequently these same managers have to initiate a restructuring program to bring down costs in line with sales. Each time a company

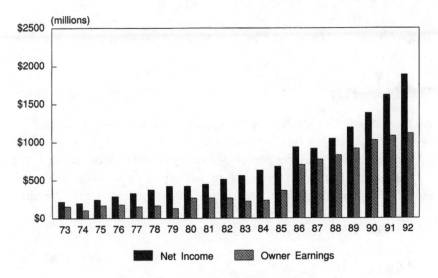

Figure 7.3 The Coca-Cola Company net income and "owner earnings."

announces a cost-cutting program, he knows this company has not fig-ured out what expenses can do to a company's owners. "The really good manager," Buffett says, "does not wake up in the morning and say, 'This is the day I'm going to cut costs,' any more than he wakes up and decides to practice breathing."[6]

Buffett understands the right size staff for any business operation and believes that for every dollar of sales there is an appropriate level of expenses. He has singled out Carl Reichardt and Paul Hazen at Wells Fargo for their relentless attack on unnecessary expenses. They "abhor having a bigger head count than is needed," he says, "and 'Attack costs as vigorously when profits are at record levels as when they are under pressure.'"[7]

Buffett himself can be tough when it comes to costs and unnecessary expenses, and he is very sensitive about Berkshire's profit margins. Of course, Berkshire Hathaway is a unique corporation. The corporate staff at Kiewit Plaza would have difficulty fielding a softball team. Berkshire Hathaway does not have a legal department, a public or investor rela-tions department. There are no strategic planning departments staffed with MBA-trained workers plotting mergers and acquisitions. The company's aftertax overhead corporate expense runs less than 1 percent of operating earnings. Compare this, says Buffett, with other companies that have similar earnings but 10 percent corporate expenses; shareholders lose 9 percent in the value of their holdings simply because of corporate overhead.

The Pampered Chef

As mentioned, Doris Christopher founded her company with $3,000 borrowed against her family's life insurance policy and she never took on further debt. Today her company has over $700 million in sales.

Customers pay for products before delivery so the company is a cash-positive business. Alan Luce, president of Luce & Associates in Orlando, Florida, a direct selling consulting firm, has estimated pretax profit margins at above 25 percent.

Coca-Cola

In 1980, Coca-Cola's pretax profit margins were a low 12.9 percent. Margins had been falling for five straight years and were substantially below the company's 1973 margins of 18 percent. In Goizueta's first year, pretax margins rose to 13.7 percent; by 1988, when Buffett bought his Coca-Cola shares, margins had climbed to a record 19 percent.

The Washington Post Company

Six months after the Post Company went public in 1971, Katherine Graham met with Wall Street security analysts. The first order of business, she told them, was to maximize profits from the company's existing operations. Profits continued to rise at the television stations and *Newsweek,* but profitability at the newspaper was leveling off. The primary reason, she said, was high production costs, namely wages.

After the Post purchased the *Times-Herald,* profits at the company had surged. Each time the unions struck the paper (1949, 1958, 1966, 1968, 1969), management had opted to pay their demands rather than risk a shutdown. During this time, Washington, DC, was still a three-newspaper town. Throughout the 1950s and 1960s, increasing wage costs dampened profits. This problem, Mrs. Graham told the analysts, was going to be solved.

As union contracts began to expire in the 1970s, Mrs. Graham enlisted labor negotiators who took a hard line with the unions. In 1974, the company defeated a strike by the Newspaper Guild and, after lengthy negotiations, the printers settled on a new contract.

In the early 1970s, *Forbes* had written, "The best that could be said about The Washington Post Company's performance was it rated a gentleman's C in profitability."[8] Pretax margins in 1973 were 10.8 percent—well below the company's historical 15 percent margins earned in the 1960s. After the successful renegotiation of the union contracts, the Post's fortunes improved. By 1978, profit margins had leaped to 19.3 percent—an 80 percent improvement within five years.

Buffett's bet had paid off. By 1988, the Post's pretax margin reached a high of 31.8 percent, which compared favorably with its newspaper group average of 16.9 percent and the Standard & Poor's Industrial average of 8.6 percent. Although the company's margins have declined somewhat in recent years, they remain substantially higher than the industry average.

THE ONE-DOLLAR PREMISE

Buffett's goal is to select companies in which each dollar of retained earnings is translated into at least one dollar of market value. This test can quickly identify companies whose managers, over time, have been able to optimally invest their company's capital. If retained earnings are invested in the company and produce above-average return, the proof will be a proportionally greater rise in the company's market value.

In time, that is. Although the stock market will track business value reasonably well over long periods, in any one year, prices can gyrate widely for reasons other than value. The same is true for retained earnings, Buffett explains. If a company uses retained earnings unproductively over an extended period, eventually the market, justifiably, will price its shares disappointingly. Conversely, if a company has been able to achieve above-average returns on augmented capital, the increased stock price will reflect that success.

Buffett believes that if he has selected a company with favorable long-term economic prospects run by able and shareholder-oriented managers, the proof will be reflected in the increased market value of the company. And he uses a quick test: The increased market value should at the very least match the amount of retained earnings, dollar for dollar. If the value goes higher than the retained earnings, so much the better. All in all, explains Buffett, "within this gigantic auction arena, it is our job to select a business with economic characteristics allowing each dollar of retained earnings to be translated into at least a dollar of market value."[9]

Coca-Cola

Since 1988, when Buffett began buying its stock, the price performance of Coca-Cola has been extraordinary. From $10 per share, the stock reached $45 in 1992. During this same period, Coca-Cola trounced the performance of the Standard & Poor's 500 Index.

Between 1989 and 1999, the market value of Coca-Cola rose from $25.8 billion to $143.9 billion. To put this growth in other terms, consider this: A $100 investment in its common stock on December 31, 1989, with dividends reinvested, grew in pretax value to $681 ten years later—an average annual compound return of 21 percent. In that same ten-year period, the company produced $26.9 billion in profits, paid out $10.5 billion in dividends to shareholders, and retained $16.4 billion for reinvestment. For every dollar the company retained, it created $7.20 in market value.

At year-end 2003, Berkshire's original $1.023 billion investment in Coca-Cola was worth more than $10 billion.

Gillette

From 1988, when Buffett first became involved with the company, to 1992, the market value of Gillette increased by $9.3 billion. During this time, the company earned $1.6 billion, distributed $582 million to shareholders, and retained $1.011 billion for reinvestment. For every dollar it retained, the market value of the company increased $9.21.

Looking deep into a company's financial structure is no easy task, and for anyone who is not Warren Buffett, it is virtually impossible to learn all these facts when the company is privately held. Nonetheless, Buffett would tell us, the effort is always worthwhile, for it reveals significant information.

As we have learned of one accounting scandal after another, it has become even more critical for investors to delve into these financial areas. There is no guarantee that through this effort you will fully uncover the truth, but you will have much greater chance of spotting phony numbers than if you do nothing. As Buffett remarks, "Managers that always promise to 'make the numbers' will at some point make *up* the numbers."[10] Your goal is to begin to learn to tell the difference.

8

Investing Guidelines

Value Tenets

All the principles embodied in the tenets described so far lead to one decision point: buying or not buying shares in a company. At that point, any investor must weigh two factors: Is this company a good value, and is this a good time to buy it—that is, is the price favorable?

The stock market establishes price. The investor determines value after weighing all the known information about a company's business, management, and financial traits. Price and value are not necessarily equal. As Warren Buffett often remarks, "Price is what you pay. Value is what you get."

If the stock market were truly efficient, prices would instantaneously adjust to all available information. Of course, we know this does not occur. Stock prices move above and below company values for numerous reasons, not all of them logical.

> It's bad to go to bed at night thinking about the price of a stock. We think about the value and company results; The stock market is there to serve you, not instruct you.[1]
>
> WARREN BUFFETT, 2003

Theoretically, investors make their decisions based on the differences between price and value. If the price is lower than its per share value, a rational investor will decide to buy. If the price is higher than value, any reasonable investor will pass.

As the company moves through its economic life cycle, a savvy investor will periodically reassess the company's value in relation to market price and will buy, sell, or hold shares accordingly.

In sum, then, rational investing has two components:

1. Determine the value of the business.
2. Buy only when the price is right—when the business is selling at a significant discount to its value.

CALCULATE WHAT THE BUSINESS IS WORTH

Through the years, financial analysts have used many formulas for determining the intrinsic value of a company. Some are fond of various shorthand methods: low price-to-earnings ratios, low price-to-book values, and high dividend yields. But the best system, according to Buffett, was determined more than sixty years ago by John Burr Williams (see Chapter 2). Buffett and many others use Williams's dividend discount model, presented in his book *The Theory of Investment Value,* as the best way to determine the value of a security.

Paraphrasing Williams, Buffett tells us that the value of a business is the total of the net cash flows (owner earnings) expected to occur over the life of the business, discounted by an appropriate interest rate. He considers it simply the most appropriate yardstick with which to measure a basket of different investment types: government bonds, corporate bonds, common stocks, apartment buildings, oil wells, and farms.

The mathematical exercise, Buffett tells us, is similar to valuing a bond. The bond market each day adds up the future coupons of a bond and discounts those coupons at the prevailing interest rate; that determines the value of the bond. To determine the value of a business, the investor estimates the "coupons" that the business will generate for a period into the future and then discounts all these coupons back to the present. "So valued," Buffett says, "all businesses, from

manufacturers of buggy whips to operators of cellular telephones, be–
come economic equals."[2]

To summarize, then, calculating the current value of a business
means, first, estimating the total earnings that will likely occur over the
life of the business; and then discounting that total backward to today.
(Keep in mind that for "earnings" Buffett uses owner earnings—net
cash flow adjusted for capital expenditures, as described in Chapter 7.)

To estimate the total future earnings, we would apply all we had
learned about the company's business characteristics, its financial
health, and the quality of its managers, using the analysis principles de–
scribed thus far. For the second part of the formula, we need only de–
cide what the discount rate should be—more on that in a moment.

Buffett is firm on one point: He looks for companies whose future
earnings are as predictable, as certain, as the earnings of bonds. If the
company has operated with consistent earnings power *and* if the busi–
ness is simple and understandable, Buffett believes he can determine its
future earnings with a high degree of certainty. If he is unable to proj–
ect with confidence what the future cash flows of a business will be, he
will not attempt to value the company. He'll simply pass.

> To properly value a business, you should ideally take all the
> flows of money that will be distributed between now and judg–
> ment day and discount them at an appropriate discount rate.
> That's what valuing businesses is all about. Part of the equation
> is how confident you can be about those cash flows occurring.
> Some businesses are easier to predict than others. We try to
> look at businesses that are predictable.[3]
>
> WARREN BUFFETT, 1988

This is the distinction of Buffett's approach. Although he admits
that Microsoft is a dynamic company and he regards Bill Gates highly
as a manager, Buffett confesses he hasn't a clue how to estimate the fu–
ture cash earnings of this company. This is what he means by "the cir–
cle of competence"; he does not know the technology industry well

enough to project the long-term earnings potential of any company within it.

This brings us to the second element in the formula: What is the appropriate discount rate? Buffett's answer is simple: the rate that would be considered risk-free. For many years, he used the rate then current for long-term government bonds. Because the certainty that the U.S. government will pay its coupon over the next thirty years is virtually 100 percent, we can say that this is a risk-free rate.

When interest rates are low, Buffett adjusts the discount rate upward. When bond yields dipped below 7 percent, Buffett upped his discount rate to 10 percent, and that is what he commonly uses today. If interest rates work themselves higher over time, he has successfully matched his discount rate to the long-term rate. If they do not, he has increased his margin of safety by three additional points.

Some academicians argue that no company, regardless of its strengths, can assure future cash earnings with the same certainty as a bond. Therefore, they insist, a more appropriate discount factor would be the risk-free rate of return *plus* an equity risk premium, added to reflect the uncertainty of the company's future cash flows. Buffett does not add a risk premium. Instead, he relies on his single-minded focus on companies with consistent and predictable earnings and on the margin of safety that comes from buying at a substantial discount in the first place. "I put a heavy weight on certainty," Buffett says. "If you do that, the whole idea of a risk factor doesn't make any sense to me."[4]

Coca-Cola

When Buffett first purchased Coca-Cola in 1988, people asked: "Where is the value in Coke?" Why was Buffett willing to pay five times book value for a company with a 6.6 percent earning yield? Because, as he continuously reminds us, price tells us nothing about value, and he believed Coca-Cola was a good value.

To begin with, the company was earning 31 percent return on equity while employing relatively little in capital investment. More important, Buffett could see the difference that Roberto Goizueta's management was making. Because Goizueta was selling off the poor-performing businesses and reinvesting the proceeds back into the higher-performing syrup business, Buffett knew the financial returns of Coca-Cola were going to improve. In addition, Goizueta was buying back shares of Coca-Cola in the market, thereby increasing the economic value of the business even more. All this went into Buffett's value calculation. Let's walk through the calculation with him.

In 1988, owner earnings of Coca-Cola equaled $828 million. The thirty-year U.S. Treasury Bond (the risk-free rate) at that time traded near a 9 percent yield. So Coca-Cola's 1988 owner earnings, discounted by 9 percent, would produce an intrinsic value of $9.2 billion. When Buffett purchased Coca-Cola, the market value was $14.8 billion, 60 percent higher, which led some observers to think he had overpaid. But $9.2 billion represents the discounted value of Coca-Cola's then-current owner earnings. If Buffett was willing to pay the higher price, it had to be because he perceived that part of the value of Coca-Cola was its future growth opportunities.

When a company is able to grow owner earnings without additional capital, it is appropriate to discount owner earnings by the difference between the risk-free rate of return and the expected growth of owner earnings. Analyzing Coca-Cola, we find that owner earnings from 1981 through 1988 grew at a 17.8 percent annual rate—faster than the risk-free rate of return. When this occurs, analysts use a two-stage discount model. This model is a way of calculating future earnings when a company has extraordinary growth for a certain number of years and then a period of constant growth at a slower rate.

We can use this two-stage process to calculate the 1988 present value of the company's future cash flows (see Table 8.1). First, assume that starting in 1988, Coca-Cola would be able to grow owner earnings at 15 percent per year for ten years. This is a reasonable assumption, since that rate is lower than the company's previous seven-year average. By the tenth year, the $828 million owner earnings that we started with would have increased to $3.349 billion. Let's further assume that starting in the eleventh year, growth rate will slow to 5 percent a year. Using a discount rate of 9 percent (the long-term bond rate at the time), we can back-calculate the intrinsic value of Coca-Cola in 1988: $48.377 billion (see Notes section at the end of this book for details of this calculation).[5]

But what happens if we decide to be more conservative, and use different growth rate assumptions? If we assume that Coca-Cola can grow owner earnings at 12 percent for ten years followed by 5 percent

Table 8.1 The Coca-Cola Company Discounted Owner Earnings Using a Two-Stage "Dividend" Discount Model (first stage is ten years)

	Year									
	1	2	3	4	5	6	7	8	9	10
Prior year cash flow	$828	$0,952	$1,095	$1,259	$1,448	1,665	1,915	2,202	2,532	2,912
Growth rate (add)	15%	15%	15%	15%	15%	15%	15%	15%	15%	15%
Cash flow	$952	$1,095	$1,259	$1,448	$1,665	1,915	2,202	2,532	2,912	3,349
Discount factor (multiply)	0.9174	0.8417	0.7722	0.7084	0.6499	0.5963	0.5470	0.5019	0.4604	0.4224
Discounted value per annum	$873	$922	972	$1,026	$1,082	$1,142	$1,204	$1,271	$1,341	$1,415
Sum of present value of cash flows					$11,248					
Residual Value										
Cash flow in year 10		$3,349								
Growth rate (g) (add)		5%								
Cash flow in year 11		$3,516								
Capitalization rate (k - g)		4%								
Value at end of year 10		$87,900								
Discount factor at end of year 10 (multiply)		0.4224								
Present Value of Residual					37,129					
Market Value of Company					$48,377					

Notes: Assumed first-stage growth rate = 15.0%; assumed second-stage growth rate = 5.0%; k = discount rate = 9.0%.
Dollar amounts are in millions.

growth, the present value of the company discounted at 9 percent would be $38.163 billion. At 10 percent growth for ten years and 5 percent thereafter, the value of Coca-Cola would be $32.497 billion. And if we assume only 5 percent throughout, the company would still be worth at least $20.7 billion [$828 million divided by (9–5 percent)].

Gillette

Berkshire, as mentioned in Chapter 4, bought $600 million worth of convertible preferred stock in July 1989. After a 2-for-1 stock split in February 1991, Berkshire converted its preferred stock and received 12 million common shares, 11 percent of Gillette's shares outstanding.

Now that Berkshire owned Gillette common yielding 1.7 percent versus the convertible preferred yielding 8.75 percent, its investment in Gillette was no longer a fixed-income security with appreciation potential but a straight equity commitment. If Berkshire were to retain its common stock, Buffett needed to be convinced that Gillette was a good investment.

We already know that Buffett understood the company and that the company's long-term prospects were favorable. Gillette's financial characteristics, including return on equity and pretax margins, were improving. The ability to increase prices thereby boosting return on equity to above-average rates signaled the company's growing economic goodwill. CEO Mockler was purposefully reducing Gillette's long-term debt and working hard to increase shareholder value.

In short, the company met all the prerequisites for purchase. What remained for Buffett was to determine the company's value, to assure that Gillette was not overpriced.

Gillette's owner earnings at year-end 1990 were $275 million and had grown at a 16 percent annual rate since 1987. Although this is too short a period to fully judge a company's growth, we can begin to make certain assumptions. In 1991, Buffett compared Gillette to Coca-Cola. "Coca-Cola and Gillette are two of the best companies in the world," he wrote, "and we expect their earnings to grow at hefty rates in the years ahead."[6]

In early 1991, the thirty-year U.S. government bond was trading at an 8.62 percent yield. To be conservative, we can use a 9 percent discount rate to value Gillette. But like Coca-Cola, Gillette's potential growth of earnings exceeds the discount rate, so again we must use the two-stage discount model. If we assume a 15 percent annual growth for ten years and 5 percent growth thereafter, discounting Gillette's 1990 owner earnings at 9 percent, the approximate value of Gillette is $16 billion. If we adjust the future growth rate downward to 12 percent, the value is approximately $12.6 billion; at 10 percent growth, the value would be $10.8 billion. At a very conservative 7 percent growth in owner earnings, the value of Gillette is at least $8.5 billion.

The Washington Post Company

In 1973, the total market value for the *Washington Post* was $80 million. Yet Buffett claims that "most security analysts, media brokers, and media executives would have estimated WPC's intrinsic value at $400 to $500 million."[7] How did Buffett arrive at that estimate? Let us walk through the numbers, using Buffett's reasoning.

We'll start by calculating owner earnings for that year: Net income ($13.3 million) plus depreciation and amortization ($3.7 million) minus capital expenditures ($6.6 million) yields 1973 owner earnings of $10.4 million. If we divide these earnings by the long-term U.S. government bond yield at the time (6.81 percent), the value of the *Washington Post* reaches $150 million, almost twice the market value of the company but well short of Buffett's estimate.

Buffett tells us that, over time, the capital expenditures of a newspaper will equal depreciation and amortization charges, and therefore net income should approximate owner earnings. Knowing this, we can simply divide net income by the risk-free rate and thus reach a valuation of $196 million.

If we stop here, the assumption is that the increase in owner earnings will equal the rise in inflation. But we know that newspapers have unusual pricing power: Because most are monopolies in their community, they can raise their prices at rates higher than inflation. If we make one last assumption—that the *Washington Post* has the ability to raise real prices by 3 percent—the value of the company is closer to $350 million. Buffett also knew that the company's 10 percent pretax margins were below its 15 percent historical average margins, and he knew that Katherine Graham was determined that the Post would once again achieve these margins. If pretax margins improved to 15 percent, the present value of the company would increase by $135 million, bringing the total intrinsic value to $485 million.

Wells Fargo

The value of a bank is the function of its net worth plus its projected earnings as a going concern. When Berkshire Hathaway began purchasing Wells Fargo in 1990, the company in the previous year had earned $600 million. The average yield on the thirty-year U.S. government bond that year was approximately 8.5 percent. To remain conservative, we can discount Wells Fargo's 1989 $600 million earnings by 9 percent and value the bank at $6.6 billion. If the bank never earned another dime over $600 million a year for the next thirty years, it was worth at least $6.6 billion. When Buffett purchased Wells Fargo in 1990, he paid $58 per share for its stock. With 52 million shares outstanding, this was equivalent to paying $3 billion for the company—a 55 percent discount to its value.

The debate in investment circles at the time centered on whether Wells Fargo, after taking into consideration all its loan problems, even had earnings power. The short sellers said it no; Buffett said yes. He knew full well that ownership of Wells Fargo carried some risk, but he felt confident in his analysis. His step-by-step thinking is a good model for everyone weighing the risk factor of an investment.

He started with what he already knew. Carl Reichardt, then chairman of Wells Fargo, had run the bank since 1983, with impressive results. Under his leadership, growth in earnings and return on equity were both above average and operating efficiencies were among the highest in the country. Reichardt had also built a solid loan portfolio.

Next, Buffett envisioned the events that would endanger the investment and came up with three possibilities, then tried to imagine the likelihood that they would occur. It is, in a real sense, an exercise in probabilities.

The first possible risk was a major earthquake, which would "wreak havoc" on borrowers and in turn on their lenders. The second risk was broader: a "systemic business contraction or financial panic so severe it would endanger almost every highly leveraged institution, no matter how intelligently run." Neither of those two could be ruled out entirely, of course, but Buffett concluded, based on best evidence, that the probability of either one was low.

The third risk, and the one getting the most attention from the market at the time, was that real estate values in the West would tumble because of overbuilding and "deliver huge losses to banks that have financed the expansion."[8] How serious would that be?

Buffett reasoned that a meaningful drop in real estate values should not cause major problems for a well-managed bank like Wells Fargo. "Consider some mathematics," he explained. Buffett knew that Wells Fargo earned $1 billion pretax annually after expensing an average $300 million for loan losses. He figured if 10 percent of the bank's $48 billion in loans—not just commercial real estate loans but all the bank's loans—were problem loans in 1991 and produced losses, including interest, averaging 30 percent of the principal value of the loan, Wells Fargo would still break even.

In Buffett's judgment, the possibility of this occurring was low. But even if Wells Fargo earned no money for a year, but merely broke even, Buffett would not flinch. "A year like that—which we consider only a low-level possibility, not a likelihood—would not distress us."[9]

The attraction of Wells Fargo intensified when Buffett was able to purchase shares at a 50 percent discount to their value. His bet paid off. By the end of 1993, Wells Fargo's share price reached $137 per share, nearly triple what Buffett originally paid.

BUY AT ATTRACTIVE PRICES

Focusing on businesses that are understandable, with enduring economics, run by shareholder-oriented managers—all those characteristics are important, Buffett says, but by themselves will not guarantee investment success. For that, he first has to buy at sensible prices, and then the company has to perform to his business expectations. The second is not always easy to control, but the first is: If the price isn't satisfactory, he passes.

Buffett's basic goal is to identify businesses that earn above-average returns, and then to purchase these businesses at prices below their indicated value. Graham taught Buffett the importance of buying a stock only when the difference between its price and its value represents a margin of safety. Today, this is still his guiding principle, even though his partner Charlie Munger has encouraged him toward occasionally paying more for outstanding companies.

> Great investment opportunities come around when excellent companies are surrounded by unusual circumstances that cause the stock to be misappraised.[10]
>
> WARREN BUFFETT, 1988

The margin-of-safety principle assists Buffett in two ways. First, it protects him from downside price risk. If he calculates that the value of a business is only slightly higher than its per share price, he will not buy the stock. He reasons that if the company's intrinsic value were to dip even slightly, eventually the stock price would also drop, perhaps below what he paid for it. But when the margin between price and value is large enough, the risk of declining value is less. If Buffett is able to purchase a company at 75 percent of its intrinsic value (a 25 percent discount) and the value subsequently declines by 10 percent, his original purchase price will still yield an adequate return.

The margin of safety also provides opportunities for extraordinary stock returns. If Buffett correctly identifies a company with above-average economic returns, the value of its stock over the long term will steadily march upward. If a company consistently earns 15 percent on equity, its share price will appreciate more each year than that of a company that earns 10 percent on equity. Additionally, if Buffett, by using the margin of safety, is able to buy this outstanding business at a significant discount to its intrinsic value, Berkshire will earn an extra bonus when the market corrects the price of the business. "The market, like the Lord, helps those who help themselves," says Buffett. "But unlike the Lord, the market does not forgive those who know not what they do."[11]

(Text continues on page 134.)

CASE IN POINT
LARSON-JUHL, 2001

Late in 2001, Warren Buffett made a handshake deal to buy Larson-Juhl, wholesale supplier of custom picture-framing materials, for $223 million in cash. It was Buffett's favorite scenario: a solid company, with good economics, strong management, and an excellent reputation in its industry, but experiencing a short-term slump that created an attractive price.

The business was owned 100 percent by Craig Ponzio, a talented designer with an equal talent for business. While in college, he worked for one of the manufacturing facilities of Larson Picture Frame, then ended up buying the company in 1981. Seven years later, he bought competitor Juhl-Pacific, creating the company now known as Larson-Juhl. When Ponzio bought Larson in 1981, its annual sales were $3 million; in 2001, Larson-Juhl's sales were more than $300 million.

That is the kind of performance that Buffett admires.

He also admires the company's operating structure. Larson-Juhl manufactures and sells the materials that custom framing shops use: fancy moldings for frames, matboard, glass, and assorted hardware. The local shops display samples of all the frame moldings available, but keep almost none of it in inventory. When a customer picks out a frame style, the shop must order the molding stock. And this is where Larson-Juhl shines. Through its network of twenty-three manufacturing and distribution facilities scattered across the United States, it is able to fill orders in record time. In the great majority of cases—industry analysts say as much as 95 percent of the time—materials are received the next day.

With that extraordinary level of service, very few shops are going to change suppliers, even if the prices are higher. And that gives Larson-Juhl what Buffett calls a moat—a clear and sustainable edge over competitors.

Further strengthening that moat, Larson-Juhl is widely known as the class act in molding. Frame shop operators order molding material in one-foot increments, and then cut it to the exact size needed for the customer's project. If the molding splits or does not cut cleanly, they cannot achieve the tight corners that they pride themselves on. Larson-Juhl molding, they say, makes perfect corners every time. That reputation for quality has made Larson-Juhl not only the largest but also the most prestigious company in its industry.

Larson-Juhl sells thousands of framing styles and finishes to its more than 18,000 customers. The leading supplier in the United States, it also operates thirty-three facilities in Europe, Asia, and Australia.

In sum, Larson-Juhl has many of the qualities Buffett looks for. The business is simple and understandable, and the company has a long and consistent history; one of the original component companies dates back 100 years. It also has a predictable future, with favorable long-term prospects. The ingredients of custom framing—molding, glass, mats—are not likely to be made obsolete by changes in technology, nor is customer demand for special treatment of favorite art likely to disappear.

What piqued Buffett's interest at this particular time, however, was the opportunity to acquire the company at an attractive price, triggered by a dip in profitability that he believed was temporary.

In fiscal 2001 (which ended in August), Larson-Juhl had $314 million in net sales and $30.8 million in cash from operations. That was down somewhat from prior years: $361 million sales and $39.1 million cash in 2000; $386 million in sales in 1999. Knowing Buffett's general approach to calculating value, we can make a good guess at his financial analysis of Larson-Juhl. Using his standard 10 percent dividend discount rate, adjusted for a very reasonable 3 percent growth rate, the company would have had a value of $440 million in 2001 ($30.8 million

(Continued)

divided by [10 minus 3 percent]). So the $223 million purchase price represented a very good value. Also, Buffett was convinced the fundamental economics of the company were sound, and that the lower numbers were a short-term response to the depressed economy at the time.

As is so often the case, Larson-Juhl approached Berkshire, not the other way around. Buffett describes the conversation: "Though I had never heard of Larson-Juhl before Craig's call, a few minutes talk with him made me think we would strike a deal. He was straightforward in describing the business, cared about who bought it, and was realistic as to price. Two days later, Craig and Steve McKenzie, his CEO, came to Omaha and in ninety minutes we reached an agreement."[12] From first contact to signed contract, the deal took just twelve days.

Coca-Cola

From the time that Roberto Goizueta took control of Coca-Cola in 1980, the company's stock price had increased every year. In the five years before Buffett purchased his first shares, the price increased an average of 18 percent every year. The company's fortunes were so good that Buffett was unable to purchase any shares at distressed prices. Still, he charged ahead. Price, he reminds us, has nothing to do with value.

In June 1988, the price of Coca-Cola was approximately $10 per share (split-adjusted). Over the next ten months, Buffett acquired 93,400,000 shares, at an average price of $10.96—fifteen times earnings, twelve times cash flow, and five times book value. He was willing to do that because of Coke's extraordinary level of economic goodwill, and because he believed the company's *intrinsic* value was much higher.

The stock market's value of Coca-Cola in 1988 and 1989, during Buffett's purchase period, averaged $15.1 billion. But Buffett was convinced its intrinsic value was higher—$20 billion (assuming 5 percent growth), $32 billion (assuming 10 percent growth), $38 billion (at 12 percent growth), perhaps even $48 billion (if 15 percent growth). Therefore Buffett's margin of safety—the discount to intrinsic value—could be as low as a conservative 27 percent or as high as 70 percent. At the same time, his conviction about the company had not changed: The probabilities of Coca-Cola's share price beating the market rate of return were going up, up, and up (see Figure 8.1)

So what did Buffett do? Between 1988 and 1989, Berkshire Hathaway purchased more than $1 billion of Coca-Cola stock, representing 35 percent of Berkshire's common stock portfolio. It was a bold move. It was Buffett acting on one of his guiding principles: When the probabilities of success are very high, make a big bet.

Gillette

From 1984 through 1990, the average annual gain in Gillette's share was 27 percent. In 1989, the share price gained 48 percent and in 1990, the year before Berkshire converted its preferred stock to common, Gillette's share price rose 28 percent (see Figure 8.2). In February 1991, Gillette's share price reached $73 per share (presplit), then a record high. At that time, the company had 97 million shares outstanding. When Berkshire converted, total shares increased to 109 million. Gillette's stock market value was $8.03 billion.

Depending on your growth assumptions for Gillette, at the time of conversion the market price for the company was at a 50 percent discount

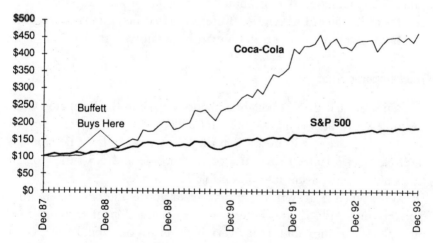

Figure 8.1 Common stock price of the Coca-Cola Company compared to the S&P 500 Index (indexed to $100 at start date).

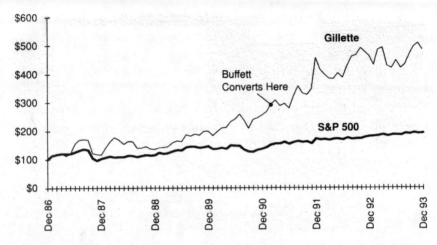

Figure 8.2   Common stock price of the Gillette Company compared to the S&P 500 Index (indexed to $100 at start date).

to value (15 percent growth in owner earnings), a 37 percent discount (12 percent growth), or a 25 percent discount (10 percent growth).

The Washington Post Company

Even the most conservative calculation of value indicates that Buffett bought the Washington Post Company for at least half of its intrinsic value. He maintains that he bought the company at less than one-quarter of its value. Either way, Buffett satisfied Ben Graham's premise that buying at a discount creates a margin of safety.

The Pampered Chef

It is reported that Buffett bought a majority stake in the Pampered Chef for somewhere between $800,000 and $900,000. With pretax margins of 20 to 25 percent, this means that the Pampered Chef was bought at a multiple of 4.3 times to 5 times pretax income and 6.5 times to 7.5 times net income, assuming full taxable earnings.

With revenue growth of 25 percent or above and net income that converts into cash at anywhere from a high fraction of earnings to a multiple of earnings, and with a very high return on capital, there is no doubt that the Pampered Chef was purchased at a significant discount.

(Text continues on page 138.)

CASE IN POINT
FRUIT OF THE LOOM, 2002

In 2001, while Fruit of the Loom was operating under the supervision of the bankruptcy court, Berkshire Hathaway offered to purchase the apparel part of the company (its core business) for $835 million in cash. As part of its bankruptcy agreement, Fruit of the Loom was required to conduct an auction for competitive offers. In January 2002, the court announced that Berkshire was the successful bidder, with the proceeds of the sale to go to creditors.

At the time of Berkshire's offer, Fruit of the Loom had a total debt of about $1.6 billion—$1.2 billion to secured lenders and bondholders and $400 million to unsecured bondholders. Under the terms of the agreement, secured creditors received an estimated 73 cents on the dollar for their claims, unsecured creditors about 10 cents.

Just before filing for bankruptcy in 1999, the company had $2.35 billion in assets, then lost money during reorganization. As of October 31, 2000, assets were $2.02 billion.

So, in simplified terms, Buffett bought a company with $2 billion in assets for $835 million, which went to pay the outstanding debt of $1.6 billion.

But there was a nice kicker. Soon after Fruit of the Loom went bankrupt, Berkshire bought its debt (both bonds and bank loans) for about 50 percent of face value. Throughout the bankruptcy period, interest payments on senior debt continued, earning Berkshire a return of about 15 percent. In effect, Buffett had bought a company that owed him money, and repaid it. As Buffett explained it, "Our holdings grew to 10 percent of Fruit's senior debt, which will probably end up returning us about 70 percent of face value. Through this investment, we indirectly reduced our purchase price for the whole company by a small amount."[13]

(Continued)

Warren Buffett is one of the few people who could charac-
terize $105 million as a "small amount," but, in fact, after tak-
ing into account these interest payments, the net purchase price
for the company was $730 million.

At the time Berkshire's offer was being reviewed by the
bankruptcy court, a reporter for the *Omaha World-Herald*
asked Travis Pascavis, a Morningstar analyst, about the deal. He
noted that companies like Fruit of the Loom usually sell for
their book value, which in this case would have been $1.4 bil-
lion. So with a bid of $835 million (ultimately, $730 million),
Berkshire would be getting the company for a bargain price.[14]

Clayton Homes

Berkshire's purchase of Clayton was not all smooth sailing; a legal battle erupted over the selling price.

At $12.50 per share, Buffett's April 2003 offer for Clayton was at
the low end of the $11.49 to $15.58 range that bankers had assigned to
the shares a month earlier. Clayton management argued that the deal
was fair considering the industry's slump at the time. But Clayton
shareholders mounted a battle in the courts, saying that Berkshire's offer
was far below the real value of Clayton's shares. James J. Dorr, general
counsel for Orbis Investment Management Ltd., which voted its 5.4
percent stake against the merger, grumbled, "The fact that it's Warren
Buffett who wants to buy from you should tell you that you shouldn't
sell, at least not at his price."[15] For a value investor, that is probably a
very high compliment.

Warren Buffett defended his offer. At the time of the shareholder
vote, he wrote, "the mobile home business was in bad shape and companies such as Clayton, which needs at least $1 billion of financing
each year and faces declining sales, would continue to have a hard time
finding funds." Clayton's board apparently agreed. Then, as evidence
of his commitment to Clayton, Buffett added that he had advanced
the company $360 million of financing since his offer.[16] Buffett and
Clayton management ended up winning the shareholder battle by a
narrow margin.

PUTTING IT ALL TOGETHER

Warren Buffett has said more than once that investing in stocks is really simple: Find great companies that are run by honest and competent people and are selling for less than they are intrinsically worth. No doubt many who have heard and read that remark over the years have thought to themselves, "Sure, simple if you're Warren Buffett. Not so simple for me."

Both sentiments are true. Finding those great companies takes time and effort, and that is never easy. But the next step—determining their real value so you can decide whether the price is right—is a simple matter of plugging in the right variables. And that is where the investment tenets described in these chapters will serve you well:

- The business tenets will keep you focused on companies that are relatively predictable. If you stick to those with a consistent operating history and favorable prospects, producing basically the same products for the same markets, you will develop a sense of how they will do in the future. The same is true if you concentrate on businesses that you understand; if not, you won't be able to interpret the impact of new developments.
- The management tenets will keep you focused on companies that are well run. Excellent managers can make all the difference in a company's future success.
- Together, the business and management tenets will give a good sense of the company's future earnings potential.
- The financial tenets will reveal the numbers you need to make a determination of the company's real value.
- The value tenets will take you through the mathematics necessary to come up with a final answer: Based on everything you have learned, is this a good buy?

The two value tenets are crucial. But don't worry too much if you are unable to address the other ten fully. Don't let yourself become paralyzed by too much information. Do the best you can, get started, and keep moving forward.

9

Investing in Fixed-Income Securities

Warren Buffett is perhaps best known in the investment world for his decisions in common stocks, and he is famous for his "buy and hold" positions in companies such as Coca-Cola, American Express, the Washington Post, and Gillette. His activities are not, however, limited to stocks. He also buys short-term and long-term fixed-income securities, a category that includes cash, bonds, and preferred stocks. In fact, fixed-income investing is one of Buffett's regular outlets, provided—as always—that there are undervalued opportunities. He simply seeks out, at any given time, those investments that provide the highest aftertax return. In recent years, this has included forays into the debt market, including corporate and government bonds, convertible bonds, convertible preferred stock, and even high-yielding junk bonds.

When we look inside these fixed-income transactions, what we see looks familiar, for Buffett has displayed the same approach that he takes with investments in stocks. He looks for margin of safety, commitment, and low prices (bargains). He insists on strong and honest management, good allocation of capital, and a potential for profit. His decisions do not depend on hot trends or market-timing factors but instead are savvy investments based on specific opportunities where Buffett believes there are undervalued assets or securities.

This aspect of Buffett's investing style doesn't receive a great deal of attention in the financial press, but it is a critical part of the overall Berkshire portfolio. Fixed-income securities represented 20 percent of Berkshire's investment portfolio in 1992; today, 14 years later, that percentage has grown to about 30 percent.

The reason for adding these fixed-income investments is simple: They were the best value at the time. Because of the absolute growth of the Berkshire Hathaway portfolio and the changing investment environment, including a lack of publicly traded stocks that he finds attractive, Buffett has often turned to buying entire companies and to acquiring fixed-income securities. He wrote in his 2003 letter to shareholders that it was hard to find significantly undervalued stocks, "a difficulty greatly accentuated by the mushrooming of the funds we must deploy."

In that same 2003 letter, Buffett explained that Berkshire would continue the capital allocation practices it had used in the past: "If stocks become cheaper than entire businesses, then we will buy them aggressively. If selected bonds become attractive, as they did in 2002, we will again load up on these securities. Under any market or economic conditions we will be happy to buy businesses that meet our standards. And, for those that do, the bigger, the better. Our capital is underutilized now. It is a painful condition to be in but not as painful as doing something stupid. (I speak from experience.)"[1]

To some extent, fixed-income investments will always be necessary for Berkshire Hathaway's portfolio because of Berkshire's concentration in insurance companies. To fulfill their obligation to policyholders, insurance companies must invest some of their assets in fixed-income securities. Still, Berkshire holds a significantly smaller percentage of fixed-income securities in its insurance investment portfolio compared with other insurance companies.

Generally speaking, Buffett has tended to avoid fixed-income investments (outside what was needed for the insurance portfolios) whenever he feared impending inflation, which would erode the future purchasing power of money and therefore the value of bonds. Even though interest rates in the late 1970s and early 1980s approximated the returns of most businesses, Buffett was not a net purchaser of long-term bonds. There always existed, in his mind, the possibility of runaway inflation. In that kind of environment, common stocks would have lost real value, but bonds outstanding would have suffered far greater losses. An insurance company heavily invested in bonds in a hyperinflationary environment has the potential to wipe out its portfolio.

Even though thinking of Buffett and bonds in the same sentence may be a new idea for you, it will come as no surprise that he applies the same principles as he does in valuing a company or stocks. He is a principle-based investor who will put his money in a deal where he sees a potential for profit, and he makes sure that the risk is priced into the deal. Even in fixed-income transactions, his business owner's perspective means that he pays close attention to the issuing company's management, values, and performance. This "bond-as-a-business" approach to fixed-income investing is highly unusual but it has served Buffett well.

BONDS

Washington Public Power Supply System

Back in 1983, Buffett decided to invest in some bonds of the Washington Public Power Supply System (WPPSS). The transaction is a clear example of Buffett's thinking in terms of the possible gains from buying the bonds compared with those if he bought the entire company.

On July 25, 1983, WPPSS (pronounced, with macabre humor, "Whoops") announced that it was in default of $2.25 billion in municipal bonds used to finance the uncompleted construction of two nuclear reactors, known as Projects 4 and 5. The state ruled that the local power authorities were not obligated to pay WPPSS for power they had previously promised to buy but ultimately did not require. That decision led to the largest municipal bond default in U.S. history. The size of the default and the debacle that followed depressed the market for public power bonds for several years. Investors moved quickly to sell their utility bonds, forcing prices lower and current yields higher.

The cloud over WPPSS Projects 4 and 5 cast a shadow over Projects 1, 2, and 3. But Buffett perceived significant differences between the terms and obligations of Projects 4 and 5 on the one hand and those of Projects 1, 2, and 3 on the other. The first three were operational utilities that were also direct obligations of Bonneville Power Administration, a government agency. However, the problems of Projects 4 and 5 were so severe that some were predicting they could weaken the credit position of Bonneville Power.

Buffett evaluated the risks of owning municipal bonds of WPPSS Projects 1, 2, and 3. Certainly there was a risk that these bonds could default and a risk that the interest payments could be suspended for a prolonged period. Still another factor was the upside ceiling on what these bonds could ever be worth. Even though he could purchase these bonds at a discount to their par value, at the time of maturity they could only be worth one hundred cents on the dollar.

Shortly after Projects 4 and 5 defaulted, Standard & Poor's suspended its ratings on Projects 1, 2, and 3. The lowest coupon bonds of Projects 1, 2, and 3 sank to forty cents on the dollar and produced a current yield of 15 to 17 percent tax-free. The highest coupon bonds fell to eighty cents on the dollar and generated a similar yield. Undismayed, from October 1983 through June the following year, Buffett aggressively purchased bonds issued by WPPSS for Projects 1, 2, and 3. By the end of June 1984, Berkshire Hathaway owned $139 million of WPPSS Project 1, 2, and 3 bonds (both low-coupon and high-coupon) with a face value of $205 million.

With WPPSS, explains Buffett, Berkshire acquired a $139 million business that could expect to earn $22.7 million annually after tax (the cumulative value of WPPSS annual coupons) and would pay those earnings to Berkshire in cash. Buffett points out there were few businesses available for purchase during this time that were selling at a discount to book value and earning 16.3 percent after tax on unleveraged capital. Buffett figured that if he set out to purchase an unleveraged operating company earning $22.7 million after tax ($45 million pretax), it would have cost Berkshire between $250 and $300 million—assuming he could find one. Given a strong business that he understands and likes, Buffett would have happily paid that amount. But, he points out, Berkshire paid half that price for WPPSS bonds to realize the same amount of earnings. Furthermore, Berkshire purchased the business (the bonds) at a 32 percent discount to book value.

Looking back, Buffett admits that the purchase of WPPSS bonds turned out better than he expected. Indeed, the bonds outperformed most business acquisitions made in 1983. Buffett has since sold the WPPSS low-coupon bonds. These bonds, which he purchased at a significant discount to par value, doubled in price while annually paying Berkshire a return of 15 to 17 percent tax-free. "Our WPPSS experience, though pleasant, does nothing to alter our negative opinion about long-term bonds," said Buffett. "It only makes us hope that we run into some other large stigmatized issue, whose troubles have caused it to be significantly misappraised by the market."[2]

RJR Nabisco

Later in the 1980s, a new investment vehicle was introduced to the financial markets. The formal name is high-yield bond, but most investors, then and now, call them junk bonds.

In Buffett's view, these new high-yield bonds were different from their predecessor "fallen angels"—Buffett's term for investment-grade bonds that, having fallen on bad times, were downgraded by ratings agencies. The WPPSS bonds were fallen angels. He described the new high-yield bonds as a bastardized form of the fallen angels and, he said, were junk before they were issued.

Wall Street's securities salespeople were able to promote the legitimacy of junk bond investing by quoting earlier research that indicated higher interest rates compensated investors for the risk of default. Buffett argued that earlier default statistics were meaningless since they were based on a group of bonds that differed significantly from the junk bonds currently being issued. It was illogical, he said, to assume that junk bonds were identical to the fallen angels. "That was an error similar to checking the historical death rate from Kool-Aid before drinking the version served at Jonestown."[3]

As the 1980s unfolded, high-yield bonds became junkier as new offerings flooded the market. "Mountains of junk bonds," noted Buffett, "were sold by those who didn't care to those that didn't think and there was no shortage of either."[4] At the height of this debt mania, Buffett predicted that certain capital enterprises were guaranteed to fail when it became apparent that debt-laden companies were struggling to meet their interest payments. In 1989, Southmark Corporation and Integrated Resources both defaulted on their bonds. Even Campeau Corporation, a U.S. retailing empire created with junk bonds, announced it was having difficulty meeting its debt obligations. Then on October 13, 1989, UAL Corporation, the target of a $6.8 billion management-union led buyout that was to be financed with high-yield bonds, announced that it was unable to obtain financing. Arbitrageurs sold their UAL common stock position, and the Dow Jones Industrial Average dropped 190 points in one day.

The disappointment over the UAL deal, coupled with the losses in Southmark and Integrated Resources, led many investors to question the value of high-yield bonds. Portfolio managers began dumping their junk bond positions. Without any buyers, the price for high-yield bonds plummeted. After beginning the year with outstanding gains, Merrill Lynch's index of high-yield bonds returned a paltry 4.2 percent compared with the 14.2 percent returns of investment-grade bonds. By the end of 1989, junk bonds were deeply out of favor with the market.

A year earlier, Kohlberg Kravis & Roberts had succeeded in purchasing RJR Nabisco for $25 billion financed principally with bank debt and junk bonds. Although RJR Nabisco was meeting its financial obligations, when the junk bond market unraveled, RJR bonds declined along with other junk bonds. In 1989 and 1990, during the junk bond bear market, Buffett began purchasing RJR bonds.

Most junk bonds continued to look unattractive during this time, but Buffett figured RJR Nabisco was unjustly punished. The company's stable products were generating enough cash flow to cover its debt payments. Additionally, RJR Nabisco had been successful in selling portions of its business at very attractive prices, thereby reducing its debt-to-equity ratio. Buffett analyzed the risks of investing in RJR and concluded that the company's credit was higher than perceived by other investors who were selling their bonds. RJR bonds were yielding 14.4 percent (a businesslike return), and the depressed price offered the potential for capital gains.

So, between 1989 and 1990, Buffett acquired $440 million in discounted RJR bonds. In the spring of 1991, RJR Nabisco announced it was retiring most of its junk bonds by redeeming them at face value. The RJR bonds rose 34 percent, producing a $150 million capital gain for Berkshire Hathaway.

Level 3 Communications

In 2002, Buffett bought up large bundles of other high-yield corporate bonds, increasing his holdings in these securities sixfold to $8.3 billion.

Of the total, 65 percent were in the energy industry and about $7 billion were bought through Berkshire insurance companies.

Describing his thinking in the 2002 letter to shareholders, Buffett wrote, "The Berkshire management does not believe the credit risks associated with the issuers of these instruments has correspondingly declined." And this comes from a man who does not take unaccounted-for (read: unpriced) risks. To that point, he added, "Charlie and I detest taking even small risks unless we feel we are being adequately compensated for doing so. About as far as we will go down that path is to occasionally eat cottage cheese a day after the expiration date on the carton."[5]

In addition to pricing his risk, he also typically bought the securities at far less than what they were worth, even at distressed prices, and waited until the asset value was realized.

What is particularly intriguing about these bond purchases is that, in all likelihood, Buffett would not have bought equity in many of these companies. By the end of 2003, however, his high-yield investments paid off to the tune of about $1.3 billion, while net income for the company that year was a total of $8.3 billion. As the high-yield market skyrocketed, some of the bonds were called or sold. Buffett's comment at the time was simply, "Yesterday's weeds are being priced as today's flowers."

In July 2002, three companies invested a total of $500 million in Broomfield, Colorado-based Level 3 Communications' ten-year convertible bonds, with a coupon of 9 percent and a conversion price of $3.41, to help the company make acquisitions and to enhance the company's capital position. The three were Berkshire Hathaway ($100 million), Legg Mason ($100 million) and Longleaf Partners ($300 million).

Technology-intensive companies are not Buffett's normal acquisition fare; he candidly admits he does not know of a way to properly value technology companies. This was an expensive deal for Level 3 but it gave them the cash and credibility when they needed it. For his part, Buffett obtained a lucrative (9 percent) investment with an equity position. At the time, Buffett was quoted as saying that investors should expect 7 to 8 percent returns from the stock market annually, so at 9 percent, he was ahead of the game.

There is another aspect to this story that is typical of Buffett—a strong component of managerial integrity and personal relationships. Level 3 Communications was a spin-off from an Omaha-based construction company, Peter Kiewit Sons; Buffett's friend Walter Scott Jr., is both chairman emeritus of Kiewit and chairman of Level 3. Often called Omaha's first citizen, Scott was the driving force behind the city's zoo, its art museum, the engineering institute, and the Nebraska Game and Parks Foundation. Scott and Buffett have close personal and professional connections: Scott sits on Berkshire's board, and the two men are only floors away from each other at Kiewit Plaza.

Even though Buffett knew Scott well and held him in high regard, he wanted the investment to be fair and transparent, with no question that the relationship between the two men unduly influenced the deal. So Buffett suggested that O. Mason Hawkins, chairman and chief executive of Southeastern Asset Management, which advises Longleaf Partners, set up the deal and negotiate the terms.

By mid-June 2003, a year later, Buffett, Legg Mason, and Longleaf Partners exchanged $500 million for a total of 174 million Level 3 common shares (including an extra 27 million shares as an incentive to convert). (Longleaf had already converted $43 million earlier in the year and then converted the rest, $457 million, in June.)

Buffett received 36.7 million shares. In June, he sold 16.8 million for $117.6 million, and in November sold an additional 18.3 million shares for $92.4 million. Sure enough, Level 3 made good on its debt payments, and by the end of 2003, Buffett had doubled his money in 16 months. On top of that, his bonds had earned $45 million of interest, and he still held on to 1,644,900 of Level 3's shares.

Qwest

In the summer of 2002, Berkshire purchased hundreds of millions of dollars of bonds issued by Qwest Communications, a struggling telecommunications company based in Denver formerly known as US West, and its regulatory operating subsidiary, Qwest Corporation. At the time, Qwest had $26 billion in debt and was in the midst of restating its 1999, 2000, and 2001 financial statements. Bankruptcy rumors were flying. Qwest corporate bonds were trading at thirty-five to forty cents on the dollar and the bonds of its operating company at eighty cents to the dollar. Some of the bonds were yielding 12.5 percent and were backed with specific assets; other, riskier bonds were not. Buffett bought both.

Most analysts at the time said that Qwest's assets had enough value for Buffett to more than recover his investment given the current trading price. And, if it had not been for the interest payments, Qwest would have had a healthy cash flow. The company's most valuable asset was the 14-state local phone service franchise, but Buffett had faith that with former Ameritech CEO, Dick Notebaert, at the helm, the company would solve its problems.

Amazon.com

In July 2002, only one week after Buffett wrote CEO Jeff Bezos a letter praising him for his decision to account for stock options as an expense, Buffett bought $98.3 million of Amazon's high-yield bonds.

Buffett clearly appreciates managers who exhibit integrity and strong values, and he has long advocated for expensing stock options, but he certainly was not on a goodwill mission when he bought the Amazon.com bonds. The Government Employees Insurance Company, the auto insurance unit of Berkshire, stood to make $16.4 million profit on the investment in high-yield bonds, a 17 percent return in nine months if Amazon repurchased the $264 million in 10 percent senior notes that were issued in 1998. Later that summer, Buffett bought an additional $60.1 million of Amazon's 6⅞ percent convertible bonds. Assuming a price of $60.00 per $1,000 bond, the yield would have been a healthy 11.46 percent and the yield to maturity would have been even higher once interest payments were calculated in.

It is well known that Buffett sticks with things he understands and shies away from technology. His involvement with the Internet is limited to three online activities: He buys books, reads the *Wall Street Journal,* and plays bridge. Buffett even made fun of his own technology avoidance in his 2000 letter to shareholders: "We have embraced the 21st century by entering such cutting-edge industries as brick, carpet and paint. Try to control your excitement."[6]

So why was he attracted to Amazon's bonds? First, he said, they were "extraordinarily cheap." Second, he had faith that the company would thrive. Buffett may also have observed that Amazon.com had a similar profile to many of his other investments in retail companies. Amazon.com generates its revenue through huge amounts of sales for low prices and although it has low margins, the company is efficient and profitable. Buffett admires the way Bezos has created a megabrand and the way he has pulled the company through some very difficult times.

ARBITRAGE

Arbitrage, in its simplest form, involves purchasing a security in one market and simultaneously selling the same security in another market. The object is to profit from price discrepancies. For example, if stock in a company was quoted as $20 per share in the London market and $20.01 in the Tokyo market, an arbitrageur could profit from simultaneously purchasing shares of the company in London and selling the same shares in Tokyo. In this case, there is no capital risk. The arbitrageur is merely profiting from the inefficiencies that occur between markets. Because this transaction involves no risk, it is appropriately called riskless arbitrage. Risk arbitrage, on the other hand, is the sale or purchase of a security in hopes of profiting from some announced value.

The most common type of risk arbitrage involves the purchase of a stock at a discount to some future value. This future value is usually based on a corporate merger, liquidation, tender offer, or reorganization. The risk an arbitrageur confronts is that the future announced price of the stock may not be realized.

To evaluate risk arbitrage opportunities, explains Buffett, you must answer four basic questions. "How likely is it that the promised event will indeed occur? How long will your money be tied up? What chance is there that something better will transpire—a competing takeover bid, for example? What will happen if the event does not take place because of antitrust action, financing glitches, etc.?"[7]

Confronted with more cash than investable ideas, Buffett has often turned to arbitrage as a useful way to employ his extra cash. The Arkata Corporation transaction in 1981, where he bought over 600,000 shares as the company was going through a leveraged buyout, was a good example. However, whereas most arbitrageurs might participate in fifty or more deals annually, Buffett sought out only a few, financially large transactions. He limited his participation to deals that were announced and friendly, and he refused to speculate about potential takeovers or the prospects for greenmail.

Although he never calculated his arbitrage performance over the years, Buffett estimated that Berkshire has averaged an annual return of about 25 percent pretax. Because arbitrage is often a substitute for short-term Treasury bills, Buffett's appetite for deals fluctuated with Berkshire's cash level.

Nowadays, however, he does not engage in arbitrage on a large scale but rather keeps his excess cash in Treasuries and other short-term liquid investments. Sometimes Buffett holds medium-term, tax-exempt bonds as cash alternatives. He realizes that by substituting medium-term bonds for short-term Treasury bills, he runs the risk of principal loss if he is forced to sell at disadvantageous time. But because these tax-free bonds offer higher aftertax returns than Treasury bills, Buffett figures that the potential loss is offset by the gain in income.

With Berkshire's historical success in arbitrage, shareholders might wonder why Buffett strayed from this strategy. Admittedly, Buffett's investment returns were better than he imagined, but by 1989 the arbitrage landscape started changing. The financial excesses brought about by the leveraged buyout market were creating an environment of unbridled enthusiasm. Buffett was not sure when lenders and buyers would come to their senses, but he has always acted cautiously when others are giddy. Even before the collapse of the UAL buyout in October 1989, Buffett was pulling back from arbitrage transactions. Another reason may be that deals of a size that would really make a difference to Buffett's very large portfolio simply do not exist.

In any case, Berkshire's withdrawal from arbitrage was made easier with the advent of convertible preferred stocks.

CONVERTIBLE PREFERRED STOCKS

A convertible preferred stock is a hybrid security that possesses characteristics of both stocks and bonds. Generally, these stocks provide investors with higher current income than common stocks. This higher yield offers protection from downside price risk. If the common stock declines, the higher yield of the convertible preferred stock prevents it from falling as low as the common shares. In theory, the convertible stock will fall in price until its current yield approximates the value of a nonconvertible bond with a similar yield, credit, and maturity.

A convertible preferred stock also provides the investor with the opportunity to participate in the upside potential of the common shares. Since it is convertible into common shares, when the common rises, the convertible stock will rise as well. However, because the convertible stock provides high income and has the potential for capital gains, it is priced at a premium to the common stock. This premium is reflected in the rate at which the preferred is convertible into common shares. Typically, the conversion premium may be 20 percent to 30 percent. This means that the common must rise in price 20 to 30 percent before the convertible stock can be converted into common shares without losing value.

In the same way that he invested in high-yield bonds, Buffett invested in convertible preferred stocks whenever the opportunity presented itself as better than other investments. In the late 1980s and 1990s, Buffett made several investments in convertible preferred stocks, including Salomon Brothers, Gillette, USAir, Champion International, and American Express.

Takeover groups were challenging several of these companies, and Buffett became known as a "white knight," rescuing companies from hostile invaders. Buffett, however, certainly did not perceive himself as a pro bono savior. He simply saw these purchases as good investments with a high potential for profit. At the time, the preferred stocks of these companies offered him a higher return than he could find elsewhere.

Some of the companies issuing the convertible preferred securities were familiar to Buffett, but in other cases he had no special insight about the business nor could he predict with any confidence what its future cash flows would be. This unpredictability, Buffett explains, is the precise reason Berkshire's investment was a convertible preferred issue rather than common stock. Despite the conversion potential, the real value of the preferred stock, in his eye, was its fixed-income characteristics.

There is one exception: MidAmerican. This is a multifaceted transaction involving convertible preferred and common stock as well as debt. Here, Buffett values the convertible preferred for its fixed-income return as well as for its future equity stake.

MidAmerican

On March 14, 2000, Berkshire acquired 34.56 million shares of convertible preferred stock along with 900,942 shares of common stock in MidAmerican Energy Holdings Company, a Des Moines-based gas and electric utility, for approximately $1.24 billion, or $35.05 per share. Two years later, in March 2002, Berkshire bought 6.7 million more shares of the convertible preferred stock for $402 million. This brought

Berkshire's holdings to over 9 percent voting interest and just over 80 percent economic interest in MidAmerican.

Since 2002, Berkshire and certain of its subsidiaries also have acquired approximately $1.728 million of 11 percent nontransferable trust preferred securities, of which $150 million were redeemed in August 2003. An additional $300 million was invested by David Sokol, MidAmerican's chairman and CEO, and Walter Scott, MidAmerican's largest individual shareholder. It was, in fact, Scott who initially approached Buffett ; it was the first major deal they had worked on together in their 50 years of friendship.

The price Buffett paid for MidAmerican was toward the low end of the scale, which according to reports was $34 to $48 per share, so he was able to achieve a certain discount. Yet Buffett also committed himself and Berkshire to MidAmerican's future growth to the extent that they would support MidAmerican's acquisition of pipelines up to $15 billion. As part of its growth strategy, MidAmerican, with Buffett's help, bought pipelines from distressed energy merchants.

One such purchase happened almost immediately. In March 2002, Buffett bought, from Tulsa-based Williams Company, the Kern River Gas Transmission project, which transported 850 million cubic feet of gas per day over 935 miles. Buffett paid $960 million, including assumption of debt and an additional $1 billion in capital expenses.

MidAmerican also went on to acquire Dynegy's Northern Natural gas pipeline later in 2002 for a bargain price of about $900 million, plus the assumption of debt. Then, as of early January 2004, Berkshire announced it would put up about 30 percent of the costs, or $2 billion, for a new natural gas pipeline tapping Alaskan North Slope natural gas reserves that would boost U.S. reserves by 7 percent. MidAmerican chairman Sokol said that without Buffett's help, the investment would have been a strain on MidAmerican.

In another but related transaction, a Berkshire subsidiary, MEHC Investment Inc., bought $275 million of Williams's preferred stock. This preferred stock does not generally vote with the common stock in the election of directors, but in this deal Berkshire Hathaway gained the right to elect 20 percent of MidAmerican's board as well as rights of approval over certain important transactions.

Later that summer, Buffett, along with Lehman Brothers, provided Williams with a one-year $900 million senior loan at over 19 percent, secured by almost all the oil and gas assets of Barrett Resources, which Williams originally acquired for about $2.8 billion. It was reported that Buffett's loan was part of a $3.4 billion package of cash and credit that Williams, still an investment-grade company, needed to stave off bankruptcy. The terms of the deal were tough and laden with conditions and fees that reportedly could have put the interest rate on the deal at 34 percent. Still, it can be argued that not only was Buffett helping an investment-grade company out of a tight spot but also protecting himself against the high risk of the situation.

Although MidAmerican was not Buffett's only foray into the then-beleaguered energy industry, it definitely was a complex, multifaceted investment. Buffett believed that the company was worth more than its then-current value in the market. He knew that the management, including Walter Scott and David Sokol, operated with great credibility, integrity, and intelligence. Finally, the energy industry can be a stable business, and Buffett was hoping it would become even more stable and profitable.

In MidAmerican, Buffett bought a fixed-income investment with an equity potential. As with all his other investments, he took a characteristic ownership approach and committed himself to the company's growth. He made some money off the Williams fixed-income instruments while protecting himself with covenants, high rates, and assets (Barrett Resources). As it turned out, by October 2003, MidAmerican had grown into the third largest distributor of electricity in the United Kingdom and was providing electricity to 689,000 people in Iowa, while the Kern River and Northern Natural pipelines carried about 7.8 percent of the natural gas in the United States. In total, the company had about $19 billion of assets and $6 billion in annual revenues from 25 states and several other countries, and was yielding Berkshire Hathaway about $300 million per year.

It is important to remember that Buffett thinks of convertible preferred stocks first as fixed-income securities and second as vehicles for appreciation. Hence the value of Berkshire's preferred stocks cannot be any less than the value of a similar nonconvertible preferred and, because of conversion rights, is probably more.

Buffett is widely regarded as the world's greatest value investor, which basically means buying stocks, bonds, and other securities, and whole companies, for a great deal less than their real worth, and waiting until the asset value is realized. So whether it is blue-chip stocks or high-yield corporate debt, Buffett applies his same principles. A value investor goes where the deals are.

Although Buffett is usually thought of as a long-term investor in common stocks, he has the capability, stamina, and capital to wade into beleaguered industries and pick out diamonds in the rough. He chooses specific companies with honest, smart managers and cash-generating products. He also chooses the instruments that make the most sense at the time. Usually, he has been right and when he's not, he admits it. As it turns out, his decision to move strongly into fixed-income instruments in 2002 and 2003 was definitely right. In 2002, Berkshire's gross realized gain from fixed-income investments was $1 billion. In 2003, that number almost tripled, to $2.7 billion.

10

Managing Your Portfolio

Up to this point, we have studied Warren Buffett's approach to making investment decisions, which is built on timeless principles codified into twelve tenets. We watched over his shoulder as he applied those principles to buy stocks and bonds, and to acquire companies. And we took the time to understand the insights from others that helped shape his philosophy about investing.

But as every investor knows, deciding which stocks to buy is only half the story. The other half is the ongoing process of managing the portfolio and learning how to cope with the emotional roller coaster that inevitably accompanies such decisions.

It is no surprise that here, too, the leadership of Warren Buffett will show us the way.

Hollywood has given us a visual cliché of what a money manager looks like: talking into two phones at once, frantically taking notes while trying to keep an eye on computer screens that blink and blip at him from all directions, tearing at his hair whenever one of those computer blinks shows a minuscule drop in stock price.

Warren Buffett is about as far from that kind of frenzy as anything imaginable. He moves with the calm that comes of great confidence. He has no need to watch a dozen computer screens at once, for the minute-by-minute changes in the market are of no interest to him. Warren Buffett doesn't think in minutes, days, or months, but years. He doesn't need to keep up with hundreds of companies, because his investments are focused in just a select few. This approach, which he calls "focus investing," greatly simplifies the task of portfolio management.

> "We just focus on a few outstanding companies. We're focus investors."[1]
>
> WARREN BUFFETT, 1994

STATUS QUO: A CHOICE OF TWO

The current state of portfolio management, as practiced by everyone else, appears to be locked into a tug-of-war between two competing strategies—active portfolio management and index investing.

Active portfolio managers are constantly at work buying and selling a great number of common stocks. Their job is to try to keep their clients satisfied. That means consistently outperforming the market so that on any given day should a client apply the obvious measuring stick—how is my portfolio doing compared with the market overall—the answer will be positive and the client will leave her money in the fund. To keep on top, active managers try to predict what will happen with stocks in the coming six months and continually churn the portfolio, hoping to take advantage of their predictions.

Index investing, on the other hand, is a buy-and-hold passive approach. It involves assembling, and then holding, a broadly diversified portfolio of common stocks deliberately designed to mimic the behavior of a specific benchmark index, such as the Standard & Poor's 500. The simplest and by far the most common way to achieve this is through an indexed mutual fund.

Proponents of both approaches have long waged combat to prove which one will ultimately yield the higher investment return.

Active portfolio managers argue that, by virtue of their superior stock-picking skills, they can do better than any index. Index strategists, for their part, have recent history on their side. In a study that tracked results in a twenty-year period, from 1977 through 1997, the percentage number of equity mutual funds that have been able to beat the Standard & Poor's 500 Index dropped dramatically, from 50 percent in the early years to barely 25 percent in the final four years. And as of November 1998, 90 percent of actively managed funds were underperforming the market (averaging 14 percent *lower* than the S&P 500), which means that only 10 percent were doing better.[2]

Active portfolio management as commonly practiced today stands a very small chance of outperforming the index. For one thing, it is grounded in a very shaky premise: Buy today whatever we predict can be sold soon at a profit, regardless of what it is. The fatal flaw in that logic is that given the complexity of the financial universe, predictions are impossible. Second, this high level of activity comes with transaction costs that diminish the net returns to investors. When we factor in these costs, it becomes apparent that the active money management business has created its own downfall.

Indexing, because it does not trigger equivalent expenses, is better than actively managed portfolios in many respects. But even the best index fund, operating at its peak, will only net you exactly the returns of the overall market. Index investors can do no worse than the market, and also no better.

Intelligent investors must ask themselves: Am I satisfied with average? Can I do better?

A NEW CHOICE

Given a choice between active and index approaches, Warren Buffett would unhesitatingly pick indexing. This is especially true for investors with a very low tolerance for risk, and for people who know very little about the economics of a business but still want to participate in the long-term benefits of investing in common stocks.

"By periodically investing in an index fund," he says in inimitable Buffett style, "the know-nothing investor can actually outperform most investment professionals."[3] Buffett, however, would be quick to point out that there is a third alternative—a very different kind of active port-folio strategy that significantly increases the odds of beating the index. That alternative is focus investing.

FOCUS INVESTING: THE BIG PICTURE

Reduced to its essence, focus investing means this: Choose a few stocks that are likely to produce above-average returns over the long haul, concentrate the bulk of your investments in those stocks, and have the fortitude to hold steady during any short-term market gyrations.

The following sections describe the separate elements in the process.

"Find Outstanding Companies"

Over the years, Warren Buffett has developed a way of determining which companies are worthy places to put his money; it rests on a notion of great common sense: If the company is doing well and is managed by smart people, eventually its stock price will reflect its inherent value. Buffett thus devotes most of his attention not to tracking share price but to analyzing the economics of the underlying business and assessing its management.

The Buffett tenets, described in earlier chapters, can be thought of as a kind of tool belt. Each tenet is one analytical tool, and in the aggregate

---

THE FOCUS INVESTOR'S GOLDEN RULES

1. Concentrate your investments in outstanding companies run by strong management.
2. Limit yourself to the number of companies you can truly understand. Ten to twenty is good, more than twenty is asking for trouble.
3. Pick the very best of your good companies, and put the bulk of your investment there.
4. Think long-term: five to ten years, minimum.
5. Volatility happens. Carry on.

they provide a method for isolating the companies with the best chance for high economic returns. Buffett uses his tool belt to find companies with a long history of superior performance and a stable management, and that stability means they have a high probability of performing in the future as they have in the past. And that is the heart of focus investing: concentrating your investments in companies with the highest probability of above-average performance.

"Less Is More"

Remember Buffett's advice to a know-nothing investor—to stay with index funds? What is more interesting for our purposes is what he said next:

"If you are a know-something investor, able to understand business economics and to find five to ten sensibly priced companies that possess important long-term competitive advantages, conventional diversification (broadly based active portfolios) makes no sense for you."[4]

What's wrong with conventional diversification? For one thing, it greatly increases the chances that you will buy something you don't know enough about. Philip Fisher, who was known for his focus portfolios, although he didn't use the term, profoundly influenced Buffett's thinking in this area. Fisher always said he preferred owning a small number of outstanding companies that he understood well to a large number of average ones, many of which he understood poorly.

"Know-something" investors, applying the Buffett tenets, would do better to focus their attention on just a few companies. How many is a few? Even the high priests of modern finance have discovered that, on average, just fifteen stocks gives you 85 percent diversification.[5] For the average investor, a legitimate case can be made for ten to twenty. Focus investing falls apart if it is applied to a large portfolio with dozens of stocks.

"Put Big Bets on High-Probability Events"

Phil Fisher's influence on Buffett can also be seen in another way—his belief that the only reasonable course when you encounter a strong opportunity is to make a large investment. Warren Buffett echoes that thinking: "With each investment you make, you should have the courage and the conviction to place at least ten percent of your net worth in that stock."[6]

You can see why Buffett says the ideal portfolio should contain no more than ten stocks, if each is to receive 10 percent. Yet focus investing is not a simple matter of finding ten good stocks and dividing your investment pool equally among them. Even though all the stocks in a focus portfolio are high-probability events, some will inevitably be higher than others, and they should be allocated a greater proportion of the investment.

Blackjack players understand this intuitively: When the odds are strongly in your favor, put down a big bet.

> I can't be involved in 50 or 75 things. That's a Noah's Ark way of investing—you end up with a zoo. I like to put meaningful amounts of money in a few things.[7]
>
> WARREN BUFFETT, 1987

Think back for a moment to Buffett's decision to buy American Express for the limited partnership, described in Chapter 1. When threat of scandal caused the company's share price to drop by almost half, Buffett invested a whopping 40 percent of the partnership's assets in this one company. He was convinced that, despite the controversy, the company was solid and eventually the stock price would return to its proper level; in the meantime, he recognized a terrific opportunity. But was it worth almost half of his total assets? It was a big bet that paid off handsomely: Two years later, he sold the much-appreciated shares for a profit of $20 million.

"Be Patient"

Focus investing is the antithesis of a broadly diversified high-turnover approach. Although focus investing stands the best chance among all active strategies of outperforming an index return over time, it requires investors to patiently hold their portfolio even when it appears that other strategies are winning.

How long is long enough? As you might imagine, there is no hard-and-fast rule (although Buffett would probably say that anything less than five years is a fool's theory). The goal is not *zero* turnover (never selling anything); that's foolish in the opposite direction, for it would prevent you from taking advantage of something better when it comes along. As a general rule of thumb, we should aim for a turnover rate between 20 and 10 percent, which means holding the stock for somewhere between five and ten years.

"Don't Panic over Price Changes"

Focus investing pursues *above*-average results, and there is strong evidence, both in academic research and actual case histories, that the pursuit is successful. There can be no doubt, however, that the ride is bumpy, for price volatility is a necessary by-product of the focus approach. Focus investors tolerate the bumpiness because they know that in the long run the underlying economics of the companies will more than compensate for any short-term price fluctuations.

Buffett is a master bump-ignorer. So is his partner, Charlie Munger, who once calculated, using a compound interest table and lessons learned playing poker, that as long as he could handle the price volatility, owning as few as three stocks would be plenty. "I knew I could handle the bumps psychologically, because I was raised by people who believe in handling bumps."[8]

Maybe you also come from a long line of people who can handle bumps. But even if you were not born so lucky, you can acquire some of their traits. It is a matter of consciously deciding to change how you think and behave. Acquiring new habits and thought patterns does not happen overnight, but gradually teaching yourself not to panic and act rashly in response to the vagaries of the market is doable—and necessary.

BUFFETT AND MODERN PORTFOLIO THEORY

Warren Buffett's faith in the fundamental ideas of focus investing puts him at odds with many other financial gurus, and also with a package of concepts that is collectively known as *modern portfolio theory*. Because this is a book about Buffett's thinking, and because Buffett himself does not subscribe to this theory, we will not spend much time describing it. But as you continue to learn about investing, you will hear about this theory, and so it is important to cover its basic elements. Then we'll give Buffett a chance to weigh in on each.

Modern portfolio theory is a combination of three seminal ideas about finance from three powerful minds. Harry Markowitz, a graduate student in economics at the University of Chicago, first quantified the relationship between return and risk. Using a mathematical tool called covariance, he measured the combined movement of a group of stocks, and used that to determine the riskiness of an entire portfolio.

Markowitz concluded that investment risk is not a function of how much the price of any individual stock changes, but how much a group of stocks changes in the same direction. If they do so, there is a good chance that economic shifts will drive them all down at the same time. The only reasonable protection, he said, was diversification.

About ten years later, another graduate student, Bill Sharpe from the University of California-Los Angeles, developed a mathematical process for measuring volatility that simplified Markowitz's approach. He called it the Capital Asset Pricing Model.

So in the space of one decade, two academicians had defined two important elements of what we would later come to call modern portfolio theory: Markowitz with his idea that the proper reward/risk balance depends on diversification, and Sharpe with his definition of risk. A third piece—the efficient market theory (EMT)—came from a young assistant professor of finance at the University of Chicago, Eugene Fama.

Fama began studying the changes in stock prices in the early 1960s. An intense reader, he absorbed all the written work on stock market behavior then available and concluded that stock prices are not predictable because the market is too efficient. In an efficient market, as information becomes available, a great many smart people aggressively apply that information in a way that causes prices to adjust instantaneously, before anyone can profit. At any given moment, stock prices reflect all available information. Predictions about the future therefore have no place in an efficient market, because the share prices adjust too quickly.

Buffett's View of Risk

In modern portfolio theory, the volatility of the share price defines risk. But throughout his career, Buffett has always perceived a drop in share prices as an opportunity to make money. In his mind, then, a dip in price actually reduces risk. He points out, "For owners of a business—and that's the way we think of shareholders—the academics' definition of risk is far off the mark, so much so that it produces absurdities."[9]

Buffett has a different definition of risk: the possibility of harm. And that is a factor of the intrinsic value of the business, not the price behavior of the stock. Financial harm comes from misjudging the future profits of the business, plus the uncontrollable, unpredictable effect of taxes and inflation.

Furthermore, Buffett sees risk as inextricably linked to an investor's time horizon. If you buy a stock today, he explains, with the intention of selling it tomorrow, then you have entered into a risky transaction. The odds of predicting whether share prices will be up or down in a short period are the same as the odds of predicting the toss of a coin; you will lose half of the time. However, says Buffett, if you extend your time horizon out to several years (always assuming that you have made a sensible purchase), then the odds shift meaningfully in your favor.

Buffett's View of Diversification

Buffett's view on risk drives his diversification strategy, and here, too, his thinking is the polar opposite of modern portfolio theory. According to that theory, the primary benefit of a broadly diversified portfolio is to mitigate the price volatility of the individual stocks. But if you are unconcerned with price volatility, as Buffett is, then you will also see portfolio diversification in a different light.

He knows that many so-called pundits would say the Berkshire strategy is riskier, but he is not swayed. "We believe that a policy of portfolio concentration may well *decrease* risk if it raises, as it should, both the intensity with which an investor thinks about a business and the comfort level he must feel with its economic characteristics before buying into it."[10] By purposely focusing on just a few select companies, you are better able to study them closely and understand their intrinsic value. The more knowledge you have about your company, the less risk you are likely taking.

"Diversification serves as protection against ignorance," explains Buffett. "If you want to make sure that nothing bad happens to you relative to the market, you should own everything. There is nothing wrong with that. It's a perfectly sound approach for somebody who doesn't know how to analyze businesses."[11]

Buffett's View of the Efficient Market Theory

Buffett's problem with the EMT rests on a central point: It makes no provision for investors who analyze all the available information, as Buffett urges them to do, which gives them a competitive advantage.

Nonetheless, EMT is still religiously taught in business schools, a fact that gives Warren Buffett no end of satisfaction. "Naturally the disservice done students and gullible investment professionals who have swallowed EMT has been an extraordinary service to us and other followers of Graham," Buffett wryly observed. "From a selfish standpoint, we should probably endow chairs to ensure the perpetual teaching of EMT."[12]

In many ways, modern portfolio theory protects investors who have limited knowledge and understanding on how to value a business. But that protection comes with a price. According to Buffett, "Modern portfolio theory tells you how to be average. But I think almost anybody can figure out how to do average in the fifth grade."[13]

THE SUPERINVESTORS OF BUFFETTVILLE

One of the greatest investment books of all time came out in 1934, during the height of the Great Depression. *Security Analysis,* by Benjamin Graham and David Dodd, is universally acclaimed a classic, and is still in print after five editions and sixty-five years. It is impossible to overstate its influence on the modern world of investing.

Fifty years after its original publication, the Columbia Business School sponsored a seminar marking the anniversary of this seminal text. Warren Buffett, one of the school's best-known alumni and the most famous modern-day proponent of Graham's value approach, addressed the gathering. He titled his speech "The Superinvestors of Graham-and-Doddsville," and in its own way, it has become as much a classic as the book it honored.[14]

He began by recapping the central argument of modern portfolio theory—that the stock market is efficient, all stocks are priced correctly, and therefore anyone who beats the market year after year is simply lucky. Maybe so, he said, but I know some folks who have done it, and their success can't be explained away as simply random chance.

And he proceeded to lay out the evidence. The examples he presented that day were all people who had managed to beat the market consistently over time, not because of luck, but because they followed principles learned from the same source: Ben Graham. They all reside, he said, in the "intellectual village" of Graham-and-Doddsville.

Nearly two decades later, I thought it might be interesting to take an updated look at a few people who exemplify the approach defined by Graham and who also share Buffett's belief in the value of a focused portfolio with a small number of stocks. I think of them as the Superinvestors of Buffettville: Charlie Munger, Bill Ruane, Lou Simpson, and of course Buffett. From their performance records, there is much we can learn.

Charlie Munger

Although Berkshire Hathaway's investment performance is usually tied to its chairman, we should never forget that vice chairman Charlie Munger is an outstanding investor. Shareholders who have attended Berkshire's annual meeting or read Charlie's thoughts in *Outstanding Investor Digest* realize what a fine intellect he has.

"I ran into him in about 1960," said Buffett, "and I told him law was fine as a hobby but he could better."[15] As you may recall, Munger at the time had a thriving law practice in Los Angeles, but gradually shifted his energies to a new investment partnership bearing his name. The results of his talents can be found in Table 10.1.

Table 10.1 Charles Munger Partnership

| Year | Annual Percentage Change | |
	Overall Partnership (%)	Dow Jones Industrial Average (%)
1962	30.1	−7.6
1963	71.7	20.6
1964	49.7	18.7
1965	8.4	14.2
1966	12.4	−15.8
1967	56.2	19.0
1968	40.4	7.7
1969	28.3	−11.6
1970	−0.1	8.7
1971	25.4	9.8
1972	8.3	18.2
1973	−31.9	−13.1
1974	−31.5	−23.1
1975	73.2	44.4
Average Return	24.3	6.4
Standard Deviation	33.0	18.5
Minimum	−31.9	−23.1
Maximum	73.2	44.4

"His portfolio was concentrated in very few securities and there-fore, his record was much more volatile," Buffett explained, "but it was based on the same discount-from-value approach." In making in-vestment decisions for his partnership, Charlie followed the Graham methodology and would look only at companies that were selling below their intrinsic value. "He was willing to accept greater peaks and valleys in performance, and he happens to be a fellow whose psy-che goes toward concentration."[16]

Notice that Buffett does not use the word *risk* in describing Charlie's performance. Using the conventional definition of risk (price volatility), we would have to say that over its thirteen-year his-tory Charlie's partnership was extremely risky, with a standard devia-tion almost twice that of the market. But beating the average annual return of the market by 18 points over those same thirteen years was not the act of a risky man, but of an astute investor.

Bill Ruane

Buffett first met Bill Ruane in 1951, when both were taking Ben Graham's Security Analysis class at Columbia. The two classmates stayed in contact, and Buffett watched Ruane's investment performance over the years with admiration. When Buffett closed his investment partnership in 1969, he asked Ruane if he would be willing to handle the funds of some of the partners, and that was the beginning of the Sequoia Fund.

It was a difficult time to set up a mutual fund. The stock market was splitting into a two-tier market, with most of the hot money gyrating toward the so-called Nifty-Fifty (the big-name companies like IBM and Xerox), leaving the "value" stocks far behind. Ruane was undeterred. Later Buffett commented, "I am happy to say that my partners, to an amazing degree, not only stayed with him but added money, with happy results."[17]

Sequoia Fund was a true pioneer, the first mutual fund run on the principles of focus investing. The public record of Sequoia's holdings demonstrates clearly that Bill Ruane and Rick Cuniff, his partner in Ruane, Cuniff & Company, managed a tightly focused, low-turnover portfolio. On average, well over 90 percent of the fund was concentrated between six and ten companies. Even so, the economic diversity of the portfolio was, and continues to be, broad.

Bill Ruane's point of view is in many ways unique among money managers. Generally speaking, most managers begin with some preconceived notion about portfolio management and then fill in the portfolio with various stocks. At Ruane, Cuniff & Company, the partners begin with the idea of selecting the best possible stocks and then let the portfolio form around these selections.

Selecting the best possible stocks, of course, requires a high level of research, and here again Ruane, Cuniff & Company stands apart from the rest of the industry. The firm eschews Wall Street's broker-fed research reports and instead relies on its own intensive company investigations. "We don't go in much for titles at our firm," Ruane once said, "[but] if we did, my business card would read Bill Ruane, Research Analyst."[18]

How well has this unique approach served their shareholders? Table 10.2 outlines the investment performance of Sequoia Fund from 1971 through 2003. During this period, Sequoia earned an average

Table 10.2 Sequoia Fund, Inc.

| Year | Annual Percentage Change | |
	Sequoia Fund	S&P 500 Index
1971	13.5	14.3
1972	3.7	18.9
1973	−24.0	−14.8
1974	−15.7	−26.4
1975	60.5	37.2
1976	72.3	23.6
1977	19.9	−7.4
1978	23.9	6.4
1979	12.1	18.2
1980	12.6	32.3
1981	21.5	−5.0
1982	31.2	21.4
1983	27.3	22.4
1984	18.5	6.1
1985	28.0	31.6
1986	13.3	18.6
1987	7.4	5.2
1988	11.1	16.5
1989	27.9	31.6
1990	−3.8	−3.1
1991	40.0	30.3
1992	9.4	7.6
1993	10.8	10.0
1994	3.3	1.4
1995	41.4	37.5
1996	21.7	22.9
1997	42.3	33.4
1998	35.3	28.6
1999	−16.5	21.0
2000	20.1	−9.1
2001	10.5	−11.9
2002	−2.6	−22.1
2003	17.1	28.7
Average Return	18.0	12.9
Standard Deviation	20.2	17.7
Minimum	−24.0	−26.4
Maximum	72.3	37.5

annual return of 18 percent, compared with the 12.9 percent of the Standard & Poor's 500 Index.

Lou Simpson

About the time Warren Buffett began acquiring the stock of the Government Employees Insurance Company (GEICO) in the late 1970s, he also made another acquisition that would have a direct benefit on the insurance company's financial health. His name was Lou Simpson.

Simpson, who earned a master's degree in economics from Princeton, worked for both Stein Roe & Farnham and Western Asset Management before Buffett lured him to GEICO in 1979. He is now CEO of Capital Operations for the company. Recalling his job interview, Buffett remembers that Lou had "the ideal temperament for investing."[19] Lou, he said, was an independent thinker who was confident of his own research and "who derived no particular pleasure from operating with or against the crowd."

Simpson, a voracious reader, ignores Wall Street research and instead pores over annual reports. His common stock selection process is similar to Buffett's. He purchases only high-return businesses that are run by able management and are available at reasonable prices. Lou also has something else in common with Buffett. He focuses his portfolio on only a few stocks. GEICO's billion-dollar equity portfolio customarily owns fewer than ten stocks.

Between 1980 and 1996, GEICO's portfolio achieved an average annual return of 24.7 percent, compared with the market's return of 17.8 percent (see Table 10.3). "These are not only terrific figures," says Buffett, "but, fully as important, they have been achieved in the right way. Lou has consistently invested in undervalued common stocks that, individually, were unlikely to present him with a permanent loss and that, collectively, were close to risk free."[20]

It is important to note that the focus strategy sometimes means enduring several weak years. Even the Superinvestors—undeniably skilled, undeniably successful—faced periods of short-term underperformance. A look at Table 10.4 shows that they would have struggled through several difficult periods.

What do you think would have happened to Munger, Simpson, and Ruane if they had been rookie managers starting their careers today in an environment that can only see the value of one year's, or even one

Table 10.3 Lou Simpson, GEICO

| | Annual Percentage Change | |
| | GEICO | |
Year	Equities (%)	S&P 500 (%)
1980	23.7	32.3
1981	5.4	−5.0
1982	45.8	21.4
1983	36.0	22.4
1984	21.8	6.1
1985	45.8	31.6
1986	38.7	18.6
1987	−10.0	5.1
1988	30.0	16.6
1989	36.1	31.7
1990	−9.1	−3.1
1991	57.1	30.5
1992	10.7	7.6
1993	5.1	10.1
1994	13.3	1.3
1995	39.7	37.6
1996	29.2	37.6
Average Return	24.7	17.8
Standard Deviation	19.5	14.3
Minimum	−10.0	−5.0
Maximum	57.1	37.6

quarter's, performance? They would probably have been canned, to their clients' profound loss.

MAKING CHANGES IN YOUR PORTFOLIO

Don't be lulled into thinking that just because a focus portfolio lags the stock market on a price basis from time to time, you are excused from the ongoing responsibility of performance scrutiny. Granted, a focus investor should not become a slave to the stock market's whims, but you should always be acutely aware of all economic stirrings of the companies in your portfolio. There will be times when buying something, selling something else, is exactly the right thing to do.

Table 10.4 The Superinvestors of Buffettville

	Number of Years of Performance	Number of Years of Underperformance	Number of Consecutive Years of Underperformance	Underperformance Years as a Percent of All Years
Munger	14	5	3	36
Ruane	29	11	4	37
Simpson	17	4	1	24

The Decision to Buy: An Easy Guideline

When Buffett considers adding an investment, he first looks at what he already owns to see whether the new purchase is any better. "What Buffett is saying is something very useful to practically any investor," Charlie Munger stresses. "For an ordinary individual, the best thing you already have should be your measuring stick."

What happens next is one of the most critical but widely overlooked secrets to increasing the value of your portfolio. "If the new thing you are considering purchasing is not better than what you already know is available," says Charlie, "then it hasn't met your threshold. This screens out 99 percent of what you see."[21]

The Decision to Sell: Two Good Reasons to Move Slowly

Focus investing is necessarily a long-term approach to investing. If we were to ask Buffett what he considers an ideal holding period, he would answer "forever"—so long as the company continues to generate above-average economics and management allocates the earnings of the company in a rational manner. "Inactivity strikes us as intelligent behavior," he explains.[22]

If you own a lousy company, you require turnover because otherwise you end up owning the economics of a subpar business for a long time. But if you own a superior company, the last thing you want to do is to sell it.

This slothlike approach to portfolio management may appear quirky to those accustomed to actively buying and selling stocks on a regular basis, but it has two important economic benefits, in addition to growing capital at an above-average rate:

1. *It works to reduce transaction costs.* This is one of those commonsense dynamics that is so obvious it is easily overlooked. Every time you buy or sell, you trigger brokerage costs that lower your net returns.
2. *It increases aftertax returns.* When you sell a stock at a profit, you will be hit with capital gain taxes, eating into your profit. The solution: Leave it be. If you leave the gain in place (this is referred to as unrealized gain), your money compounds more forcefully. Overall, investors have too often underestimated the enormous value of this unrealized gain—what Buffett calls an "interest-free loan from the Treasury."

To make his point, Buffett asks us to imagine what happens if you buy a $1 investment that doubles in price each year. If you sell the investment at the end of the first year, you would have a net gain of $.66 (assuming you're in the 34 percent tax bracket). Now you reinvest the $1.66, and it doubles in value by year-end. If the investment continues to double each year, and you continue to sell, pay the tax, and reinvest the proceeds, at the end of twenty years you would have a net gain of $25,200 after paying taxes of $13,000. If, on the other hand, you purchased a $1 investment that doubled each year and *never* sold it until the end of twenty years, you would gain $692,000 after paying taxes of approximately $356,000.

The best strategy for achieving high aftertax returns is to keep your average portfolio turnover ratio somewhere between 0 and 20 percent. Two strategies lend themselves best to low turnover rates. One is to stick with an index mutual fund; they are low turnover by definition. Those who prefer a more active style of investing will turn to the second strategy: a focus portfolio.

THE CHALLENGE OF FOCUS INVESTING

My goal so far has been to lay out the argument for adopting the focus investing approach that Warren Buffett uses with such great success. I would be doing you less than full service if I did not also make it plain that an unavoidable consequence of this approach is heightened volatility. When your portfolio is focused on just a few companies, a price change in any one of them is all the more noticeable and has greater overall impact.

The ability to withstand that volatility without undue second-guessing is crucial to your peace of mind, and ultimately to your financial success. Coming to terms with it is largely a matter of understanding the emotional side effects of investing, which is the topic of Chapter 11.

Money matters are about the most emotional issues of all, and that will never change. But at the same time, you need not be constantly at the mercy of those emotions, to the point that sensible action is handicapped. The key is to keep your emotions in appropriate perspective, and that is much easier if you understand something of the basic psychology involved.

THE CHALLENGE OF SUCCESS

Warren Buffett's challenge is not psychology; he understands the emotional side of investing as well as anyone and better than most. His challenge is maintaining the level of returns that others have come to expect from him. Two factors are involved: First, in very recent years, Buffett hasn't found very many stocks that meet his price criteria. That's a problem of the market. Second, when you're driving a $100 billion company, it takes a significant level of economic return to move the needle. That's a problem of size.

Buffett explains it this way: "Some years back, a good $10 million idea could do wonders for us. Today, the combination of *ten* such ideas and a triple in the value of *each* would increase the net worth of Berkshire by only one quarter of one percent. We need 'elephants' to make significant gains now—and they are hard to find." [23] That was in early 2002. Berkshire's net worth has continued to grow since then, and, presumably, these elephants are even harder to find today.

The good news for most investors is that they can put their elephant guns away. The other good news is that, regardless of the size of their pocketbook, the fundamentals of focus investing still apply. No matter how much money you have to work with, you will want to do the same thing Buffett does: When you find a high-probability event, put down a big bet.

11

The Psychology of Money

The study of what makes us all tick is endlessly fascinating. It is especially intriguing to me that it plays such a strong role in investing, a world that people generally perceive to be dominated by cold numbers and soulless data. When it comes to investment decisions, our behavior is sometimes erratic, often contradictory, and occasionally goofy. Sometimes our illogical decisions are consistently illogical, and sometimes no pattern is discernible. We make good decisions for inexplicable reasons, and bad decisions for no good reason at all.

What is particularly alarming, and what all investors need to grasp, is that they are often unaware of their bad decisions. To fully understand the markets and investing, we have to understand our own irrationalities. That is every bit as valuable to an investor as being able to analyze a balance sheet and income statement.

It is a complex, puzzling, intriguing study. Few aspects of human existence are more emotion-laden than our relationship to money. And the two emotions that drive decisions most profoundly are fear and greed. Motivated by fear or greed, or both, investors frequently buy or sell stocks at foolish prices, far above or below a company's intrinsic value. To say this another way, investor sentiment has a more pronounced impact on stock prices than a company's fundamentals.

Much of what drives people's decisions about stock purchases can be explained only by principles of human behavior. And since the market is, by definition, the collective decisions made by all stock purchasers, it is not an exaggeration to say that psychological forces push and pull the entire market.

Anyone who hopes to participate profitably in the market, therefore, must allow for the impact of emotion. It is a two-sided issue: keeping your own emotional profile under control as much as possible and being alert for those times when other investors' emotion-driven decisions present you with a golden opportunity.

> Success in investing doesn't correlate with IQ once you're above the level of 125. Once you have ordinary intelligence, what you need is the temperament to control the urges that get other people into trouble in investing.[1]
>
> WARREN BUFFETT, 1999

The first step in properly weighting the impact of emotion in investing is understanding it. Fortunately, there is good information at hand. In recent years, psychologists have turned their attention to how established principles of human behavior play out when the dynamic is money. This blending of economics and psychology is known as behavioral finance, and it is just now moving down from the universities' ivory towers to become part of the informed conversation among investment professionals—who, if they look over their shoulders, will find the shadow of a smiling Ben Graham.

THE TEMPERAMENT OF A TRUE INVESTOR

Ben Graham, as we know, fiercely urged his students to learn the basic difference between an investor and a speculator. The speculator, he said, tries to anticipate and profit from price changes; the investor seeks only to acquire companies at reasonable prices. Then he explained further: The successful investor is often the person who has achieved a certain temperament—calm, patient, rational. Speculators have the opposite temperament: anxious, impatient, irrational. Their worst enemy is not the stock market, but themselves. They may well have superior abilities in mathematics, finance, and accounting, but if they cannot master their emotions, they are ill suited to profit from the investment process.

Graham understood the emotional quicksand of the market as well as any modern psychologist, maybe better. His notion that true investors can be recognized by their temperament as well as by their skills holds as true today as when first expressed.

Investors have the following characteristics:

• *True investors are calm.* They know that stock prices, influenced by all manner of forces both reasonable and unreasonable, will fall as well as rise, and that includes stocks they own. When that happens, they react with equanimity; they know that as long as the company retains the qualities that attracted them as investors in the first place, the price will come back up. In the meantime, they do not panic.

On this point, Buffett is blunt: Unless you can watch your stock holdings decline by 50 percent without becoming panic-stricken, you should not be in the stock market. In fact, he adds, as long as you feel good about the businesses you own, you should welcome lower prices as a way to profitably increase your holdings.

At the opposite end of the spectrum, true investors also remain calm in the face of what we might call the mob influence. When one stock or one industry or one mutual fund suddenly lands in the spotlight, the mob rushes in that direction. The trouble is, when everyone is making the same choices because "everyone" knows it's the thing to do, then no one is in a position to profit. In remarks reported in *Fortune* at the end of 1999, Buffett talked about the "can't-miss-the-party" factor that has infected so many bull-market investors.[2] His caution seems to be this: True investors don't worry about missing the party; they worry about coming to the party unprepared.

• *True investors are patient.* Instead of being swept along in the enthusiasm of the crowd, true investors wait for the right opportunity. They say no more often than yes. Buffett recalls that when he worked for Graham-Newman, analyzing stocks for possible purchase, Ben Graham turned down his recommendations most of the time. Graham, Buffett says, was never willing to purchase a stock unless all the facts were in his favor. From this experience, Buffett learned that the ability to say no is a tremendous advantage for an investor.

> We don't have to be smarter than the rest; we have to be more
> disciplined than the rest.[3]
>
> WARREN BUFFETT, 2002

Buffett believes that too many of today's investors feel a need to purchase too many stocks, most of which are certain to be mediocre, instead
of waiting for the few exceptional companies. To reinforce Graham's lesson, Buffett often uses the analogy of a punch card. "An investor," he
says, "should act as though he had a lifetime decision card with just
twenty punches on it. With every investment decision his card is
punched, and he has one fewer available for the rest of his life."[4] If investors were restrained in this way, Buffett figures that they would be
forced to wait patiently until a great investment opportunity surfaced.

• *True investors are rational.* They approach the market, and the
world, from a base of clear thinking. They are neither unduly pessimistic
nor irrationally optimistic; they are, instead, logical and rational.

Buffett finds it odd that so many people habitually dislike markets
that are in their best interests and favor those markets that continually
put them at a disadvantage. They feel optimistic when market prices are
rising, pessimistic when prices are going down. If they go the next step
and put those feelings into action, what do they do? Sell at lower prices
and buy at higher prices—not the most profitable strategy.

Undue optimism rears its head when investors blithely assume that
somehow the fates will smile on them and their stock choice will be the
one in a hundred that really takes off. It is especially prevalent in bull
markets, when high expectations are commonplace. Optimists see no
need to do the fundamental research and analysis that would illuminate
the real long-term winners (e.g., finding the few keepers among all the
look-alike dot-coms) because the short-term numbers are so seductive.

Undue pessimism, whether directed at one company or the market
in general, motivates investors to sell at exactly the wrong time. In
Buffett's view, true investors are pleased when the rest of the world turns
pessimistic, because they see it for what it really is: a perfect time to buy

good companies at bargain prices. Pessimism, he says, is "the most common cause of low prices. . . . We want to do business in such an environment, not because we like pessimism but because we like the prices it produces. It's optimism that is the enemy of the rational buyer."[5]

Whether an investor feels optimistic or pessimistic is a statement of what that investor thinks about the future. Forecasting what is going to happen next is tricky at best, and downright foolish when optimism (or pessimism) is based more on emotion than on research. Buffett, who once remarked that "the only value of stock forecasters is to make fortune tellers look good," makes no attempt to anticipate the periods in which the market is likely to go up or down.[6] Instead, he keeps an eye on the general emotional tenor of the overall market, and acts accordingly. "We simply attempt," he explains, "to be fearful when others are greedy and to be greedy only when others are fearful."[7]

INTRODUCING MR. MARKET

To show his students how powerfully emotions are tied to stock market fluctuations, and to help them recognize the folly of succumbing to emotion, Graham created an allegorical character he named "Mr. Market." Buffett has frequently shared the story of Mr. Market with Berkshire's shareholders.

Imagine that you and Mr. Market are partners in a private business. Each day without fail, Mr. Market quotes a price at which he is willing to either buy your interest or sell you his. The business that you both own is fortunate to have stable economic characteristics, but Mr. Market's quotes are anything but. For you see, Mr. Market is emotionally unstable. Some days, he is cheerful and enormously optimistic, and can only see brighter days ahead. On these days, he offers a very high price for shares in your business. At other times, Mr. Market is discouraged and terribly pessimistic; seeing nothing but trouble ahead, he quotes a very low price for your shares in the business.

Mr. Market has another endearing characteristic, Graham said: He does not mind being snubbed. If Mr. Market's quotes are ignored, he will be back again tomorrow with a new quote. Graham warned his students that it is Mr. Market's pocketbook, not his wisdom, that is useful. If Mr. Market shows up in a foolish mood, you are free to ignore him or take advantage of him, but it will be disastrous if you fall under his influence.

"The investor who permits himself to be stampeded or unduly worried by unjustified market declines in his holdings is perversely transforming his basic advantage into a basic disadvantage," Graham wrote. "That man would be better off if his stocks had no market quotation at all, for he would then be spared the mental anguish caused him by other persons' mistakes of judgment."[8]

To be successful, investors need good business judgment and the ability to protect themselves from the emotional whirlwind that Mr. Market unleashes. One is insufficient without the other. An important factor in Buffett's success is that he has always been able to disengage himself from the emotional forces of the stock market. He credits Ben Graham and Mr. Market with teaching him how to remain insulated from the silliness of the market.

MR. MARKET, MEET CHARLIE MUNGER

It was more than sixty years ago that Ben Graham introduced Mr. Market, sixty years since he began writing about the irrationality that exists in the market. Yet in all the years since, there has been little apparent change in investor behavior. Investors still act irrationally. Foolish mistakes are still the order of the day. Fear and greed still permeate the marketplace.

We can, through numerous academic studies and surveys, track investor foolishness. We can, if we follow Warren Buffett's lead, turn other people's fear or greed to our advantage. But to fully understand the dynamics of emotion in investing, we turn to another individual: Charlie Munger.

Munger's understanding of how psychology affects investors, and his insistence on taking it into account, have greatly influenced the operations of Berkshire Hathaway. It is one of his most profound contributions. In particular, he stresses what he calls the psychology of misjudgment: What is it in human nature that draws people to mistakes of judgment?

Munger believes a key problem is that our brain takes shortcuts in analysis. We jump too quickly to conclusions. We are easily misled and are prone to manipulation. To compensate, Munger has developed a

> I came to the psychology of misjudgment almost against my
> will; I rejected it until I realized my attitude was costing me a
> lot of money.[9]
>
> CHARLIE MUNGER, 1995

mental habit that has served him well. "Personally, I've gotten so that I
now use a kind of two-track analysis," he said in a 1994 speech reprinted
in *Outstanding Investor Digest*. "First, what are the factors that really
govern the interests involved, rationally considered. And second, what
are the subconscious influences where the brain at a subconscious level is
automatically doing these things—which by and large are useful, but
which often misfunction."[10]

BEHAVIORAL FINANCE

In many ways, Charlie Munger is a genuine pioneer. He was thinking
about, and talking about, the psychological aspects of market behavior
long before other investment professionals gave it serious attention. But
that is beginning to change. Behavioral finance is now an accepted area
of study in the economics department at major universities, including
the work done by Richard Thaler at the University of Chicago.

Observing that people often make foolish mistakes and illogical assumptions when dealing with their own financial affairs, academics, including Thaler, began to dig deeper into psychological concepts to explain
the irrationalities in people's thinking. It is a relatively new field of study,
but what we are learning is fascinating, as well as eminently useful to
smart investors.

Overconfidence

Several psychological studies have pointed out that errors in judgment
occur because people in general are overconfident. Ask a large sample
of people how many believe their skills at driving a car are above average, and an overwhelming majority will say they are excellent driv-
ers. Another example: When asked, doctors believe they can diagnose

pneumonia with 90 percent confidence when in fact they are right only 50 percent of the time.

Confidence per se is not a bad thing. But *over*confidence is another matter, and it can be particularly damaging when we are dealing with our financial affairs. Overconfident investors not only make silly decisions for themselves but also have a powerful effect on the market as a whole.

Overconfidence explains why so many investors make wrong calls. They have too much confidence in the information they gather and think they are more right than they actually are. If all the players think that their information is correct and they know something that others do not, the result is a great deal of trading.

Overreaction Bias

Thaler points to several studies that demonstrate people put too much emphasis on a few chance events, thinking they spot a trend. In particular, investors tend to fix on the most recent information they received and extrapolate from it; the last earnings report thus becomes in their mind a signal of future earnings. Then, believing that they see what others do not, they make quick decisions from superficial reasoning.

Overconfidence is at work here; people believe they understand the data more clearly than others do and interpret it better. But there is more to it. Overreaction exacerbates overconfidence. The behaviorists have learned that people tend to overreact to bad news and react slowly to good news. Psychologists call this *overreaction bias*. Thus if the short-term earnings report is not good, the typical investor response is an abrupt, ill-considered overreaction, with its inevitable effect on stock prices.

Thaler describes this overemphasis on the short term as investor "myopia" (the medical term for nearsightedness) and believes most investors would be better off if they didn't receive monthly statements. In a study conducted with other behavioral economists, he proved his idea in dramatic fashion.

Thaler and colleagues asked a group of students to divide a hypothetical portfolio between stocks and Treasury bills. But first, they sat the students in front of a computer and simulated the returns of the portfolio over a trailing twenty-five-year period. Half the students were given mountains of information, representing the market's volatile nature with ever-changing prices. The other group was only given periodic performance measured in five-year time periods. Thaler then asked each group to allocate their portfolio for the next forty years.

The group that had been bombarded by lots of information, some of which inevitably pointed to losses, allocated only 40 percent of its money to the stock market; the group that received only periodic information allocated almost 70 percent of its portfolio to stocks. Thaler, who lectures each year at the Behavioral Conference sponsored by the National Bureau of Economic Research and the John F. Kennedy School of Government at Harvard, told the group, "My advice to you is to invest in equities and then don't open the mail."[11]

This experiment, as well as others, neatly underscores Thaler's notion of investor myopia—shortsightedness leading to foolish decisions. Part of the reason myopia provokes such an irrational response is another bit of psychology: our innate desire to avoid loss.

Loss Aversion

According to behaviorists, the pain of a loss is far greater than the enjoyment of a gain. Many experiments, by Thaler and others, have demonstrated that people need twice as much positive to overcome a negative. On a 50/50 bet, with precisely even odds, most people will not risk anything unless the potential gain is twice as high as the potential loss.

This is known as *asymmetrical loss aversion:* The downside has a greater impact than the upside, and it is a fundamental aspect of human psychology. Applied to the stock market, it means that investors feel twice as bad about losing money as they feel good about picking a winner.

This aversion to loss makes investors unduly conservative, at great cost. We all want to believe we made good decisions, so we hold onto bad choices far too long in the vague hope that things will turn around. By not selling our losers, we never have to confront our failures. But if you don't sell a mistake, you are potentially giving up a gain that you could earn by reinvesting smartly.

Mental Accounting

A final aspect of behavioral finance that deserves our attention is what psychologists have come to call *mental accounting.* It refers to our habit of shifting our perspective on money as surrounding circumstances change. We tend to mentally put money into different "accounts," and that determines how we think about using it.

A simple situation will illustrate. Let us imagine that you have just returned home from an evening out with your spouse. You reach for your wallet to pay the babysitter, but discover that the $20 bill you thought was there, is not. So, when you drive the sitter home, you stop by an ATM and get another $20. Then the next day, you discover the original $20 bill in your jacket pocket.

If you're like most people, you react with something like glee. The $20 in the jacket is "found" money. Even though the first $20 and the second $20 both came from your checking account, and both represent money you worked hard for, the $20 bill you hold in your hand is money you didn't expect to have, and you feel free to spend it frivolously.

Once again, Richard Thaler provides an interesting academic experiment to demonstrate this concept. In his study, he started with two groups of people. People in the first group were given $30 in cash and told they had two choices: (1) They could pocket the money and walk away, or (2) they could gamble on a coin flip. If they won they would get $9 extra and if they lost they would have $9 deducted. Most (70 percent) took the gamble because they figured at the very least they would end up with $21 of found money. Those in the second group were offered a different choice: (1) They could gamble on a coin toss— if they won, they would get $39 and if they lost they would get $21; or (2) they could get an even $30 with no coin toss. More than half (57 percent) decided to take the sure money. Both groups of people stood to win the exact same amount of money with the exact same odds, but they perceived the situation differently.[12]

Risk Tolerance

In the same way that a strong magnet pulls together all the nearby pieces of metal, your level of risk tolerance pulls together all the elements of the psychology of finance. The psychological concepts are abstract; where they get real is in the day-to-day decisions that you make about buying and selling. And the common thread in all those decisions is how you feel about risk.

In the last dozen or so years, investment professionals have devoted considerable energy to helping people assess their risk tolerance. At first, it seemed like a simple task. By using interviews and questionnaires, they could construct a risk profile for each investor. The trouble is, people's tolerance for risk is founded in emotion, and that means it changes with changing circumstances. When the market declines drastically, even those with an aggressive profile will become very cautious. In a booming market, supposedly conservative investors add more stocks just as quickly as aggressive investors do.

A true picture of risk tolerance requires digging below the surface of the standard assessment questions and investigating issues driven by psychology. A few years ago, in collaboration with Dr. Justin Green of Villanova University, I developed a risk analysis tool that focuses on personality as much as on the more obvious and direct risk factors.

Summarizing our research, we found that propensity for risk taking is connected to two demographic factors: gender and age. Women are typically more cautious than men, and older people are less willing to assume risk than younger people. Looking at personality factors, we learned that the investor with a high degree of risk tolerance will be someone who sets goals and believes he or she has control of the environment and can affect its outcome. This person sees the stock market as a contingency dilemma in which information combined with rational choices will produce winning results.

For investors, the implications of behavioral finance are clear: How we decide to invest, and how we choose to manage those investments, has a great deal to do with how we think about money. Mental accounting has been suggested as a further reason people don't sell stocks that are doing badly: In their minds, the loss doesn't become real until they act on it. Another powerful connection has to do with risk. We are far more likely to take risks with found money. On a broader scale, mental accounting emphasizes one weakness of the efficient market hypothesis: It demonstrates that market values are determined not solely by the aggregated information but also by how human beings process that information.

THE PSYCHOLOGY OF FOCUS INVESTING

Everything we have learned about psychology and investing comes together in the person of Warren Buffett. He puts his faith in his own research, rather than in luck. His actions derive from carefully thought-out goals, and he is not swept off course by short-term events. He understands the true elements of risk and accepts the consequences with confidence.

Long before behavioral finance had a name, it was understood and accepted by a few renegades like Warren Buffett and Charlie Munger. Charlie points out that when he and Buffett left graduate school, they "entered the business world to find huge, predictable patterns of extreme irrationality."[13] He is not talking about predicting the timing, but rather the idea that when irrationality does occur it leads to predictable patterns of subsequent behavior.

When it comes to investing, emotions are very real, in the sense that they affect people's behavior and thus ultimately affect market prices. You have already sensed, I am sure, two reasons understanding the human dynamic is so valuable in your own investing:

1. You will have guidelines to help you avoid the most common mistakes.
2. You will be able to recognize other people's mistakes in time to profit from them.

All of us are vulnerable to individual errors of judgment that can affect our personal success. When a thousand or a million people make errors of judgment, the collective impact is to push the market in a destructive direction. Then, so strong is the temptation to follow the crowd, accumulated bad judgment only compounds itself. In a turbulent sea of irrational behavior, the few who act rationally may well be the only survivors.

Successful focus investors need a certain kind of temperament. The road is always bumpy, and knowing the right path to take is often counterintuitive. The stock market's constant gyrations can be unsettling to investors and make them act in irrational ways. You need to be on the lookout for these emotions and be prepared to act sensibly even when your instincts may strongly call for the opposite behavior. But as we have learned, the future rewards focus investing significantly enough to warrant our strong effort.

12

The Unreasonable Man

eorge Bernard Shaw wrote, "The reasonable man adapts himself to the world. The unreasonable one persists in trying to adapt the world to himself. Therefore all progress depends on the unreasonable man."[1]

Shall we conclude that Buffett is "the unreasonable man"? To do so, we must presume that his investment approach represents progress in the financial world, an assumption I freely make. For when we look at the recent achievements of the "reasonable" men, we see at best unevenness, at worst disaster.

The 1980s are likely to be remembered as the *Future Shock* decade of financial management. Program trading, leveraged buyouts, junk bonds, derivative securities, and index futures frightened many investors. The distinctions between money managers faded. The grind of fundamental research was replaced by the whirl of computers. Black boxes replaced management interviews and investigation. Automation replaced intuition.

The late 1990s were, if anything, worse. That frenzied, overvalued marketplace phenomenon generally known as the dot-com boom went disastrously bust. Warren Buffett called it "The Great Bubble." And we all know what happens to bubbles when they get too big—they burst, dripping sticky residue on everyone within range.

Many investors have become disenchanted and estranged from the financial marketplace. The residue of the three-year bear market of 2000 through 2002 left many with a particularly bitter taste in their mouths. Even now, with so many money managers unable to add value to client portfolios, it is easy to understand why passive investing has gained popularity.

Throughout the past few decades, investors have flirted with many different investment approaches. Periodically, small capitalization, large capitalization, growth, value, momentum, thematic, and sector rotation have proven financially rewarding. At other times, these approaches have stranded their followers in periods of mediocrity. Buffett, the exception, has not suffered periods of mediocrity. His investment performance, widely documented, has been consistently superior. As investors and speculators alike have been distracted by esoteric approaches to investing, Buffett has quietly amassed a multi-billion-dollar fortune. Throughout, businesses have been his tools, common sense his philosophy.

How did he do it?

Given the documented success of Buffett's performance coupled with the simplicity of his methodology, the more appropriate question is, why don't other investors apply his approach? The answer may lie in how people think about investing.

When Buffett invests, he sees a business. Most investors see only a stock price. They spend far too much time and effort watching, predicting, and anticipating price changes and far too little time understanding the business they are part owner of. Elementary as this may be, it is the root that distinguishes Buffett.

Stocks are simple. All you do is buy shares in a great business for less than the business is intrinsically worth, with management of the highest integrity and ability. Then you own those shares forever.[2]

WARREN BUFFETT, 1990

While other professional investors are busy studying capital asset pricing models, beta, and modern portfolio theory, Buffett studies income statements, capital reinvestment requirements, and the cash-generating capabilities of his companies. His hands-on experience with a wide variety of businesses in many industries separates Buffett from all other professional investors. "Can you really explain to a fish what it's like to walk on land?" Buffett asks. "One day on land is worth a thousand years of talking about it and one day running a business has exactly the same kind of value."[3]

According to Buffett, the investor and the businessperson should look at the company in the same way, because they both want essentially the same thing. The businessperson wants to buy the entire company and the investor wants to buy portions of the company. Theoretically, the businessperson and the investor, to earn a profit, should be looking at the same variables.

If adapting Buffett's investment strategy required only changing perspective, then probably more investors would become proponents. However, applying Buffett's approach requires changing not only perspective but also how performance is evaluated and communicated. The traditional yardstick for measuring performance is price change: the difference between what you originally paid for a stock and its market price today.

In the long run, the market price of a stock should approximate the change in value of the business. However, in the short run, prices can swoop widely above and below a company's value for any number of illogical reasons. The problem remains that most investors use these short-term price changes to gauge the success or failure of their investment approach, even though the changes often have little to do with the changing economic value of the business and much to do with anticipating the behavior of other investors.

To make matters worse, clients require professional money to report performance in quarterly periods. Knowing that they must improve short-term performance or risk losing clients, professional investors become obsessed with chasing stock prices.

The market is there only as a reference point to see if anybody is offering to do anything foolish.[4]

WARREN BUFFETT, 1988

Buffett believes it is foolish to use short-term prices to judge a company's success. Instead, he lets his companies report their value to him by their economic progress. Once a year, he checks several variables:

- Return on beginning shareholder's equity
- Change in operating margins, debt levels, and capital expenditure needs
- The company's cash-generating ability

If these economic measurements are improving, he knows the share price, over the long term, should reflect this. What happens to the stock price in the short run is inconsequential.

INVESTING THE WARREN BUFFETT WAY

The major goal of this book is to help investors understand and employ the investment strategies that have made Buffett successful. It is my hope that, having learned from his past experiences, you will be able to go forward and apply his methods. Perhaps in the future you may see examples of "Buffett-like" purchases and will be in a position to profit from his teachings.

For instance . . .

- When the stock market forces the price of a good business downward, as it did to the *Washington Post,* or
- When a specific risk temporarily punishes a business, as it did Wells Fargo, or
- When investor indifference allows a superior business such as Coca-Cola to be priced at half of its intrinsic value

. . . investors who know how to think and act like Buffett will be rewarded.

The Warren Buffett Way is deceptively simple. There are no computer programs to learn, no cumbersome investment banking manuals to decipher. There is nothing scientific about valuing a business and then paying a price that is below this business value. "What we do is not beyond anybody else's competence," says Buffett. "It is just not necessary to do extraordinary things to get extraordinary results."[5]

The irony is that Buffett's success lies partly in the failure of others. "It has been helpful to me," he explains, "to have tens of thousands (students) turned out of business schools taught that it didn't do any good to think."[6] I do not mean to imply that Buffett is average, far from it. He is unquestionably brilliant. But the gap between Buffett and other professional investors is widened by their own willingness to play a loser's game that Buffett chooses not to play. Readers of this book have the same choice.

Whether you are financially able to purchase 10 percent of a company or merely one hundred shares, the Warren Buffett Way can help you achieve profitable investment returns. But this approach will help only those investors who are willing to help themselves. To be successful, you must be willing to do some thinking on your own. If you need constant affirmation, particularly from the stock market, that your investment decisions are correct, you will diminish your benefits. But if you can think for yourself, apply relatively simple methods, and have the courage of your convictions, you will greatly increase your chances for profit.

Whenever people try something new, there is initial apprehension. Adopting a new and different investment strategy will naturally evoke some uneasiness. In the Warren Buffett Way, the first step is the most challenging. If you can master this first step, the rest of the way is easy.

Step One: Turn off the Stock Market

Remember that the stock market is manic-depressive. Sometimes it is wildly excited about future prospects, and at other times it is unreasonably depressed. Of course, this behavior creates opportunities, particularly when shares of outstanding businesses are available at irrationally low prices. But just as you would not take direction from an advisor who exhibited manic-depressive tendencies, neither should you allow the market to dictate your actions.

The stock market is not a preceptor; it exists merely to assist you with the mechanics of buying or selling shares of stock. If you believe that the stock market is smarter than you are, give it your money by investing in index funds. But if you have done your homework and understand your business and are confident that you know more about your business than the stock market does, turn off the market.

Buffett does not have a stock quote machine in his office and he seems to get by just fine without it. If you plan on owning shares in an outstanding business for a number of years, what happens in the market on a day-to-day basis is inconsequential. You *do* need to check in regularly, to see if something has happened that presents you with a nifty opportunity, but you will find that your portfolio weathers nicely even if you do not look constantly at the market.

"After we buy a stock, we would not be disturbed if markets closed for a year or two," says Buffett. "We don't need a daily quote on our 100 percent position in See's or H.H. Brown to validate our well being. Why, then, should we need a quote on our 7 percent interest [today, more than 8 percent] in Coke?"[7]

Buffett is telling us that he does not need the market's prices to validate Berkshire's common stock investments. The same holds true for individual investors. You know you have approached Buffett's level when your attention turns to the stock market and the only question on your mind is: "Has anybody done anything foolish lately that will give me an opportunity to buy a good business at a great price?"

Step Two: Don't Worry about the Economy

Just as people spend fruitless hours worrying about the stock market so, too, do they worry needlessly about the economy. If you find yourself discussing and debating whether the economy is poised for growth or tilting toward a recession, whether interest rates are moving up or down, or whether there is inflation or disinflation, STOP! Give yourself a break.

Often investors begin with an economic assumption and then go about selecting stocks that fit neatly within this grand design. Buffett considers this thinking to be foolish. First, no one has economic predictive powers any more than they have stock market predictive powers. Second, if you select stocks that will benefit by a particular economic environment, you inevitably invite turnover and speculation, as you continuously adjust your portfolio to benefit in the next economic scenario.

Buffett prefers to buy a business that has the opportunity to profit in any economy. Macroeconomic forces may affect returns on the margin, but overall, Buffett's businesses are able to profit nicely despite vagaries in the economy. Time is more wisely spent locating and owning a business that can profit in *all* economic environments than by renting a group of stocks that do well only if a guess about the economy happens to be correct.

Step Three: Buy a Business, Not a Stock

Let's pretend that you have to make a very important decision. Tomorrow you will have an opportunity to pick one business to invest in. To make it interesting, let's also pretend that once you have made your decision, you can't change it and, furthermore, you have to hold the investment for ten years. Ultimately, the wealth generated from this business ownership will support you in your retirement. Now, what are you going to think about?

Probably many questions will run through your mind, bringing a great deal of confusion. But if Buffett were given the same test, he would begin by methodically measuring the business against his basic tenets, one by one:

- Is the business simple and understandable, with a consistent operating history and favorable long-term prospects?
- Is it run by honest and competent managers, who allocate capital rationally, communicate candidly with shareholders, and resist the institutional imperative?
- Are the company's economics in good shape—with high profit margins, owners' earnings, and increased market value that matches retained earnings?
- Finally, is it available at a discount to its intrinsic value? Take note: Only at this final step does Buffett look at the stock market price.

Calculating the value of a business is not mathematically complex. However, problems arise when we wrongly estimate a company's future cash flow. Buffett deals with this problem in two ways. First, he increases his chances of correctly predicting future cash flows by sticking with businesses that are simple and stable in character. Second, he insists on a margin of safety between the company's purchase price and its determined value. This margin of safety helps create a cushion that will protect him—and you—from companies whose future cash flows are changing.

Step Four: Manage a Portfolio of Businesses

Now that you are a business owner as opposed to a renter of stocks, the composition of your portfolio will change. Because you are no longer measuring your success solely by price change or comparing annual price change to a common stock benchmark, you have the liberty to select the best businesses available. There is no law that says you must include every major industry within your portfolio, nor do you have to include 30, 40, or 50 stocks in your portfolio to achieve adequate diversification.

Buffett believes that wide diversification is required only when investors do not understand what they are doing. If these "know-nothing" investors want to own common stocks, they should simply put their money in an index fund. But for the "know-something" investors, conventional diversification into dozens of stocks makes little sense. Buffett asks you to consider: If the best business you own presents the least financial risk and has the most favorable long-term prospects, why would you put money into your twentieth favorite business instead of adding money to the top choice?

Now that you are managing a portfolio of businesses, many things begin to change. First, you are less likely to sell your best businesses just because they are returning a profit. Second, you will pick new businesses for purchase with much greater care. You will resist the temptation to purchase a marginal company just because you have cash reserves. If the company does not pass your tenet screen, don't purchase it. Be patient and wait for the right business. It is wrong to assume that if you're not buying and selling, you're not making progress. In Buffett's mind, it is too difficult to make hundreds of smart decisions in a lifetime. He would rather position his portfolio so he only has to make a few smart decisions.

The Essence of Warren Buffett

The driving force of Warren Buffett's investment strategy is the rational allocation of capital. Determining how to allocate a company's earnings is the most important decision a manager will make. Rationality—displaying rational thinking when making that choice—is the quality Buffett most admires. Despite underlying vagaries, a line of reason permeates the financial markets. Buffett's success is the result of locating that line of reason and never deviating from its path.

Buffett has had his share of failures and no doubt will have a few more in the years ahead. But investment success is not synonymous with infallibility, but it comes about by doing more things right than wrong. The Warren Buffett Way is no different. Its success depends as much on eliminating those things you can get wrong, which are many and per-plexing (predicting markets, economies, and stock prices), as on getting things right, which are few and simple (valuing a business).

When Buffett purchases stocks, he focuses on two simple variables: the price of the business and its value. The price of a business can be found by looking up its quote. Determining value requires some calcula-tion, but it is not beyond the comprehension of those willing to do some homework.

> Investing is not that complicated. You need to know account-ing, the language of business. You should read *The Intelligent Investor*. You need the right mind-set, the right temperament. You should be interested in the process and be in your circle of competence. Read Ben Graham and Phil Fisher, read annual reports and trade reports, but don't do equations with Greek letters in them.[8]
>
> WARREN BUFFETT, 1993

Because you no longer worry about the stock market, the economy, or predicting stock prices, you are now free to spend more time under-standing your businesses. You can spend more productive time reading annual reports and business and industry articles that will improve your knowledge as an owner. In fact, the more willing you are to investigate your own business, the less dependent you will be on others who make a living advising people to take irrational action.

Ultimately, the best investment ideas will come from doing your own homework. However, you should not feel intimidated. The Warren Buffett Way is not beyond the comprehension of most serious investors. You do not have to become an MBA-level authority on business valua-tion to use it successfully. Still, if you are uncomfortable applying these tenets yourself, nothing prevents you from asking your financial advisor these same questions. In fact, the more you enter into a dialogue on price and value, the more you will begin to understand and appreciate the Warren Buffett Way.

Buffett, over his lifetime, has tried different investment gambits. At a young age he even tried his hand at stock charting. He has studied with the brightest financial mind of the twentieth century, Benjamin Graham, and managed and owned a host of businesses with his partner, Charlie Munger. Over the past five decades, Buffett has experienced double-digit interest rates, hyperinflation, and stock market crashes. Through all the distractions, he found his niche, that point where all things make sense: where investment strategy cohabits with personality. "Our (investment) attitude," said Buffett, "fits our personalities and the way we want to live our lives."[6]

Buffett's attitude easily reflects this harmony. He is always upbeat and supportive. He is genuinely excited about coming to work every day. "I have in life all I want right here," he says. "I love every day. I mean, I tap dance in here and work with nothing but people I like."[7] "There is no job in the world," he says, "that is more fun than running Berkshire and I count myself lucky to be where I am."[8]

Afterword

Managing Money the Warren Buffett Way

I began my money management career at Legg Mason in the summer of 1984. It was a typical hot and humid day in Baltimore. Fourteen newly minted investment brokers, including myself, walked into an open-windowed conference room to begin our training. Sitting down at our desks, we all received a copy of *The Intelligent Investor* by Benjamin Graham (a book I had never heard of) and a photocopy of the 1983 Berkshire Hathaway annual report (a company I had never heard of) written by Warren Buffett (a man I had never heard of).

The first day of class included introductions and welcomes from top management, including some of the firm's most successful brokers. One after another, they proudly explained that Legg Mason's investment philosophy was 100 percent value-based. Clutching *The Intelligent Investor,* each took a turn at reciting chapter and verse from this holy text. Buy stocks with low price-to-earnings ratios (P/E), low price-to-book value, and high dividends, they said. Don't pay attention to the stock market's daily gyrations, they said; its siren song would almost certainly pull you in the wrong direction. Seek to become a contrarian, they said. Buy stocks that are down in price and unpopular so you can later sell them at higher prices when they again become popular.

The message we received throughout the first day was both consistent and logical. We spent the afternoon analyzing Value Line research reports and learning to distinguish between stocks that were down in price and appeared to be cheap and stocks that were up in price and appeared to be expensive. By the end of our first training session, we all believed we were in possession of the Holy Grail of investing. As we packed up our belongings, our instructor reminded us to take the Berkshire Hathaway annual report with us and read it before tomorrow's class. "Warren Buffett," she cheerily reminded us, "was Benjamin Graham's most famous student, you know."

Back in my hotel room that night, I was wrung out with exhaustion. My eyes were blurry and tired, and my head was swimming with balance sheets, income statements, and accounting ratios. Quite honestly, the last thing I wanted to do was to spend another hour or so reading an annual report. I was sure if one more investing factoid reached my inner skull, it would certainly explode. Reluctantly and very tiredly, I picked up the Berkshire Hathaway report.

It began with a salutation *To the Shareholders of Berkshire Hathaway Inc.* Here Buffett outlined the company's major business principles: "Our long-term economic goal is to maximize the average annual rate of gain in intrinsic value on a per share basis," he wrote. "Our preference would be to reach this goal by directly owning a diversified group of businesses that generate cash and consistently earn above-average returns on capital." He promised, "We will be candid in our reporting to you, emphasizing the pluses and minuses important in appraising business value. Our guideline is to tell you the business facts that we would want to know if our positions were reversed."

The next fourteen pages outlined Berkshire's major business holdings including Nebraska Furniture Mart, *Buffalo Evening News,* See's Candy Shops, and the Government Employees Insurance Company. And true to his word, Buffett proceeded to tell me everything I would want to know about the economics of these businesses, and more. He listed the common stocks held in Berkshire's insurance portfolio, including Affiliated Publications, General Foods, Ogilvy & Mather, R.J. Reynolds Industries, and the *Washington Post.* I was immediately struck by how seamlessly Buffett moved back and forth between describing the stocks in the portfolio and the business attributes of Berkshire's major holdings. It was as if the analyses of stocks and of businesses were one and the same.

Granted, I had spent the entire day in class analyzing stocks, which I knew were partial ownership interests in businesses, but I had not made this most important analytical connection. When I studied Value Line reports I saw accounting numbers and financial ratios. When I read the Berkshire Hathaway report I saw businesses, with products and customers. I saw economics and cash earnings. I saw competitors and capital expenditures. Perhaps I should have seen all that when I analyzed the Value Line reports, but for whatever reason, it did not resonate in the same way. As I continued to read the Berkshire report, the entire world of investing, which was still somewhat mysterious to me, began to open. That night, in one epiphanic moment, Warren Buffett revealed the inner nature of investing.

The next morning, I was bursting with a newly discovered passion for investing, and when the training class was completed, I quickly returned to Philadelphia with a single-minded purpose: I was going to invest my clients' money in the same fashion as did Warren Buffett.

I knew I needed to know more, so I started building a file of background information. First I obtained all the back copies of Berkshire Hathaway annual reports. Then I ordered the annual reports of all the publicly traded companies Buffett had invested with. Then I collected all the magazine and newspaper articles on Warren Buffett I could find.

When the file was as complete as I could get it, I dove in. My goal was to first become an expert on Warren Buffett and then share those insights with my clients.

Over the ensuing years, I built a respectable investment business. By following Buffett's teachings and stock picks, I achieved for my clients more investment success than failure. Most of my clients intellectually bought into the approach of thinking about stocks as businesses and trying to buy the best businesses at a discount. The few clients who did not stick around left not because the Buffett approach was unsound, but because being contrarian was too much of an emotional challenge. And a few left simply because they did not have enough patience to see the process succeed. They were impatient for activity, and the constant itch to do something—anything—drove them off the track. Looking back, I don't believe I dealt with anyone who openly disagreed with the logic of Buffett's investment approach, yet there were several who could not get the psychology right.

All the while, I continued to collect Buffett data. Annual reports, magazine articles, interviews—anything having to do with Warren Buffett and Berkshire Hathaway, I read, analyzed, and filed. I was like a kid following a ballplayer. He was my hero, and each day I tried to swing the bat like Warren.

As the years passed, I had a growing and powerful urge to become a full-time portfolio manager. At the time, investment brokers were compensated on their purchases and sales; it was largely a commission-based system. As a broker, I was getting the "buy" part of the equation right, but Buffett's emphasis on holding stocks for the long-term made the "sell" part of the equation more difficult. Today, most financial service businesses allow investment brokers and financial advisors to manage money for their clients for a fee instead of a commission—if they choose. Eventually I met several portfolio managers who were compensated for performance regardless of whether they did a lot of buying or selling. This arrangement appeared to me to be the perfect environment in which to apply Buffett's teachings.

Initially, I gained some portfolio management experience at a local bank trust department in Philadelphia, and along the way obtained the obligatory Chartered Financial Analyst designation. Later, I joined a small investment counseling firm where I managed client portfolios for a fee. Our objective was to help our clients achieve a reasonable rate of return within an acceptable level of risk. Most had already achieved their financial goals, and now they wanted to preserve their wealth. Because of this, many of the portfolios in our firm were balanced between stocks and bonds.

It was here that I began to put my thoughts about Buffett down on paper, to share with our clients the wisdom of his investment approach. After all, Buffett, who had been investing for forty years, had built up a pretty nice nest egg; learning more about how he did it certainly couldn't hurt. These collected writings ultimately became the basis for *The Warren Buffett Way*.

The decision to start an equity mutual fund based on the principles described in *The Warren Buffett Way* came from two directions. First, our investment counseling firm needed an instrument to manage those accounts that were not large enough to warrant a separately managed portfolio. Second, I wanted to establish a discretionary performance record that was based on the teachings of the book. I wanted to demonstrate that what Buffett had taught and what I had written, if followed, would allow an investor to generate market-beating returns. The proof would be in the performance.

The new fund was established on April 17, 1995. Armed with the knowledge gained by having studied Warren Buffett for over ten years, coupled with the experience of managing portfolios for seven of those years, I felt we were in a great position to help our clients achieve above-average results. Instead, what we got was two very mediocre years of investment performance.

What happened?

As I analyzed the portfolio and the stock market during this period, I discovered two important but separate explanations. First, when I started the fund, I populated the portfolio mostly with Berkshire Hathaway-type stocks: newspapers, beverage companies, other consumer nondurable businesses, and selected financial service companies. I even bought shares of Berkshire Hathaway.

Because my fund was a laboratory example of Buffett's teachings, perhaps it was not surprising that many of the stocks in the portfolio were stocks Buffett himself had purchased. But the difference between Buffett's stocks in the 1980s and those same stocks in 1997 was striking. Many of the companies that had consistently grown owner earnings at a double-digit rate in the 1980s were slowing to a high single-digit rate in the late 1990s. In addition, the stock prices of these companies had steadily risen over the decade and so the discount to intrinsic value was smaller compared with the earlier period. When the economics of your business slow and the discount to intrinsic value narrows, the future opportunity for outsized investment returns diminishes.

If the first factor was lack of high growth level inside the portfolio, the second factor was what happening outside the portfolio. At the same time that the economics of the businesses in the fund were slowing, the economics of certain technology companies—telecommunications, software, and Internet service providers—were sharply accelerating. Because these new industries were taking a larger share of the market capitalization of the Standard & Poor's 500 Index, the stock market itself was rising at a faster clip. What I soon discovered was that the economics of what I owned in the fund were no match for the newer, more powerful technology-based companies then revving up in the stock market.

In 1997, my fund was at the crossroads. If I continued to invest in the traditional Buffett-like stocks, it was likely I would continue to generate just average results. Even Buffett was telling Berkshire Hathaway shareholders they could no longer expect to earn the above-average investment gains the company had achieved in the past. I knew if I continued to own the same stocks Buffett owned in his portfolio at these elevated prices, coupled with moderating economics, I was unlikely to generate above-average investment results for my shareholders. And in that case, what was the purpose? If a mutual fund cannot generate, over time, investment results better than the broad market index, then its shareholders would be better off in an index mutual fund.

Standing at the investment crossroads during this period was dramatic. There were questions about whether the fund should continue. There were questions about whether Buffett could compete against the newer industries and still provide above-average results. And there was the meta-question of whether the whole philosophy of thinking about stocks as businesses was a relevant approach when analyzing the newer technology-oriented industries.

I knew in my heart that the Buffett approach to investing was still valid. I knew without question that this business-analytical approach would still provide the opportunity for investors to spot mispricing and thus profit from the market's narrower view. I knew all these things and more, yet I momentarily hesitated at the shoreline, unable to cross into the new economic landscape.

I was fortunate to become friends with Bill Miller when I first began my career at Legg Mason. At the time, Bill was comanaging a value fund with Ernie Kiehne. Bill periodically spent time with the newer investment brokers sharing his thoughts about the stock market, about companies, and ideas from the countless books he had read. After I left Legg Mason to become a portfolio manager, Bill and I remained friends. After *The Warren Buffett Way* was published, we circled back for more intense discussions about investing and the challenges of navigating the economic landscape.

In the book, I pointed out that Buffett did not rely solely on low P/E ratios to select stocks. The driving force in value creation was owner earnings and a company's ability to generate above-average returns on capital. Sometimes a stock with a low P/E ratio did generate cash and achieve high returns on capital and subsequently became a great investment. Other times, a stock with a low P/E ratio consumed cash and generated below-average returns on capital and so became a poor investment. Stocks with low P/E ratios might be a nice pond to fish in for ideas, Buffett said, but what makes them go up is the cash and high returns on invested capital.

Bill had figured this out a few years earlier, and he was already steering his value fund in this direction. He had already chalked up four consecutive years of outperformance and was turning heads in the investment community.

With my fund struggling to gain a footing, I met with Bill to discuss strategies and opportunities. I told him Buffett's investment approach was solid. He agreed. I told him the only way to outwit the stock market was to analyze stocks as businesses in order to discover the deep-rooted fundamental changes that occur in a businesses before the market's pricing mechanism picks it up. He agreed. I told him I was certain Buffett's approach could be applied to the new industries but I was unsure how to proceed. He said, "Come work with us at Legg Mason and I'll show you how it works."

Bill, using a valuation approach that focused not on P/E ratios but on cash earnings and return on capital, had already been pursuing the newer companies in the technology space. He purchased Dell Computer in 1996 at six times earnings with a 40 percent return on capital. Other value managers also bought Dell but then they sold at twelve times earnings because the conventional wisdom dictated you always bought PC manufacturers at six times earnings and sold them at twelve times earnings. Bill instead studied the business model and soon discovered that Dell's return on capital was quickly rising to an astonishing triple-digit rate of return. So while other value managers sold their Dell Computer at twelve times earnings, Bill held on at twenty times, thirty times, and forty times earnings, believing that the company was still deeply undervalued relative to its rapidly growing intrinsic value. And he was right. His investment in Dell Computer produced a 3,000 percent return for his fund's shareholders.

Bill has not shied away from making additional investments in the New Economy landscape. He hit a home run with AOL. He invested in telecommunications, generating outsized returns in Nokia and Nextel Communications. Legg Mason Capital Management is the second largest shareholder in Amazon.com—second only to CEO Jeff Bezos. Most recently, Bill added eBay to his fund's portfolio, reasoning that it is at an economic starting gate very similar to Microsoft's in 1993.

Back then Microsoft was a $22 billion business that most value investors thought was significantly overvalued. By the end of 2003, Microsoft had grown to a $295 billion business. The company went up in price over 1,000 percent, while the S&P 500 Index advanced 138 percent during the same time period.

Was Microsoft a value stock in 1993? It certainly looks like it was, yet no value investor would touch it. Is eBay a value stock today? We obviously believe it is, but we will not know for certain for some years to come. But one thing is clear to us: You cannot determine whether eBay is a value stock by looking at its P/E any more than you could determine Microsoft's valuation by looking at its P/E.

At the heart of all Bill's investment decisions is the requirement of understanding a company's business model. What are the value creators? How does the company generate cash? What level of cash can a company produce and what rate of growth can it expect to achieve? What is the company's return on capital? If it achieves a return above the cost of capital, the company is creating value. If it achieves a rate of return below the cost of capital, the company is destroying value.

In the end, Bill's analysis gives him a sense of what the business is worth, based largely on the discounted present value of the company's future cash earnings. Although Bill's fund owns companies that are different from those in Buffett's Berkshire Hathaway portfolio, no one can deny that they are approaching the investment process in the same way. The only difference is that Bill has decided to take the investment philosophy and apply it to the New Economy franchises that are rapidly dominating the global economic landscape.

When Bill asked me to join Legg Mason Capital Management and bring my fund along, it was clear to me our philosophical approach was identical. The more important advantage of joining Bill's team was that now I was part of an organization that was dedicated to applying a business-valuation approach to investing wherever value-creation opportunities appeared. I was no longer limited to looking at just the stocks Buffett had purchased. The entire stock market was now open for analysis. I guess you could say it forced me to expand my circle of competence.

One of my earliest thinking errors in managing my fund was the mistaken belief that because Buffett did not own high-tech companies, these businesses must have been inherently unanalyzable. Yes, these newly created businesses possessed more economic risk than many of the companies Buffett owned. The economics of soda pop, razor blades, carpets, paint, candy, and furniture are much easier to predict than the economics of computer software, telecommunications, and the Internet.

But "difficult to predict" is not the same as "impossible to analyze." Certainly the economics of a technology company are more variant than those of consumer nondurable businesses. But a thoughtful study of how any business operates should still allow us to determine a range of valuation possibilities. And keeping with the Buffett philosophy, it is not critical that we determine precisely what the value of the company is, only that we are buying the company at a significant price discount (margin of safety) from the range of valuation possibilities.

What some Buffettologists miss in their thinking is that the payoff of being right in the analysis of technology companies more than compensates for the risk. All we must do is analyze each stock as a business, determine the value of the business and, to protect against higher economic risk, demand a greater margin of safety in the purchase price.

We should not forget that over the years many devotees of Warren Buffett's investment approach have taken his philosophy and applied it to different parts of the stock market. Several prominent investors have bought stocks not found anywhere in Berkshire's portfolio. Others have bought smaller-capitalization stocks. A few have taken Buffett's approach into the international market and purchased foreign securities. The important takeaway is this: Buffett's investment approach is applicable to all types of businesses, regardless of industry, regardless of market capitalization, regardless of where the business is domiciled.

Since becoming part of Legg Mason Capital Management in 1998, my growth fund has enjoyed a remarkable period of superior investment performance. The reason for this much better performance is not that the philosophy or process changed, but that the philosophy and process were applied to a larger universe of stocks. When portfolio managers and analysts are willing to study all types of business models, regardless of industry classification, the opportunity to exploit the market's periodic mispricing greatly expands, and this translates into better returns for our shareholders.

This does not mean we do not have an occasional bad year, bad quarter, or bad month. It simply means when you add up all the times we lost money relative to the market, using any time period, the amount of money we lost was smaller than the amount of money we made when we outperformed the market.

In this respect, the record of this fund is not far different from other focused portfolios. Think back to the performance of Charlie Munger, Bill Ruane, and Lou Simpson. Each one achieved outstanding long-term performance but endured periods of short-term underperformance. Each one employed a business valuation process to determine whether stocks were mispriced. Each one ran concentrated, low-turnover portfolios. The process they used enabled them to achieve superior long-term results at the expense of a higher standard deviation.

Michael Mauboussin, the chief investment strategist at Legg Mason Capital Management, conducted a study of the best-performing mutual funds between 1992 and 2002.[1] He screened for funds that had one manager during the period, had assets of at least $1 billion, and beat the Standard & Poor's 500 Index over the ten-year period. Thirty-one mutual funds made the cut.

Then he looked at the process each manager used to beat the market, and isolated four attributes that set this group apart from the majority of fund managers.

1. *Portfolio turnover.* As a whole, the market-beating mutual funds had an average turnover ratio of about 30 percent. This stands in stark contrast to the turnover for all equity funds—110 percent.
2. *Portfolio concentration.* The long-term outperformers tend to have higher portfolio concentration than the index or other general equity funds. On average, the outperforming mutual funds placed 37 percent of their assets in their top ten names.
3. *Investment style.* The vast majority of the above-market performers espoused an intrinsic-value approach to selecting stocks.
4. *Geographic location.* Only a small fraction of the outperformers hail from the East Coast financial centers, New York or Boston. Most of the high-alpha generators set up shop in cities like Chicago, Salt Lake City, Memphis, Omaha, and Baltimore. Michael suggests that perhaps being away from the frenetic pace of New York and Boston lessens the hyperactivity that permeates so many mutual fund portfolios.

A common thread for outperformance, whether it be for the Super-investors of Graham-and-Doddsville, the Superinvestors of Buffettville, or those who lead the funds that Michael's research identified, is a port-folio strategy that emphasizes concentrated bets and low turnover and a stock-selection process that emphasizes the discovery of a stock's intrin-sic value.

Still, with all the evidence on how to generate above-average long results, a vast majority of money managers continue to underperform the stock market. Some believe this is evidence of market efficiency. Perhaps with the intense competition among money managers, stocks are more accurately priced. This may be partly true. We believe the market has become more efficient, and there are fewer opportunities to extract profits from the stock market using simple-minded techniques to determine value. Surely no one still believes the market is going to allow you to pick its pocket simply by calculating a P/E ratio.

Analysts who understand the deep-rooted changes unfolding in a business model will likely discover valuation anomalies that appear in the market. Those analysts will have a different view of the duration and magnitude of the company's cash-generating ability compared with the market's view. "That the S&P 500 has also beaten other active money managers is not an argument against active money management," said Bill Miller; "it is an argument against the methods employed by most active money managers."[2]

It has been twenty years since I read my first Berkshire Hathaway an-nual report. Even now, when I think about Warren Buffett and his phi-losophy, it fills me with excitement and passion for the world of investing. There is no doubt in my mind that the process is sound and, if consistently applied, will generate above-average long-term results. We have only to observe today's best-in-class money managers to see that they are all using varied forms of Buffett's investment approach.

Although companies, industries, markets, and economies will al-ways evolve over time, the value of Buffett's investment philosophy lies in its timelessness. No matter what the condition, investors can apply Buffett's approach to selecting stocks and managing portfolios.

When Buffett first started managing money in the 1950s and 1960s, he was thinking about stocks as businesses and managing focused portfolios. When he added the new economic franchises to Berkshire's portfolio in the 1970s and 1980s, he was still thinking about stocks as businesses and managing a focused portfolio. When Bill Miller bought technology and Internet companies for his value fund in the 1990s and into the first half of this decade, he was thinking about stocks as businesses and managing a focused portfolio.

Were the companies purchased in the 1950s different from the companies in the 1980s? Yes. Were the companies purchased in the 1960s different from those purchased in 1990s? Of course they were. Businesses change, industries unfold, and the competitiveness of markets allows new economic franchises to be born while others slowly wither. Throughout the constant evolution of markets and companies, it should be comforting for investors to realize there is an investment process that remains robust even against the inevitable forces of change.

At Berskhire's 2004 annual meeting, a shareholder asked Warren whether, looking back, he would change anything about his approach. "If we were to do it over again, we'd do it pretty much the same way," he answered. "We'd read everything in sight about businesses and industries. Working with far less capital, our investment universe would be far broader than it is currently. I would continually learn the basic principles of sound investing which are Ben Graham's, affected in a significant way by Charlie and Phil Fisher in terms of looking at better businesses." He paused for a moment, then added, "There's nothing different, in my view, about analyzing securities today versus fifty years ago."

Nor will there be anything different five, ten, or twenty years from now. Markets change, prices change, economic environments change, industries come and go. And smart investors change their day-to-day behavior to adapt to the changing context. What does not change, however, are the fundamentals.

Those who follow Buffett's way will still analyze stocks (and companies) according to the same tenets; will maintain a focus portfolio; and will ignore bumps, dips, and bruises. They believe, as I do, that the principles that have guided Warren Buffett's investment decisions for some sixty years are indeed timeless, and provide a foundation of solid investment wisdom on which all of us may build.

Appendix

Table A.1   Berkshire Hathaway 1977 Common Stock Portfolio

Number of Shares	Company	Cost	Market Value
934,300	The Washington Post Company	$ 10,628	$ 33,401
1,969,953	GEICO Convertible Preferred	19,417	33,033
592,650	Interpublic Group of Companies	4,531	17,187
220,000	Capital Cities Communications, Inc.	10,909	13,228
1,294,308	GEICO Common Stock	4,116	10,516
324,580	Kaiser Aluminum and Chemical Corp.	11,218	9,981
226,900	Knight-Ridder Newspapers	7,534	8,736
170,800	Ogilvy & Mather International	2,762	6,960
1,305,800	Kaiser Industries, Inc.	778	6,039
	Total	$ 71,893	$139,081
	All other common stocks	34,996	41,992
	Total common stocks	$106,889	$181,073

Source: Berkshire Hathaway 1977 Annual Report.
Note: Dollar amounts are in thousands.

Table A.2 Berkshire Hathaway 1978 Common Stock Portfolio

Number of Shares	Company	Cost	Market Value
934,000	The Washington Post Company	$ 10,628	$ 43,445
1,986,953	GEICO Convertible Preferred	19,417	28,314
953,750	SAFECO Corporation	23,867	26,467
592,650	Interpublic Group of Companies	4,531	19,039
1,066,934	Kaiser Aluminum and Chemical Corp.	18,085	18,671
453,800	Knight-Ridder Newspapers	7,534	10,267
1,294,308	GEICO Common Stock	4,116	9,060
246,450	American Broadcasting Companies	6,082	8,626
	Total	$ 94,260	$163,889
	All other common stocks	39,506	57,040
	Total common stocks	$133,766	$220,929

Source: Berkshire Hathaway 1978 Annual Report.
Note: Dollar amounts are in thousands.

Table A.3 Berkshire Hathaway 1979 Common Stock Portfolio

Number of Shares	Company	Cost	Market Value
5,730,114	GEICO Corp. (common stock)	$ 28,288	$ 68,045
1,868,000	The Washington Post Company	10,628	39,241
1,007,500	Handy & Harman	21,825	38,537
953,750	SAFECO Corporation	23,867	35,527
711,180	Interpublic Group of Companies	4,531	23,736
1,211,834	Kaiser Aluminum and Chemical Corp.	20,629	23,328
771,900	F.W. Woolworth Company	15,515	19,394
328,700	General Foods, Inc.	11,437	11,053
246,450	American Broadcasting Companies	6,082	9,673
289,700	Affiliated Publications	2,821	8,800
391,400	Ogilvy & Mather International	3,709	7,828
282,500	Media General,Inc.	4,545	7,345
112,545	Amerada Hess	2,861	5,487
	Total	$156,738	$297,994
	All other common stocks	28,675	36,686
	Total common stocks	$185,413	$334,680

Source: Berkshire Hathaway 1979 Annual Report.
Note: Dollar amounts are in thousands.

Table A.4 Berkshire Hathaway 1980 Common Stock Portfolio

Number of Shares	Company	Cost	Market Value
7,200,000	GEICO Corporation	$ 47,138	$105,300
1983,812	General Foods	62,507	59,889
2,015,000	Handy & Harman	21,825	58,435
1,250,525	SAFECO Corporation	32,063	45,177
1,868,600	The Washington Post Company	10,628	42,277
464,317	Aluminum Company of America	25,577	27,685
1,211,834	Kaiser Aluminum and Chemical Corp.	20,629	27,569
711,180	Interpublic Group of Companies	4,531	22,135
667,124	F.W. Woolworth Company	13,583	16,511
370,088	Pinkerton's, Inc.	12,144	16,489
475,217	Cleveland-Cliffs Iron Company	12,942	15,894
434,550	Affiliated Publications, Inc.	2,821	12,222
245,700	R.J. Reynolds Industries	8,702	11,228
391,400	Ogilvy & Mather International	3,709	9,981
282,500	Media General	4,545	8,334
247,039	National Detroit Corporation	5,930	6,299
151,104	The Times mirror Company	4,447	6,271
881,500	National Student Marketing	5,128	5,895
	Total	$298,848	$497,591
	All other common stocks	26,313	32,096
	Total common stocks	$325,161	$529,687

Source: Berkshire Hathaway 1980 Annual Report.
Note: Dollar amounts are in thousands.

Table A.5 Berkshire Hathaway 1981 Common Stock Portfolio

Number of Shares	Company	Cost	Market Value
7,200,000	GEICO Corporation	$ 47,138	$199,800
1,764,824	R.J. Reynolds Industries	76,668	83,127
2,101,244	General Foods	66,277	66,714
1,868,600	The Washington Post Company	10,628	58,160
2,015,000	Handy & Harman	21,825	36,270
785,225	SAFECO Corporation	21,329	31,016
711,180	Interpublic Group of Companies	4,531	23,202
370,088	Pinkerton's, Inc.	12,144	19,675
703,634	Aluminum Company of America	19,359	18,031
420,441	Arcata Corporation	14,076	15,136
475,217	Cleveland-Cliffs Iron Company	12,942	14,362
451,650	Affiliated Publications, Inc.	3,297	14,362
441,522	GATX Corporation	17,147	13,466
391,400	Ogilvy & Mather International	3,709	12,329
282,500	Media General	4,545	11,088
	Total	$335,615	$616,490
	All other common stocks	16,131	22,739
	Total common stocks	$351,746	$639,229

Source: Berkshire Hathaway 1981 Annual Report.
Note: Dollar amounts are in thousands.

Table A.6 Berkshire Hathaway 1982 Common Stock Portfolio

Number of Shares	Company	Cost	Market Value
7,200,000	GEICO Corporation	$ 47,138	$309,600
3,107,675	R.J. Reynolds Industries	142,343	158,715
1,868,600	The Washington Post Company	10,628	103,240
2,101,244	General Foods	66,277	83,680
1,531,391	Time, Inc.	45,273	79,824
908,800	Crum & Forster	47,144	48,962
2,379,200	Handy & Harman	27,318	46,692
711,180	Interpublic Group of Companies	4,531	34,314
460,650	Affiliated Publications, Inc.	3,516	16,929
391,400	Ogilvy & Mather International	3,709	17,319
282,500	Media General	4,545	12,289
	Total	$402,422	$911,564
	All other common stocks	21,611	34,058
	Total common stocks	$424,033	$945,622

Source: Berkshire Hathaway 1982 Annual Report.
Note: Dollar amounts are in thousands.

Table A.7 Berkshire Hathaway 1983 Common Stock Portfolio

Number of Shares	Company	Cost	Market Value
6,850,000	GEICO Corporation	$ 47,138	$ 398,156
5,618,661	R.J. Reynolds Industries	268,918	314,334
4,451,544	General Foods	163,786	228,698
1,868,600	The Washington Post Company	10,628	136,875
901,788	Time, Inc.	27,732	56,860
2,379,200	Handy & Harman	27,318	42,231
636,310	Interpublic Group of Companies	4,056	33,088
690,975	Affiliated Publications, Inc.	3,516	26,603
250,400	Ogilvy & Mather International	2,580	12,833
197,200	Media General	3,191	11,191
	Total	$558,863	$1,260,869
	All other common stocks	7,485	18,044
	Total common stocks	$566,348	$1,278,913

Source: Berkshire Hathaway 1983 Annual Report.
Note: Dollar amounts are in thousands.

Table A.8 Berkshire Hathaway 1984 Common Stock Portfolio

Number of Shares	Company	Cost	Market Value
6,850,000	GEICO Corporation	$ 47,138	$ 397,300
4,047,191	General Foods	149,870	226,137
3,895,710	Exxon Corporation	173,401	175,307
1,868,600	The Washington Post Company	10,628	149,955
2,553,488	Time, Inc.	89,237	109,162
740,400	American Broadcasting Companies	44,416	46,738
2,379,200	Handy & Harman	27,318	38,662
690,975	Affiliated Publications, Inc.	3,516	32,908
818,872	Interpublic Group of Companies	2,570	28,149
555,949	Northwest Industries	26,581	27,242
	Total	$573,340	$1,231,560
	All other common stocks	11,634	37,326
	Total common stocks	$584,974	$1,268,886

Source: Berkshire Hathaway 1984 Annual Report.
Note: Dollar amounts are in thousands.

Table A.9 Berkshire Hathaway 1985 Common Stock Portfolio

Number of Shares	Company	Cost	Market Value
6,850,000	GEICO Corporation	$ 45,713	$ 595,950
1,727,765	The Washington Post Company	9,731	205,172
900,800	American Broadcasting Companies	54,435	108,997
2,350,922	Beatrice Companies, Inc.	106,811	108,142
1,036,461	Affiliated Publications, Inc.	3,516	55,710
2,553,488	Time, Inc.	20,385	52,669
2,379,200	Handy & Harman	27,318	43,718
	Total	$267,909	$1,170,358
	All other common stocks	7,201	27,963
	Total common stocks	$275,110	$1,198,321

Source: Berkshire Hathaway 1985 Annual Report.
Note: Dollar amounts are in thousands.

Table A.10 Berkshire Hathaway 1986 Common Stock Portfolio

Number of Shares	Company	Cost	Market Value
2,990,000	Capital Cities/ABC, Inc.	$515,775	$ 801,694
6,850,000	GEICO Corporation	45,713	674,725
1,727,765	The Washington Post Company	9,731	269,531
2,379,200	Handy & Harman	27,318	46,989
489,300	Lear Siegler, Inc.	44,064	44,587
	Total	$642,601	$1,837,526
	All other common stocks	12,763	36,507
	Total common stocks	$655,364	$1,874,033

Source: Berkshire Hathaway 1986 Annual Report.
Note: Dollar amounts are in thousands.

Table A.11 Berkshire Hathaway 1987 Common Stock Portfolio

Number of Shares	Company	Cost	Market Value
3,000,000	Capital Cities/ABC, Inc.	$517,500	$1,035,000
6,850,000	GEICO Corporation	45,713	756,925
1,727,765	The Washington Post Company	9,731	323,092
	Total common stocks	$572,944	$2,115,017

Source: Berkshire Hathaway 1987 Annual Report.
Note: Dollar amounts are in thousands.

Table A.12 Berkshire Hathaway 1988 Common Stock Portfolio

Number of Shares	Company	Cost	Market Value
3,000,000	Capital Cities/ABC, Inc.	$ 517,500	$1,086,750
6,850,000	GEICO Corporation	45,713	849,400
14,172,500	The Coca-Cola Company	592,540	632,448
1,727,765	The Washington Post Company	9,731	364,126
2,400,000	Federal Home Loan Mortgage Corp.	71,729	121,200
	Total common stocks	$1,237,213	$3,053,924

Source: Berkshire Hathaway 1988 Annual Report.
Note: Dollar amounts are in thousands.

Table A.13 Berkshire Hathaway 1989 Common Stock Portfolio

Number of Shares	Company	Cost	Market Value
23,350,000	The Coca-Cola Company	$1,023,920	$1,803,787
3,000,000	Capital Cities/ABC, Inc.	517,500	1,692,375
6,850,000	GEICO Corporation	45,713	1,044,625
1,727,765	The Washington Post Company	9,731	486,366
2,400,000	Federal Home Loan Mortgage Corp.	71,729	161,100
	Total common stocks	$1,668,593	$5,188,253

Source: Berkshire Hathaway 1989 Annual Report.
Note: Dollar amounts are in thousands.

Table A.14 Berkshire Hathaway 1990 Common Stock Portfolio

Number of Shares	Company	Cost	Market Value
46,700,000	The Coca-Cola Company	$1,023,920	$2,171,550
3,000,000	Capital Cities/ABC, Inc.	517,500	1,377,375
6,850,000	GEICO Corporation	45,713	1,110,556
1,727,765	The Washington Post Company	9,731	342,097
2,400,000	Federal Home Loan Mortgage Corp.	71,729	117,000
	Total common stocks	$1,958,024	$5,407,953

Source: Berkshire Hathaway 1990 Annual Report.
Note: Dollar amounts are in thousands.

Table A.15 Berkshire Hathaway 1991 Common Stock Portfolio

Number of Shares	Company	Cost	Market Value
46,700,000	The Coca-Cola Company	$1,023,920	$3,747,675
6,850,000	GEICO Corporation	45,713	1,363,150
24,000,000	The Gillette Company	600,000	1,347,000
3,000,000	Capital Cities/ABC, Inc.	517,500	1,300,500
2,495,200	Federal Home Loan Mortgage Corp.	77,245	343,090
1,727,765	The Washington Post Company	9,731	336,050
31,247,000	Guinness plc	264,782	296,755
5,000,000	Wells Fargo & Company	289,431	290,000
	Total common stocks	$2,828,322	$9,024,220

Source: Berkshire Hathaway 1991 Annual Report.
Note: Dollar amounts are in thousands.

Table A.16 Berkshire Hathaway 1992 Common Stock Portfolio

Number of Shares	Company	Cost	Market Value
93,400,000	The Coca-Cola Company	$1,023,920	$ 3,911,125
34,250,000	GEICO Corporation	45,713	2,226,250
3,000,000	Capital Cities/ABC, Inc.	517,500	1,523,500
24,000,000	The Gillette Company	600,000	1,365,000
16,196,700	Federal Home Loan Mortgage Corp.	414,527	783,515
6,358,418	Wells Fargo & Company	380,983	485,624
4,350,000	General Dynamics	312,438	450,769
1,727,765	The Washington Post Company	9,731	396,954
38,335,000	Guinness plc	333,019	299,581
	Total common stocks	$3,637,831	$11,442,318

Source: Berkshire Hathaway 1992 Annual Report.
Note: Dollar amounts are in thousands.

Table A.17 Berkshire Hathaway 1993 Common Stock Portfolio

Number of Shares	Company	Cost	Market Value
93,400,000	The Coca-Cola Company	$1,023,920	$ 4,167,975
34,250,000	GEICO Corporation	45,713	1,759,594
24,000,000	The Gillette Company	600,000	1,431,000
2,000,000	Capital Cities/ABC, Inc.	345,000	1,239,000
6,791,218	Wells Fargo & Company	423,680	878,614
13,654,600	Federal Home Loan Mortgage Corp.	307,505	681,023
1,727,765	The Washington Post Company	9,731	440,148
4,350,000	General Dynamics	94,938	401,287
38,335,000	Guinness plc	333,019	270,822
	Total common stocks	$3,183,506	$11,269,463

Source: Berkshire Hathaway 1993 Annual Report.
Note: Dollar amounts are in thousands.

Table A.18 Berkshire Hathaway 1994 Common Stock Portfolio

Number of Shares	Company	Cost	Market Value
93,400,000	The Coca-Cola Company	$1,023,920	$ 5,150,000
24,000,000	The Gillette Company	600,000	1,797,000
20,000,000	Capital Cities/ABC, Inc.	345,000	1,705,000
34,250,000	GEICO Corporation	45,713	1,678,250
6,791,218	Wells Fargo & Company	423,680	984,272
27,759,941	American Express Company	723,919	818,918
13,654,600	Federal Home Loan Mortgage Corp.	270,468	644,441
1,727,765	The Washington Post Company	9,731	418,983
19,453,300	PNC Bank Corporation	503,046	410,951
6,854,500	Gannett Co., Inc.	335,216	365,002
	Total common stocks	$4,280,693	$13,972,817

Source: Berkshire Hathaway 1994 Annual Report.
Note: Dollar amounts are in thousands.

Table A.19 Berkshire Hathaway 1995 Common Stock Portfolio

Number of Shares	Company	Cost	Market Value
49,456,900	American Express Company	$1,392.70	$ 2,046.30
20,000,000	Capital Cities/ABC, Inc.	345.00	2,467.50
100,000,000	The Coca-Cola Company	1,298.90	7,425.00
12,502,500	Federal Home Loan Mortgage Corp.	260.10	1,044.00
34,250,000	GEICO Corporation	45.70	2,393.20
48,000,000	The Gillette Company	600.00	2,502.00
6,791,218	Wells Fargo & Company	423.70	1,466.90
	Total common stocks	$4,366.10	$19,344.90

Source: Berkshire Hathaway 1995 Annual Report.
Note: Dollar amounts are in millions.

Table A.20 Berkshire Hathaway 1996 Common Stock Portfolio

Number of Shares	Company	Cost	Market Value
49,456,900	American Express Company	$1,392.70	$ 2,794.30
200,000,000	The Coca-Cola Company	1,298.90	10,525.00
24,614,214	The Walt Disney Company	577.00	1,716.80
64,246,000	Federal Home Loan Mortgage Corp.	333.40	1,772.80
48,000,000	The Gillette Company	600.00	3,732.00
30,156,600	McDonald's Corporation	1,265.30	1,368.40
1,727,765	The Washington Post Company	10.60	579.00
7,291,418	Wells Fargo & Company	497.80	1,966.90
	Total common stocks	$5,975.70	$24,455.20

Source: Berkshire Hathaway 1996 Annual Report.
Note: Dollar amounts are in millions.

Table A.21 Berkshire Hathaway 1997 Common Stock Portfolio

Number of Shares	Company	Cost	Market Value
49,456,900	American Express Company	$1,392.70	$ 4,414.00
200,000,000	The Coca-Cola Company	1,298.90	13,337.50
21,563,414	The Walt Disney Company	381.20	2,134.80
63,977,600	Freddie Mac	329.40	2,683.10
48,000,000	The Gillette Company	600.00	4,821.00
23,733,198	Travelers Group Inc.	604.40	1,278.60
1,727,765	The Washington Post Company	10.60	840.60
6,690,218	Wells Fargo & Company	412.60	2,270.90
	Total common stocks	$5,029.80	$31,780.50

Source: Berkshire Hathaway 1997 Annual Report.
Note: Dollar amounts are in millions.

Table A.22 Berkshire Hathaway 1998 Common Stock Portfolio

Shares	Company	Cost*	Market
50,536,900	American Express Company	$1,470	$ 5,180
200,000,000	The Coca-Cola Company	1,299	13,400
51,202,242	The Walt Disney Company	281	1,536
60,298,000	Freddie Mac	308	3,885
96,000,000	The Gillette Company	600	4,590
1,727,765	The Washington Post Company	11	999
63,595,180	Wells Fargo & Company	392	2,540
	Others	2,683	5,135
	Total Common Stocks	$7,044	$37,265

*Represents tax-basis cost which, in aggregate, is $1.5 billion less than GAAP cost.

Source: Berkshire Hathaway Annual Report, 1998.

Note: Dollar amounts are in millions.

Table A.23 Berkshire Hathaway 1999 Common Stock Portfolio

Shares	Company	Cost*	Market
50,536,900	American Express Company	$1,470	$ 8,402
200,000,000	The Coca-Cola Company	1,299	11,650
59,559,300	The Walt Disney Company	281	1,536
60,298,000	Freddie Mac	294	2,803
96,000,000	The Gillette Company	600	3,954
1,727,765	The Washington Post Company	11	960
59,136,680	Wells Fargo & Company	349	2,391
	Others	4,180	6,848
	Total Common Stocks	$8,203	$37,008

*Represents tax-basis cost which, in aggregate, is $691 million less than GAAP cost.

Source: Berkshire Hathaway Annual Report, 1999.

Note: Dollar amounts are in millions.

Table A.24 Berkshire Hathaway 2000 Common Stock Portfolio

Shares	Company	Cost	Market
151,610,700	American Express Company	$ 1,470	$ 8,329
200,000,000	The Coca-Cola Company	1,299	12,188
96,000,000	The Gillette Company	600	3,468
1,727,765	The Washington Post Company	11	1,066
55,071,380	Wells Fargo & Company	319	3,067
	Others	6,703	9,501
	Total Common Stocks	$10,402	$37,619

Source: Berkshire Hathaway Annual Report, 2000.
Note: Dollar amounts are in millions.

Table A.25 Berkshire Hathaway 2001 Common Stock Portfolio

Shares	Company	Cost	Market
151,610,700	American Express Company	$1,470	$5,410
200,000,000	The Coca-Cola Company	1,299	9,430
96,000,000	The Gillette Company	600	3,206
15,999,200	H&R Block, Inc.	255	715
24,000,000	Moody's Corporation	499	957
1,727,765	The Washington Post Company	11	916
53,265,080	Wells Fargo & Company	306	2,315
	Others	4,103	5,726
	Total Common Stocks	$8,543	$28,675

Source: Berkshire Hathaway Annual Report, 2001.
Note: Dollar amounts are in millions.

Table A.26 Berkshire Hathaway 2002 Common Stock Portfolio

Shares	Company	Cost	Market
151,610,700	American Express Company	$1,470	$5,359
200,000,000	The Coca-Cola Company	1,299	8,768
15,999,200	H&R Block, Inc.	255	643
24,000,000	Moody's Corporation	499	991
1,727,765	The Washington Post Company	11	1,275
53,265,080	Wells Fargo & Company	306	2,497
	Others	4,621	5,383
	Total Common Stocks	$9,146	$28,363

Source: Berkshire Hathaway Annual Report, 2002.
Note: Dollar amounts are in millions.

Table A.27 Berkshire Hathaway 2003 Common Stock Portfolio

Shares	Company	Cost	Market
151,610,700	American Express Company	$1,470	$7,312
200,000,000	The Coca-Cola Company	1,299	10,150
96,000,000	The Gillette Company	600	3,526
14,610,900	H&R Block, Inc.	227	809
15,476,500	HCA Inc.	492	665
6,708,760	M&T Bank Corporation	103	659
24,000,000	Moody's Corporation	499	1,453
2,338,961,000	PetroChina Company Limited	488	1,340
1,727,765	The Washington Post Company	11	1,367
56,448,380	Wells Fargo & Company	463	3,324
	Others	2,863	4,682
	Total Common Stocks	$8,515	$35,287

Source: Berkshire Hathaway Annual Report, 2003.
Note: Dollar amounts are in millions.

Notes

Chapter 1   The World's Greatest Investor

1. Carol J. Loomis, "The Inside Story of Warren Buffett," *Fortune* (April 11, 1988), 30.
2. Warren Buffett, "The Superinvestors of Graham-and-Doddsville," *Hermes* (Fall 1984).
3. Berkshire Hathaway Annual Report, 1999, 3.

Chapter 2   The Education of Warren Buffett

1. Adam Smith, *Supermoney* (New York: Random House, 1972), 178.
2. Benjamin Graham and David Dodd, *Security Analysis,* 3rd ed. (New York: McGraw-Hill, 1951), 38.
3. Ibid., 13.
4. Address by Warren Buffett to New York Society of Security Analysts, December 6, 1994, quoted in Andrew Kilpatrick, *Of Permanent Value: The Story of Warren Buffett* (Birmingham, AL: AKPE, 2004), 1341.
5. John Train, *The Money Masters* (New York: Penguin Books, 1981), 60.
6. Philip Fisher, *Common Stocks and Uncommon Profits* (New York: Harper & Brothers, 1958), 11.
7. Ibid., 33.
8. Philip Fisher, *Developing an Investment Philosophy,* The Financial Analysts Research Foundation, monograph number 10, 1.
9. I am grateful to Peter Bernstein and his excellent book, *Capital Ideas: The Improbable Origins of Modern Wall Street* (New York: The Free Press, 1992), for this background information on Williams.

10. Ibid., 151.
11. Ibid., 153.
12. Quoted on www.moneychimp.com.
13. Bernstein, *Capital Ideas,* 162.
14. Andrew Kilpatrick, *Of Permanent Value: The Story of Warren Buffett* (Birmingham, AL: AKPE, 2000), 89.
15. Munger's sweeping concept of the "latticework of mental models" is the subject of Robert Hagstrom's book *Investing: The Last Liberal Art* (New York: Texere, 2000).
16. A frequent comment, widely quoted.
17. Robert Lenzner, "Warren Buffett's Idea of Heaven: 'I Don't Have to Work with People I Don't Like,' " *Forbes* (October 18, 1993), 43.
18. L. J. Davis, "Buffett Takes Stock," *New York Times* magazine (April 1, 1990), 61.
19. Ibid.
20. Berkshire Hathaway Annual Report, 1987, 15.
21. Berkshire Hathaway Annual Report, 1990, 17.
22. Benjamin Graham, *The Intelligent Investor,* 4th ed. (New York: Harper & Row, 1973), 287.
23. *Adam Smith's Money World,* PBS, October 21, 1993, quoted in Kilpatrick, *Of Permanent Value* (2004), 1337.
24. Warren Buffett, "What We Can Learn from Philip Fisher," *Forbes* (October 19, 1987), 40.
25. "The Money Men—How Omaha Beats Wall Street," *Forbes* (November 1, 1969), 82.

Chapter 3   "Our Main Business Is Insurance": The Early Days of Berkshire Hathaway

1. Berkshire Hathaway Annual Report, 1985, 8.
2. Warren Buffett, "The Security I Like Best," *The Commercial and Financial Chronicle* (December 6, 1951); reprinted in Andrew Kilpatrick, *Of Permanent Value: The Story of Warren Buffett,* rev. ed. (Birmingham, AL: AKPE, 2000), 302.
3. Berkshire Hathaway Annual Report, 1999, 9.
4. The purchase price is often quoted as $22 billion, and in a sense that is true. The two companies announced in June 1998 that Berkshire would acquire all General Re shares at a 29 percent premium over the closing share price, by trading an equivalent value in Berkshire stock. But six months passed before the deal finally closed, and by that time both share prices had declined. General Re shareholders received $204.40 for each share they owned, rather than the $276.50 value the shares had back in June. The actual purchase

price was thus approximately $16 billion in Berkshire stock, instead of $22 billion. Kilpatrick, *Of Permanent Value* (2000), 18.

5. Andrew Kilpatrick, *Of Permanent Value: The Story of Warren Buffett* (Birmingham, AL: AKPE, 2004), 354.
6. Berkshire Hathaway Annual Report, 2000.
7. Special letter to shareholders, Berkshire Hathaway Quarterly Report, 2001.
8. Berkshire Hathaway Annual Report, 2003.
9. Robert Miles, *The Warren Buffett CEO* (Hoboken, NJ: Wiley, 2003), 70, quoted in Kilpatrick, *Of Permanent Value* (2004).
10. Quoted in Kilpatrick, *Of Permanent Value* (2004), 375.
11. Berkshire Hathaway Annual Report, 2001.
12. Berkshire Hathaway annual meeting 2001, quoted in Kilpatrick, *Of Permanent Value* (2004), 1358.
13. Berkshire Hathaway Annual Report, 1999, 6.

Chapter 4   Buying a Business

1. *Fortune,* October 31, 1994, quoted in Andrew Kilpatrick, *Of Permanent Value: The Story of Warren Buffett* (Birmingham, AL: AKPE, 2004), 1340.
2. Quoted in Andrew Kilpatrick, *Of Permanent Value: The Story of Warren Buffett* (Birmingham, AL: AKPE, 2000), 14.
3. Kilpatrick, *Of Permanent Value* (2004), 498.
4. Berkshire Hathaway Annual Report, 2003, 19.
5. Monte Burke, "Trailer King," *Forbes* (September 30, 2002), 72.
6. Berkshire Hathaway Annual Report, 2003, 5.
7. Ibid.
8. *Daily Nebraskan* (April 10, 2003), quoted in Kilpatrick, *Of Permanent Value* (2004), 728.
9. Berkshire Hathaway Annual Report, 2003, 6.
10. Berkshire Hathaway Annual Report, 2002, 5.
11. From a talk given at the University of Florida, quoted in the *Miami Herald* (December 27, 1998), quoted in Kilpatrick, *Of Permanent Value* (2004), 1350.
12. Berkshire Hathaway Annual Report, 1989, 17.
13. Robert Lenzner, "Warren Buffett's Idea of Heaven: 'I Don't Have to Work with People I Don't Like,'" *Forbes* (October 18, 1993), 43.
14. Mary Rowland, "Mastermind of a Media Empire," *Working Woman* (November 11, 1989), 115.
15. Kilpatrick, *Of Permanent Value* (2004), 398.
16. Ibid.

17. Ibid., 393.

18. Lenzner, "Warren Buffett's Idea of Heaven," 43.

Chapter 5   Investing Guidelines: Business Tenets

1. Berkshire Hathaway Annual Report, 1987, 14.

2. *Fortune,* April 11, 1988, quoted in Andrew Kilpatrick, *Of Permanent Value: The Story of Warren Buffett* (Birmingham, AL: AKPE, 2004), 1329.

3. Carol J. Loomis, "The Inside Story of Warren Buffett," *Fortune* (April 11, 1988), 30.

4. *Fortune* (November 11, 1993), 11.

5. Berkshire Hathaway Annual Report, 1991, 15.

6. Berkshire Hathaway Annual Report, 1987, 7.

7. *BusinessWeek,* July 5, 1999, quoted in Kilpatrick, *Of Permanent Value* (2004), 1353.

8. Berkshire Hathaway Annual Report, 1989, 22.

9. Berkshire Hathaway Annual Report, 1996, 15.

10. Quoted in Berkshire Hathaway Annual Report, 1993, 14.

11. Monte Burke, "Trailer King," *Forbes* (September 30, 2002), 72.

12. Berkshire Hathaway annual meeting, 1995, quoted in Kilpatrick, *Of Permanent Value* (2004), 1342.

13. *St. Petersburg Times* (December 15, 1999), quoted in Kilpatrick, *Of Permanent Value* (2004), 1356.

14. *Fortune* (November 22, 1999), quoted in Kilpatrick, *Of Permanent Value* (2004), 1356.

15. *U.S. News & World Report* (June 20, 1994), quoted in Kilpatrick, *Of Permanent Value* (2004), 1340.

16. Berkshire Hathaway annual meeting, 1996, quoted in Kilpatrick, *Of Permanent Value* (2004), 1344.

17. John Train, *The Money Masters* (New York: Penguin Books, 1981), 60.

18. Maria Halkias, "Berkshire Hathaway to Buy Maker of Tony Lama Boots," *Dallas Morning News* (June 20, 2000), 1D.

19. Maria Haklias, "CEO of Justin Industries to Retire," *Dallas Morning News* (March 17, 1999).

20. Halkias, "Berkshire Hathaway to Buy Tony Lama Boots."

21. "Berkshire Hathaway to Purchase Texas-Based Manufacturer," *Fort Worth-Star Telegram* (June 21, 2000).

22. Andrew Kilpatrick, *Warren Buffett: The Good Guy of Wall Street* (New York: Donald Fine, 1992), 123.

23. Art Harris, "The Man Who Changed the Real Thing," *Washington Post* (July 22, 1985), B1.

24. Berkshire Hathaway Annual Report, 1984, 8.

Chapter 6   Investing Guidelines: Management Tenets

1. Berkshire Hathaway Annual Report, 1989.
2. Berkshire Hathaway Annual Report, 1986.
3. Berkshire Hathaway Annual Report, 2000, 6.
4. SellingPower.com, October 2001, quoted in Andrew Kilpatrick, *Of Permanent Value: The Story of Warren Buffett* (Birminghan, AL: AKPE, 2004), 659.
5. Ibid., 661.
6. Carol J. Loomis, "The Inside Story of Warren Buffett," *Fortune* (April 11, 1988), 32.
7. Berkshire Hathaway Annual Report, 2001, 5.
8. "Puns Fly as Buffett Buys Fruit of the Loom," *Toronto Star* (May 7, 2002).
9. The Washington Post Company Annual Report, 1992, 5.
10. Berkshire Hathaway Annual Report, 1991, 8.
11. Berkshire Hathaway Annual Report, 1988, 5.
12. Berkshire Hathaway Annual Report, 2002.
13. Berkshire Hathaway Annual Report, 2003.
14. Berkshire Hathaway Annual Report, 1986, 5.
15. "Strategy for the 1980s," The Coca-Cola Company.
161.Berkshire Hathaway Annual Report, 1989, 22.
17. Ibid.
18. Linda Grant, "The $4 Billion Regular Guy," *Los Angeles Times Magazine* (April 7, 1991), 36.
19. Monte Burke, "Trailer King," *Forbes* (September 30, 2002), 72.
20. William Stern, "The Singing Mobile Home Salesman," *Forbes* (October 26, 1992), 240.
21. Burke, "Trailer King," 72.
22. Berkshire Hathaway Annual Report, 1985, 19.
23. Jim Rasmussen, "Buffett Talks Strategy with Students," *Omaha World-Herald* (January 2, 1993), 26.
24. Berkshire Hathaway Annual Report, 2001, 3.
25. Berkshire Hathaway Annual Report, 2003.
26. Berkshire Hathaway Annual Report, 2003, p7–8.
27. Reported by Greg Miles, *Bloomberg News* (April 2003).
28. Berkshire Hathaway Annual Report, 1991, quoted in Kilpatrick, *Of Permanent Value* (2004), 1333.
29. Berkshire Hathaway Annual Report, 2002, 3.
30. Ibid., 16.
31. Berkshire Hathaway Annual Report, 2003, 9.
32. Berkshire Hathaway annual meeting, 1993, quoted in Kilpatrick, *Of Permanent Value* (2004), 1335.
33. Berkshire Hathaway Annual Report, 2002, 21.

Chapter 7   Investing Guidelines: Financial Tenets

1. Berkshire Letters to Shareholders, 1977–1983, 43.
2. Berkshire Hathaway Annual Report, 1987.
3. "Strategy for the 1980s," The Coca-Cola Company.
4. Berkshire Hathaway Annual Report, 1984, 15.
5. Berkshire Hathaway Annual Report, 1986, 25.
6. Carol J. Loomis, "The Inside Story of Warren Buffett," *Fortune* (April 11, 1988), 34.
7. Berkshire Hathaway Annual Report, 1990, 16.
8. Chalmers M. Roberts, *The Washington Post: The First 100 Years* (Boston: Houghton Mifflin, 1977), 449.
9. Ibid., 426.
10. Berkshire Hathaway Annual Report, 2002, quoted in Andrew Kilpatrick, *Of Permanent Value: The Story of Warren Buffett* (Birmingham, AL: AKPE, 2004), 1361.

Chapter 8   Investing Guidelines: Value Tenets

1. Berkshire Hathaway annual meeting, 2003, quoted in Kilpatrick, *Of Permanent Value* (2004), 1362.
2. Berkshire Hathaway Annual Report, 1989, 5.
3. Berkshire Hathaway annual meeting, 1988, quoted in Kilpatrick, *Of Permanent Value* (2004), 1330.
4. Jim Rasmussen, "Buffett Talks Strategy with Students," *Omaha World-Herald* (January 2, 1994), 26.
5. The first stage applies 15 percent annual growth for ten years, starting in 1988. In year one, 1988, owner earnings were $828 million; by year ten, they will be $4.349 billion. Starting with year eleven, growth will slow to 5 percent per year, the second stage. In year eleven, owner earnings will equal $3.516 billion ($3.349 billion × 5 percent + $3.349 billion). Now, we can subtract this 5 percent growth rate from the risk-free rate of return (9 percent) and reach a capitalization rate of 4 percent. The discounted value of a company with $3.516 billion in owner earnings capitalized at 4 percent is $87.9 billion. Since this value, $87.9 billion, is the discounted value of Coca-Cola's owner earnings in year eleven, we next have to discount this future value by the discount factor at the end of year ten [1/(1+.09)10] = .4224. The present value of the residual value of Coca-Cola in year ten is $37.129 billion. The value of Coca-Cola then equals its residual value ($37.129 billion) plus the sum of the present value of cash flows during this period ($11.248 billion), for a total of $48.377 billion.

6. Berkshire Hathaway Annual Report, 1991, 5.
7. Berkshire Hathaway Annual Report, 1985, 19.
8. Berkshire Hathaway Annual Report, 1990, 16.
9. Berkshire Hathaway Annual Report, 1993, 16.
10. *Fortune* (December 19, 1988), quoted in Kilpatrick, *Of Permanent Value* (2004), 1331.
11. Berkshire Letters to Shareholders, 1977–1983, 53.
12. Berkshire Hathaway Annual Report, 2001, 5.
13. Berkshire Hathaway Annual Report, 2001, 15.
14. Grace Shim, "Berkshire Hathaway to Buy Fruit of the Loom," *Omaha World-Herald* (November 4, 2001).
15. Dean Foust, "This Trailer Deal Could Get Trashed," *BusinessWeek* (September 8, 2003), 44.
16. David Wells, "Buffett Says He Will Not Increase Bid for Clayton," *The Financial Times,* USA ed. (July 10, 2003), 19.

Chapter 9 Investing in Fixed-Income Securities

1. Berkshire Hathaway Annual Report, 2003.
2. Berkshire Hathaway Annual Report, 1988, 14.
3. Berkshire Hathaway Annual Report, 1990, quoted in Lawrence A. Cunningham, *The Essays of Warren Buffett: Lessons for Corporate America,* rev. ed. (privately printed), 105.
4. Berkshire Hathaway Annual Report, 1990, 18.
5. Berkshire Hathaway Annual Report, 2002.
6. Berkshire Hathaway Annual Report, 2000.
7. Berkshire Hathaway Annual Report, 1988, 15.

Chapter 10 Managing Your Portfolio

1. Personal communication to author, August 1994.
2. Andrew Barry, "With Little Cheery News in Sight, Stocks Take a Break," *Barron's* (November 16, 1998), MW1.
3. Berkshire Hathaway Annual Report, 1993, 15.
4. Ibid.
5. Ronald Surz, "R-Squareds and Alphas Are Far from different Alpha-Bets," *The Journal of Investing* (Summer 1998).
6. Interview with Warren Buffett, August 1994.
7. *Wall Street Journal* (September 30, 1987), quoted in Andrew Kilpatrick, *Of Permanent Value: The Story of Warren Buffett* (Birmingham, AL: AKPE, 2004), 1328.

8. *Outstanding Investor Digest* (August 10, 1995), 63.
9. Berkshire Hathaway Annual Report, 1993, 18.
10. Ibid., 13.
11. *Outstanding Investor Digest* (August 8, 1996), 29.
12. Berkshire Hathaway Annual Report, 1988, 18.
13. *Outstanding Investor Digest* (August 8, 1996), 29.
14. The speech was adapted as an article in the Columbia Business School's publication *Hermes* (Fall 1984), with the same title. The remarks directly quoted here are from that article.
15. Warren Buffett, "The Superinvestors of Graham-and-Doddsville," *Hermes* (Fall 1984). The superinvestors Buffett presented in the article include Walter Schloss, who worked at Graham-Newman Corporation in the mid-1950s, along with Buffett; Tom Knapp, another Graham-Newman alumnus, who later formed Tweedy-Browne Partners with Ed Anderson, also a Graham follower; Bill Ruane, a former Graham student who went on to establish the Sequoia Fund; Buffett's partner Charlie Munger; Rick Guerin of Pacific Partners; and Stan Perlmeter of Perlmeter Investments.
16. Ibid.
17. Ibid.
18. Sequoia Fund Annual Report, 1996.
19. Solveig Jansson, "GEICO Sticks to Its Last," *Institutional Investor* (July 1986), 130.
20. Berkshire Hathaway Annual Report, 1986, 15.
21. *Outstanding Investor Digest* (August 8, 1996), 10.
22. Berkshire Hathaway Annual Report, 1996.
23. Berkshire Hathaway Annual Report, 2001, 4.

Chapter 11 The Psychology of Money

1. *BusinessWeek* (July 5, 1999), quoted in Andrew Kilpatrick, *Of Permanent Value: The Story of Warren Buffett* (Birmingham, AL: AKPE, 2004), 1353.
2. Carol Loomis, ed., "Mr. Buffett on the Stock Market," *Fortune* (November 22, 1999).
3. Berkshire Hathaway annual meeting, 2002, quoted in Kilpatrick, *Of Permanent Value* (2004), 1360.
4. Mark Hulbert, "Be a Tiger Not a Hen," *Forbes* (May 25, 1992), 298.
5. Berkshire Hathaway Annual Report, 1990, 17.
6. Berkshire Hathaway Annual Report, 1992, 6.
7. Berkshire Hathaway Annual Report, 1986, 16.
8. Benjamin Graham, *The Intelligent Investor: A Book of Practical Counsel* (New York: Harper & Row, 1973), 107.

9. *Outstanding Investor Digest* (May 5, 1995), 51.
10. Graham, *The Intelligent Investor,* 107.
11. Brian O'Reilly, "Why Can't Johnny Invest?" *Fortune* (November 9, 1998), 73.
12. Fuerbringer, "Why Both Bulls and Bears Can Act So Bird-Brained," *New York Times* (March 30, 1997), section 3, 6.
13. Andrew Kilpatrick, *Of Permanent Value: The Story of Warren Buffett* (Birmingham, AL: AKPE, 1998), 683.

Chapter 12   The Unreasonable Man

1. This quote was used to describe Warren Buffett in V. Eugene Shahan's article, "Are Short-Term Performance and Value Investing Mutually Exclusive?" *Hermes* (Spring 1986).
2. Carol J. Loomis, "The Inside Story of Warren Buffett," *Fortune* (April 11, 1988), 30.
3. Ibid., 34.
4. *Fortune* (January 4, 1988), quoted in Andrew Kilpatrick, *Of Permanent Value: The Story of Warren Buffett* (Birmingham, AL: AKPE, 2004), 1329.
5. Loomis, "Inside Story," 28.
6. Linda Grant, "The $4 Billion Regular Guy," *Los Angeles Times Magazine,* 36.
7. Berkshire Hathaway Annual Report, 1993, 15.
8. Berkshire Hathaway annual meeting, 1993, quoted in Kilpatrick, *Of Permanent Value* (2004), 1335.
9. Berkshire Hathaway Annual Report, 1987, 15.
10. Robert Lenzner, "Warren Buffett's Idea of Heaven: 'I Don't Have to Work with People I Don't Like,'" *Forbes* (October 18, 1993), 40.
11. Berkshire Hathaway Annual Report, 1992, 6.

Afterword: Managing Money the Warren Buffett Way

1. "Investing: Profession or Business? Thoughts on Beating the Market Index," *The Consilient Observer,* vol. 2, no. 14 (July 15, 2003).
2. Legg Mason quarterly market commentary, January 25, 1999.

Acknowledgments

To begin, I want to express my deep gratitude to Warren Buffett for his teachings and for allowing me to use his copyrighted material. It is next to impossible to improve on what Warren has already said. This book is the better for being able to use his own words instead of subjecting you to a second-best paraphrase.

Thanks also to Charlie Munger for his contributions to the study of investing. His ideas on the "psychology of misjudgment" and the "latticework of mental models" are extremely important and should be examined by all. My appreciation to Charlie also includes thanks for his thoughtful conversations and his earliest word of encouragement and support.

In the development of my investment skills, no one has been more important in moving me from the theoretical to the practical than Bill Miller. Bill has been my friend and intellectual coach for over twenty years. His generosity is unmatched. As CEO of Legg Mason Capital Management, Bill has taken me by the hand and showed me how to apply Warren Buffett's approach to all types of companies, including those participating in the landscapes of the New Economy. What is particularly exciting for me is that Bill is not only a friend and teacher, but also a colleague.

I am also fortunate to work in an environment that supports and promotes rational investing. And so I would like to thank all my colleagues at Legg Mason including Nancy Dennin, Mary Chris Gay, Ernie Kiehne, Kyle Legg, Ira Malis, Michael Mauboussin, Jennifer Murphy,

David Nelson, Randy Befumo, Scot Labin, Jay Leopold, Samantha McLemore, Mitchell Penn, Dale Wettflaufer, and Jean Yu.

Over the years, I have benefited greatly from sharing numerous conversations about Warren Buffett with many thoughtful people. The list includes Bob Coleman, Tom Russo, Chris Davis, David Winters, Jamie Clark, Bill Ruane, Bob Goldfarb, Lou Simpson, Ajit Jain, Lisa Rapuano, Alice Schroeder, Chuck Akre, Al Barr, David Braverman, Wally Weitz, Mason Hawkins, Larry Pidgeon, and Ed Thorp.

Several people assisted me in the research for sections of the book. Thank you, Justin Green, Joan Lamm-Tennant, Pat Shunk, Michael Levitan, Stewart Davis, Mary Mclaugh, John Fitzgerald, and Linda Penfold.

Several prominent investors supported the book in its earliest period. My great thanks to Peter Lynch, John Rothchild, Jack Bogle, Phil Fisher, Ken Fisher, and Ed Haldeman.

Over the years, I have had the pleasure of interacting with several writers who in their own way are also Buffett experts. A special thanks to Andy Kilpatrick, who in my judgment is the official historian of Berkshire Hathaway. Thanks also to Roger Lowenstein, Henry Emerson, Janet Lowe, Carol Loomis, and Larry Cunningham.

Three talented and supersmart young women have been extraordinarily helpful in the creation in the book, each doing a specialized piece of research and manuscript development. Warm thanks to Ericka Peterson, Cathy Coladonato, and Victoria Larson.

With all the appreciation I have previously given, none could match the gratitude I owe my writing partner, Maggie Stuckey. Although we work at opposite ends of the continent, Maggie has an uncanny knack of getting inside my head and knowing exactly what I wish to communicate, often before I do. She is a dedicated professional who worked tirelessly to improve this book; I am fortunate to have her on my side.

My relationship with John Wiley & Sons has been always pleasurable. Myles Thompson, my friend and editor, championed *The Warren Buffett Way* when nobody had heard about it and not one copy had been sold. Thanks, Myles. I also thank Joan O'Neil, Pamela van Giessen, Mary Daniello, and the other publishing professionals at John Wiley for their care and attention to my writings on Warren Buffett.

I am greatly indebted to my agent, Laurie Harper at Sebastian Literary Agency. Laurie is, in a word, special. She does her job with honesty, loyalty, integrity, intelligence, and warm humor. I could not be in better hands. A word of appreciation, too, to the late Michael Cohn for taking a chance on a first-time writer ten years ago.

Anyone who has sat down to write a book knows that means countless hours spent alone that otherwise could be spent with family. My wife Maggie is a constant source of love and support. On the first day I told her I was going to write this book, she smiled and convinced me that it could be done. Over the following months, she cared for our family, giving me the luxury of time to write. Love without end to my children, Kim, Robert, and John, and to my wife, who makes all things possible for me. Even though they come last in this list, they are forever first in my heart.

For all that is good and right about this book, you may thank the people I have mentioned. For any errors or omissions, I alone am responsible.

R. G. H.

Index